INCOME DIFFERENTIALS & GENDER INEQUALITY

Wives earning more than husbands in Dar es Salaam, Tanzania

Published by Mkuki na Nyota Publishers,
P.O.BOX 4246, Dar Es Salaam, Tanzania
6 Muhonda Street, Mission Quarter, Kariakoo, Dar Es Salaam
http://www.mkukinanyota.com
contact@mkukinanyota.com

ISBN 9987-417-54-X

This and other Mkuki na Nyota Publishers' titles are available outside Africa from:
African Books Collective, Oxford, U.K
www.africanbookscollective.com

Michigan State University Press
East Lansing, Michigan, USA
www.msupress.msu.edu

Cover Design by: Mkuki B. Bgoya

PREFACE

Gender relations in the urban setting of Dar es Salaam by Luce Cloutier is an inspiring, long awaited account and analysis that will interest scientists and development workers at all levels and far beyond the African context. While we have understood that urbanization is one of the most challenging issues of these decades and that gender matters, the literature is scarce with regards to comprehensive analyses of gender determinants in the highly dynamic social and political tissue of an urban area, particularly in African countries where urbanization is still in its exponential phase.

The present book started with a very ambitious idea to capture how urbanisation shapes gender relations and how growing feminist movements in academia and in the civil society within different socio-economic strata govern urbanisation and particularly social action. The ambitions were met and provided us was fascinating realities.

The late Jorge Hardoy summarized the urban future in 1990 by saying, "where government policies become rooted in making best use of local skills, knowledge, culture and resources. This requires that governments turn to the capacities of the people who are already the most active city builders - individual citizens and the community organizations they form." We certainly agree with his statement and are also happy to realize how much this guiding principle has governed many different approaches of urban development, but we remain puzzled that his statement did not make any reference to the determinants of gender in this crucial process of building and rebuilding the cities of our world. The present book now bridges this gap and provides a sound series of analyses of gender relations in Dar es Salaam. This urban setting is deeply shaped by political stability for many decades and is rooted in the African socialism as conceptualized and lived by the first Tanzanian president Julius Nyerere. The research leading to this book took place when Tanzania was undergoing many changes. From the mid-nineties onwards, the various steps of structural adjustment policies led to an "opening" of the country with the growth of the private sector and the emerging middle class, particularly in urban areas. It was also the start of the cost-recovery approaches and the community contributions to social, health and educational services. These socio-political changes had a profound impact on the situation for the poorer segments as many policies and strategies that ensured equity and gender principles were no longer and/or could no longer be maintained. The societal gaps widened and hence the vulnerability of many households rapidly increased and led to an unprecedented situation for Tanzania. It is in this crucial period of social and political reconstruction that Luce Cloutier examined gender as the determinant of the "city builders" on the basis of an analytical framework and nicely illustrated by relevant case studies - trajectories of life in a highly dynamic and changing environment.

The analyses end with the conceptualization of Luce Cloutier's "new women" in Dar es Salaam and their commitment to building the society and hence the city based on their understanding and the subsequent daily translation into action of their concepts of equity, empowerment and self-determination.

The book not only generates understanding and provides insight, but also leaves us with the hope that the "new women" not only exist, but will be the driving force and Hardoy's "city builders" that governments as well as development agencies and workers should no longer ignore or even cannot afford to ignore if we truly wish to tackle urbanization as one of the most crucial development issue of our time.

FOREWORD

I have been working at the Dar es Salaam Urban Health Project (DUHP) for six years, from 1994 to 2001. As an anthropologist, I was a freelance consultant performing social research, evaluation and training in the health sector, especially in the field of Information, Education and Communication (IEC). The Swiss Development Cooperation funded the Dar es Salaam Urban Health Project. The Swiss Tropical Institute implemented the project for more than ten years.

It is through my work experience that I had the idea of conducting this personal research on gender relations, by focusing on women who earn more money than their husbands. Many questions remained unexplored, while others became of great interest to the understanding of the representations and discourses of both women and men. For example, women still do not have power in the decision-making process. Even in the case of children's illnesses, the husband or his relatives must authorise action, and the delay can substantially affect children's health. Nevertheless, women are held responsible if something goes wrong. There are, thus, many limitations on women's lives and much remains to be changed before full equality between women and men is attained. My analysis is limited to the ways in which women in Dar es Salaam are creating opportunities for greater equality within currently hegemonic global patriarchal and capitalist systems.

My approach to studying gender relations in Dar es Salaam relies on a "feminist political economy" that combines elements of liberal, Marxist, socialist and radical feminism. It recognises the continuing influence of patriarchy that reflects the durability of the hierarchical sexual organisation of society (Eisenstein, 1981)[1]. There is a complex interaction between the economic, political and ideological aspects of the society; although the sex/gender system is closely related to relations of production, it is separate from and not reducible to them. As argued by Gordon (1996:21), a point of

[1] Zillah Eisenstein, *The Radical Future of Liberal Feminism*, New York: Longman, 1981.

disjuncture between capitalism and patriarchy has been reached that requires changes in gender relations.

To focus on differences in experience and systems of meanings, I used a mixed feminist approach to theories of social action. It focuses on structural analysis and individual *agency* that shapes men and women's lives through their everyday perceptions and representations. Nowadays, both women and men are confronted with many social contradictions and they create, innovate and struggle. My view is that we need to incorporate the diversity of women's experiences and perceptions in feminist research.

The findings reflect the point of view of "ordinary people," some of whom could claim membership of the middle class. Quotations from men and women informants are included to facilitate an understanding of their perspectives, ideas and voices. They provide empirical evidence that exposes the discriminatory nature of the sex/gender system.

Women living in a hostile environment have learnt to struggle and to distance themselves from old social models and stereotypes. They open dynamic spaces of social trajectories in contrast to stabilised ones. Reflectivity produces more autonomous women who develop greater individual initiative. Some of these "new" women want to choose their own truth and morality and to establish their own social links. They ask for more democracy.

ACKNOWLEDGEMENTS

The making of this work has been a collective endeavour involving many individuals and institutions. First, this study would have been impossible without the participation of the women and men who so kindly agreed to take part in it.

I would like to mention the contributions of the various people who were involved in the process of the research. I am very thankful and wish to express my sincere gratitude to Dr. Deo Mtasiwa, the Regional/City Medical Officer for Health, for his help and encouragement for conducting this research. I also offer my special thanks to M. Pierre Pichette, the Chief Technical Advisor of the Dar es Salaam Urban Health Project, for his critique, guidance and tolerance during the study process. Special thanks are also reserved for Professor Marcel Tanner, Director of the Swiss Tropical Institute for his support and encouragement. I offer my thanks to the whole team of the DUHP.

I am grateful to Ms. Tabu Dorah Haule for her assistance in the first part of the research. She carried out many interviews and her mature approach was essential to the work. Special thanks to Chacha Wilson. He participated in the research process by conducting many interviews with men in Dar es Salaam and Tarime. He also allowed his students to produce dissertations on special issues. This work has been particularly useful in clarifying the point of view of young men and women. Finally, special thanks to Audrey Njelekela for her assistance in conducting special life story interviews with different women.

I express my gratitude to Mrs. Jackie Scully for the linguistic revision of the text. I say thank you to external readers for their comments and critique of the manuscript: Professor Trudy Harpham, South Bank University, United Kingdom; Professor Paul Charest, Department of Anthropology, Université Laval, Quebec, Canada; Dr. Nick Lorenz, Director of the Support Centre for International Development of the Swiss Tropical Institute, Basel and Andrée Côté for the revision of the manuscript.

CONTENTS

LIST OF TABLES

Introduction

Daily life in Dar es Salaam is a struggle for many, both old residents and newcomers. Since the 1980s Tanzania has gone through a deep economic crisis followed, in 1986, by the imposition of Structural Adjustment Programme (SAP) conditions in an effort to reform and liberalise the economy. These SAPs are viewed as the visible signs of the effects of globalisation. Hence, government priorities have shifted from human and social interests to economic development. Citizens are now expected to pay for health and social services, education and local infrastructures on the basis of cost-sharing principles. Privatisation, deregulation and liberalisation have increased competition between all kinds of producers. An ever-widening gap between rich and poor has sharpened the conflict between social classes, and ethnic and religious groups, and has polarised gender relations. As indicated by Mikell, the contemporary African state is reticent about broaching topics of women's interests and involvement because gender topics pull back the covers that conceal societal instability, flux, inequitable relations, structural duality, and social indeterminacy just below the superficial layer of visible government (1997:31).

What is the impact of these developments on the everyday life of women? According to Afshar and Barrientos (1999:5) globalisation represents both possibilities of empowerment and disempowerment. For example, as Steenbeek, Ypeij and Reysoo (2002) observed, among various changes, the dismantling of social services obliges women to intensify their domestic tasks and their participation in community life as the main actors of non paid work in the domestic and community sphere. Rising costs, the urban economy and men's low salaries oblige women to develop various survival strategies, and their implication in economic activities causes men's resistance towards the new sexual division of labour. This situation is conceptualised by the expression "feminisation of poverty."

Women enter this competitive area at a disadvantage. For instance, they do not have access to property. Marriage and inheritance rules continue to reflect a patriarchal[2] society. Most men still benefit from these rules even if in today's city, they are hard put to earn a living. Women's involvement in productive activities has become a necessity, and in some cases it means they earn more money than their husbands. How does this affect gender relation in an urban area, and what do men and women do to adjust their relationships? These questions form the core of this study.

This book assesses the influence of society on the daily life of women. In the context of an economic crisis marked by impoverishment and proletarianisation, women still carry the burden of ensuring a good life for their children. Women's self-perception compared with men's representation of women's roles and of gender relations in an urban area, is used to contrast traditional and new patterns. Women's lives are discussed within the general framework of constraints and opportunities, to give an assessment of the force of gender ideology.

Gender relations are constructed through interactions, not fixed in advance. They are made and remade through social practices situated in a given environment. Undoubtedly some structural and social features lead to particular perceptions and representations of gender roles, which in turn command particular behaviours and determine people's actions. We can presume that the urban environment has an

---

[2] Patriarchy refers to a system of social structures and practices in which men dominate, oppress, and exploit women (Walby, 1996:21). One strand of thought defines patriarchy in terms of men's domination over women in the household, often including a generational aspect in which the oldest man in the household dominates all the members, including young men (Hartmann, 1979; Moghadan, 1992; Weber, 1947). Others have preferred not to tie the definition of patriarchy to any particular household form, and have left open questions as to the relationship of the household to gender inequality (Mies, 1986). Mies argues that many other categories of men are involved in the subordination of women (for example, male bosses). Other writers include the appropriation of women's labour as the chief way in which patriarchal control is maintained (Hartman, 1979), while others suggest male violence (Browmiller, 1976), sexuality (MacKinnon, 1989), reproduction (Firestone, 1974), and various other areas of the basic structure as elements of patriarchy.

impact on gender relations and inequalities. This research considers the adaptation of women and men to a changing urban environment and asks: How is the relation to other political, economic and social processes reflected in the social construction of femininity and masculinity? In particular, is the Tanzanian gender regime affected by women's involvement in production and social reproduction? To what extent are social practices, norms and values changed and at what level are the changes taking place? Is it at the individual, household, community or national level? Are women becoming more empowered? Is the interaction between economic, legal, political, cultural, health and psychological factors affecting women's social status?

Our study focuses on women with higher salaries than their husbands. The implications are related to women's subordination to and subjection by the male group, and to women's rejection of this situation. The research exposes the social construction of gender relations in everyday life, and outlines the contradictory and dynamic character of those gender relations in an urban and social context that is undergoing continual transformation. The survey does not focus on macro-economic data and broad generalisation. It investigates the interstices of the daily life, the small exchanges between men and women, which reveal changes in gender relations that cannot be seen at the macro-level (Parpart, 1996:149). It provides a more careful attention to context and locales in which people's lives are played out.

Debate on gender relations in Tanzania

Gender has a long history in Tanzania. During the colonial period, "the colonial constructions of colonised African women were (mis)informed by basic assumptions about African women in their 'natural', that is, rural, 'tribal' setting, and with men, furthered by an ideology in which problems of control and extraction figured centrally" (Geiger, 1997:22). Control over women "was narrowly focused on their sexuality and their role in social and biological reproduction" as for "the African man," the colonial state's interests "assumed that the twin requirements of control and extraction had to cover all aspects of his life, from how and where he might work, to what crops he should produce; and from what associations he could form, to how many cattle he could own" (idem). This way of thinking was based on the assumption that women were subordinate to men and on the approach of leaving the control of women to colonised men (fathers, husbands, brothers, uncles). Women in Tanzania, as in many other African countries, as in the case of Nigeria quoted by Egbo (2000:3), were excluded from educational opportunities, wage labour, politics and government, "colonialism increased and consolidated (at great costs) the gender-based social chasm that may have existed, leaving women unprepared for the emergent world order of which their societies were fast becoming an integral part. At least such was the case up until the late fifties."

At Independence, the country subscribed to an alternative non-capitalist development strategy, based on rural socialism and self-reliance, which was formalised in the Arusha Declaration in 1967. Nyerere's philosophy of *Ujamaa* socialism and the consequent strategy is touted in his particular vision of African communal traditions, political, economic and social organisation prior to colonialism, from which flowed three central principles—mutual respect, the sharing of joint production and work by all. He isolated two basic inadequacies of traditional society such as its poverty and the subordinate position of women, both of which he believed could be rectified by the strategy of *Ujamaa* socialism (Ship, 1988:6). While acknowledging women's subordination, Nyerere did not attempt to explain the causes of this subordination, nor did he explore how patterns of women's subordination varied according to class or ethnic group. Furthermore, he did not specify what concrete steps had to be taken to eradicate women's subordination. It was assumed that it would disappear with the implementation of *Ujamaa* socialism (idem:8).

Some progressive legislation and policies were implemented to promote women's advancement in areas such as education, political recruitment and maternity legislation. Educational expansion became a priority, as universal primary education was perceived as the key to accelerate social development. A campaign for adult literacy was started. Party directives were issued for increased women's participation in management. The Umoja Wa Wanawake Wa Tanzania (UWT), the national women's organisation has been taking a more active role in the enhancement of women's equality through the institutionalisation of increased day-care and income-generating projects (Ship, 1988:9). However, most studies pointed out the subordinate position of women in the household and society, as outlined in the analytical bibliography done by Mascarenhas and Mbilinyi (1983).

The 60s were declared as the first decade for development by the United Nations. Governments and international organisations began to identify the reasons why the participation of women was deficient in public life and in productive activities.

During the second decade for development (1975-1985), the United Nations declaration of the Decade for Women at the World Conference of the Women's International Year held in Mexico City in 1975 brought the issue of the subordinate condition of women in Sub-Saharan countries to the collective awareness of the world community. The fundamentals were built around the themes of Equality (efforts to eliminate all forms of discrimination and inequalities based on gender), Development (aimed at the advancement of women's political, economic and cultural positions in society along with the development of the whole society) and Peace (to bring harmony in society by eliminating all forms of violence against women and children, and combating sexual harassment at national and local levels). This awareness, in turn, resulted in a deliberate focus on the status and welfare of women by various world organisations. Through direct funding and technical advice, UN organisations instituted educational and social policies that specifically targeted women. The UN decade for Women also provided stimulation for the formation of a cross-cultural platform and international coalitions among feminist scholars, women's rights advocates and NGOs with a special interest in the development and advancement of women.

Various theoretical frameworks have been elaborated in order to explain the continuing subordination of women. They grossly refer to radical, Marxist, socialist and liberal frameworks. They are opposed in their definition of women's oppression and on the development of political strategies.

Most comments on Women in Development (WID) and Women and Development (WAD) approaches, seen as belonging to the liberal current, concentrate on the fact that they are neglecting the existing social structures that disadvantage women. They demonstrate that economic and social development cut women from their traditional resources allowing them subsistence, and increase their workload and responsibilities towards ensuring the family's survival. Poverty is increasing and it has been proven that women are more affected by it. Women's poverty is perpetuated by the nature of power relations between men and women, as women have limited access to the resources they need for their increasing responsibilities.

Women in Development (WID) and Women and Development (WAD) approaches have been assessed as policies pointing at half of the population, indicating that the problems related to development originated from women. Women were seen as isolated subjects, without taking into account the complexity of social relations in which they live.

Changing gender categories have been subjects of discussions and debates in Tanzania. Many explanations have been offered for the continual subordination of women. Some explained it by the persistence of ideological and cultural barriers to women's advancement, such as inadequate law, and others by women's mental attitudes. It was seen as a female problem; the constancy of male resistance to changes that could benefit women was ignored. These points of view failed to confront the material bases of women's subordination—the social order and structures which generate and maintain attitudes of female inferiority and passivity, as well as the differential ways in which men and women are integrated into the productive and reproductive spheres in Tanzania (Ship, 1988:11).

In the 80s, the living standards of women were getting considerably worse. Illiteracy, unemployment, lack of health services, inapplicability of laws that would guarantee equality between men and women were showing a reality full of contradictions. WID and

WAD approaches were evaluated as legitimising feminine role, and in certain cases, as giving more work and responsibilities to women. Thus, the Gender and Development (GAD) approach helped to question the apparent immutability of social roles and to explain the end of the universal subordination of women. The relations of power and subordination between men and women in their political, economic, ethnic and cultural contexts were viewed as central to the formation, analysis and change in the organisation of social processes.

During the 80s (the third decade for development), the feminist approach influenced the analysis of gender relations, which were viewed as social, historically specific, rather than immutable and natural. Women's oppression has been related to the sexual division of labour. In Tanzania, the sexual division of labour expresses women's oppression in remunerated and non-remunerated work and is a persistent fact that works to the detriment of women. Domestic work performed by women is undervalued, is time-consuming and "forces women to work for longer hours than men to achieve low standard of living" (Ship, 1988:21). Women are segregated from the industrial sector (they represented 10 percent of the labour force in the industrial sector) and confined in lower paid, labour intensive, non-supervisory positions which are identified as less skilled, with inferior work conditions (idem). Educated women are generally found in traditional feminine occupations such as teachers and nurses.

The socially constructed sexual division of labour allocated household tasks and the work in the sphere of the reproduction of human life. Women are in charge of domestic maintenance, childcare, care of the sick and elderly, as well as subsistence food production. These tasks are the consequence of a generalised social system, a gender system that is based on unequal gender relations and gender subordination, rooted in the sexual division of labour and perpetuated through its continual reconstitution (Ship, 1988:22). Women's roles continue to be defined by their biological capacity to bear children. Women's roles as domestic caretakers and nurturers are viewed as immutable and natural, when in fact they are socially constructed.

GAD allows a more efficient analysis of this concept and identifies reasons for impediments, resistances, complementarities and conflicts between men and women. It favours a better and more adapted planning and evaluation development to the reality.

In the 90s, the concept of empowerment and mainstreaming emerged to introduce the principles of equality between men and women in the elaboration of policies and in the processes linked to development. Originating from the experiences and analysis of feminists from developing countries, the empowerment approach outlines the role played by the colonial and neo-colonial oppression in the subordination of women. The approach distinguishes between short-term strategies (answers to the crisis in food production, and in formal and informal employment sectors) and long-term strategies (identification of the structures of inequality between genders, classes and nations in order to overcome them) and is based on realities that are determined by gender. This political approach does not receive enough attention from governments and international agencies. The mainstreaming[3] approach tends to introduce the principle of equality between men and women at the inception of policies and in the whole processes of development.

The Tanzania Gender Networking Programme (TGNP) has adopted a critical gender analysis, coupled with a multidisciplinary and multisectoral approach. It recognises that women and their problems are not isolated from the rest of the society. The focus is on the gender relations between men and women, at all levels of the society, and the relationships between gender and other social relationships, such as class, race or ethnicity, and the North or South (TGNP,

---

[3] From the UN Economic and Social Council's definition: "mainstreaming a gender perspective is the process of assessing the implications for women and men of any planned action, including legislation, policies or programmes in all areas and at all levels. It is a strategy for making women as well as men's concerns and experiences an integral dimension of the design, implementation, monitoring and evaluation policies and programmes in all political, economic and societal spheres so that women and men benefit equally and inequality is not perpetuated. The ultimate goal is to achieve gender equality" (UNICEF, 2001:39).

1993:16). The interaction among different factors and sectors, and different levels of the society can be demonstrated.

As discussed by the Tanzania Gender Networking Programme[4] in its 1993 publication entitled *Gender Profile of Tanzania* (1993), the majority of Tanzanian women have not been empowered in the sense of participating in a process of transformation of social relations in the economy and politics. Most women have not acquired ownership or control over basic resources. They lack adequate skills to support many of their activities, and most of them are low-income producers who have to work hard to support themselves and their families. This leaves little time for childcare, support for relatives or any other community obligations, and contributes to the poor health status of women.

Gender relations ensure that women have less ownership of, access to, and control over cultural, educational, political or economic resources (TGNP, 1993: 40). Furthermore, women lack control in the decision-making and planning processes. They remain unable to participate fully in employment, continue to be discriminated against in employment and on-the-job training, and face sexual harassment. The majority of women are employed informally. They are left without the protection of government regulations or access to such worker benefits as minimum wages, paid annual and maternity leave, or maximum length of working day. Women entrepreneurs and small

---

[4] The Tanzania Gender Networking Programme (TGNP) started its activities in December 1992, as a result of preparations for the Review Workshop held in December 1992, which focused on Women's Conditions in Tanzania. TGNP recognised the persistence of gender inequality and women's oppression, in spite of many steps taken by the government and other development agencies to change the situation. The broad aim of TGNP is to facilitate the process of gender equity, the empowerment of women in Tanzania (and worldwide), and the transformation of society at all levels—individual, household, community, national and international. The emphasis of TGNP is on *process*, not projects. The major areas of action for TGNP are: education and training; animation workshops; action-oriented, participatory research; lobbying and networking; publications, communication and dissemination; documentation and library; exhibitions, publicity and sales; fund-raising, operations and logistics (TGNP, 1993:2-13).

traders face institutionalised gender discrimination in the allocation of credit, trading permits, property rights and other kinds of networks.

Under the present conditions of job insecurity, women are less willing to challenge discriminatory practices because they fear losing the little they have. There has often been a male backlash against organised women's groups, especially when the groups are successful in acquiring major resources. For example, the marginalisation of women who participated actively in the mobilisation for the Independence through Tanzanian historiography reflects an androcentric bias. Women's political action and history "disappeared" in a cumulative process whereby successive written accounts reinforce and echo the silence of previous ones (Geiger, 1997:9-10).

Nevertheless, women have succeeded in opening up some avenues of political participation. It is through their efforts that the Government has begun to reassess traditional laws by setting up the Law Reform Commission that identified three priorities for review: the Law of Marriage Act of 1971, the Law of Succession and Inheritance, the Children and Young Persons Ordinance, and other laws that discriminate against women. Many institutions and organisations have increased legal literacy, and legal clinics have been active in creating space for legal action in civil society. Furthermore, women have taken advantage of political liberalisation to demand greater female leadership and stronger representation of women's issues.

The urban context and gender relations

Many questions remain on the changing gender relations in the urban context, under the impact of economic restructuring upon gender relations. Two books *Gender, Family and Household in Tanzania* (1995) and *Gender, Family and Work in Tanzania* (2000) assess the impact of social change at the community and family level after two decades of severe economic problems, resulting in major changes in government policies designed to liberalise and restructure the economy. They have borne heavily upon daily life, gender and family relations.

The analysis of different themes and views of different authors present both pessimistic and optimistic points of view on changes in the gender relations. Most of them noted that generalisations are not easy to make as outcomes vary so much with circumstances and the imputation of causality is always problematic.

According to the more optimistic view:
Considering the economic aspects of changes between men and women, many authors (Bryceson, 1995; Koda, 1995; Tripp, 1992) acknowledge women's increasing workload because of their implication in income-generating activities and little access to resources. However, it has brought significant gains for women. First, women have expanded their activities in the informal sector and have access to cash income. It has given them greater bargaining power and more independence from men, both within and outside the home. Women display more confidence and a greater determination to control their lives. They have constructed a wider range of social networks for mutual support outside the home and many make their own decisions over how to spend or save their earnings. Indeed, it has helped women escape men's control over their labour-modifying power relations within the household and, in some cases, alter patterns of socialisation processes. Women manage on their own as they do not see themselves only as passive victims (Caplan, 1995:62).

According to the pessimistic view:
The lack of access to resources; poor availability of economic resources and little control over household expenditure; the dearth of negotiating power on important issues such as fertility, birth control (Caplan, 1995; Omari, 1995) still demonstrate the unequal gender relations. Too many limitations for expanding income-generating projects exist as these are mostly small-scale and service-oriented, requiring little capital investment and chosen to fit in with family responsibilities (Rutashobya, 1995). All these elements point out the low status of women in the society.

Socio-cultural variables act as impediments to women's independence. For example, women's greater contribution to household expenditure is forced, as husbands attempt to control all purchases. Campbell noted that women are forced to buy cheaper cooking tools and materials that require more labour. Such attempts by men to shift expenditures for which they were previously responsible onto women have been noted previously by other authors. Men monopolise decision making on cash expenditure even where women's contribution is higher (Mbilinyi, 1991:34-35). Women can be obliged to ask permission before spending savings (Campbell, Mwami and Ntukula, 1995). This showed the lack of democracy at the household level. Violence against women is still rampant and is sometimes seen as a necessity and natural. Thus, men manipulate "tradition" and "modernity" to suit their own interests.

The Participatory Poverty Assessment (PPA) study that was conducted in rural Tanzania can be used to expose the continuity of patterns. It demonstrated that women identified different priorities and social problems than men, reflecting the different worldviews and realities in rural Tanzania[5] (Creighton and Omari, 1995; Rwebengira, 1994, Ferreira, 1994, UNICEF, 1990 in Narayan, 1997:30-31).

The study demonstrated that female-headed households are considerably more vulnerable[6] than their male-headed counterparts because they possess fewer capital assets and experience social isolation. The predominance of customary law and prevailing cultural norms leave women destitute, following divorce or death of the husband. Most women avoid legal action, as most do no believe

---

[5] Among the top-ranked problems as expressed by men: transportation (28%), farming (22%), drunkenness (15%), health (10%), water (8%) and deforestation (7%). Women mentioned: food shortage (21%), water (20%), health (16%), drunkenness (16%), farming (9%) and transportation (4%). These findings highlight the importance of gender-disaggregated data (Narayan, 1997:31).

[6] According to Moser (1996) and Chambers (1989), the concept of vulnerability is viewed as more dynamic for capturing the processes of change and introduces more complex aspects of "livelihood security" relating to survival, security, and self-respect, as well as people's subjective perceptions of their poverty—what it means to the poor.

that the legal system would benefit them. Only a few younger and educated women in some villages fought for their rights with the support of women's organisations to receive some of the material property (Narayan, 1997:33-37). Even when married, women own few possessions—mostly the ones they use for their daily activities (kitchen utensils, gourds, vegetables, necklaces and bracelets). Furthermore, they are denied the right to decide to sell anything or keep the earnings from the sale. They can only use what is needed for home consumption, the surplus being men's possession.

Rural poor have more immediate survival needs such as food, water, and health. Education is not given the highest priority, since these fundamental needs are not satisfied. People are dissatisfied with the rising costs of education, the perceived low return on investment in education, and the impossibility of sending their children to secondary school. Girls are more often pulled out of school than boys for different reasons. Educating girls is not seen as an investment because they would get married and leave home (25 percent), might become pregnant (24 percent), or are viewed as a waste of money since they do not bring any income (7 percent). The study also revealed a pattern of periodic dropout from school to cope with economic stress, rather than a permanent withdrawal. For example, parents pulled children out of school seasonally when there was insufficient food or cash to pay for school-related expenses. The pattern obviously undermines learning and the retention of knowledge (Narayan, 1997:33-34).

Women have greater difficulty in buying land and getting credit because of social and cultural practices. Customary laws, which limit women's control over assets, thereby also limit their access to collateral and credit. Saving is also quite an impossible aim for female-headed households as they have less knowledge about formal savings institutions.

Masculinity and femininity are constructed and expressed through socialisation processes, social rules, and the sexual division of labour. Femininity is linked to tradition whereas masculinity is associated to modernity. For example, the code of modesty imposes more restrictions on women. Women and young girls are taught to be more concerned about the proper way to dress than young men. The respect expressed towards seniors by young women, whose bodies are covered properly with "appropriate" dress, also signals their socially constrained and controlled sexuality. It refers to male domination and female subordination in a society that overwhelmingly constructs gender in heterosexual terms (Hansen, 2000:33). The case of the arrival of the miniskirt in Tanzania reported by Lewinson is instructive. The authorities condemned the fashion "as violating 'African' culture, and groups from the Youth league of TANU began to roam the streets, harassing and even beating women who were wearing mini-skirts." Lewinson added that:

> *By violating the rules of modesty, revealing clothes implied that the wearer was inclined to defy "traditional" sexual norms, so women's attire expressed their commitment or lack thereof to "African values." Feminine actions embodied aspects of "traditional" Tanzanian culture, which the state wished to preserve (2000:271).*

The debate is related in certain cases to tradition and modernity. Women are the bearers of tradition, as men are of modernity. Some hail change as making society more equal, developing human potential and bringing a better standard of living. Others perceive the changes as disrupting culture, endangering moral values, and going against the "proper" (received) social order (Lewinston, 2000:271).

Bryceson, in her analysis of marriage and cohabitation, noted that contradictions in women's position have increased under the reformulation of laws, educational opportunities and greater freedom of movement. In formal terms their legal and social position has improved, but in some respects their material position has declined, while the ideological legacy of the past has hardly been dented. Men's desire to appropriate and control women's sexuality has not changed. Indeed there are signs of male backlash in rural and urban area, and the high degree of instrumentality that has long characterised gender relations in Tanzania shows little sign of weakening (Creighton and Omari, 1995:24; Lugalla, 1990). Poverty and insecurity have made marriage more fragile and have affected the formation of relationships and the nature of sexual bargaining. It cannot be assumed that women will benefit from this change (Bryceson, 1995:20).

Insecurity in marriage has led to a rise in female-headed households. Many interpretations prevail, as some researchers have seen this as a protest against patriarchal relations (Bryceson, 1980), especially at the level of the individual (Vuorela, 1987) while Bader (1975) has argued that independent women are in a stronger position than married ones. Similarly, Brand in a recent study done on fertility and demographic change in Mali, mentioned that, "Women who were most capable of regulating their own fertility were those with the highest degree of autonomy: the single women. These single women had the least to lose, but the most to gain through birth control" (2001:310). This is also the point of view expressed by many women participants in this research when they declare that marriage is no longer a security for women. Most of the older women who experienced married life want their daughters to gain independence through education and the development of professional skills. Education is seen as a priority to escape dependence in marriage.

Acquiring genuine economic independence is a new prospect for women. For example, as shown in the study of women engaged in prostitution in Nairobi, Rodriguez-Torres (1999) exposed the situation of prostitutes having money to invest. Usually, they would be confronted by many constraints such as traditional laws denying women access to land without the authorisation of a husband. To these constraints social stigma is also present. In these cases, prostitutes who want to invest develop new strategies, the most common being to hide their activities to give legitimacy to their earnings. They also multiply their activities, and some succeed, using this way to enter the formal economy.

For example, successful prostitutes in Kenya possess houses and pieces of land in the countryside, which is seen as the most important symbol of success. Others invest money in transportation in the city (owners of buses, taxis). The ones who earn less cannot invest in the formal channels of the economy. They chose to invest in the informal sector. Prostitution generates profits allowing individual or collective survival. As mentioned by Rodriguez-Torres (1999:145), if we consider the relative “success” of prostitutes, we could make the hypothesis that prostitution, as many other illegal activities, is one of the rare sectors of the Kenyan economy which profits from the actual evolution of the economic policy—free entrepreneurship is growing in illegality. Prostitution, as an element of the informal economy, is contributing to the urban growth, as the majority of investments coming from this job are done in the city. We are confronted by the logic of an economic alternative that is inserted in the dominant economy, but in the world of illegality through which investments are done, jobs are created, and a redistribution of richness is realised.

However, as Geisler (2000) demonstrated in the case of Zambia, many women still internalise the idea of subordination. The reproduction of initiation rites is one example. The debate is led by urban traditionalists in their opposition to young professional urban women (2000:73).

Initiation ceremonies are perceived as reaffirming gender inequalities. The ultimate objective seems to be the perpetuation of men’s domination and women’s subordination (idem: 66). Women are viewed as guardians of the “tradition” that could “stop the rot.” In the urban context, a recourse to the initiation of girls proved a powerful tool in aligning older women to male interests, in that it offered a seemingly “natural” way of blaming and dividing women, diverting attention away from the immorality and the incompetence of men, because girl’s initiations are about women enticing other women to accept the dominance of men (idem: 80).

The AIDS crisis reveals much about inequalities in gender relations. As pointed out in the study on *AIDS, Sexuality and Gender in Africa* edited by Baylies and Bujra (2000) many barriers still exist to women’s empowerment in the field of sexuality and gender relations even if many collective strategies and struggles are elaborated in Tanzania and Zambia. They observed that:

> *It is one thing for women to organise collectively to raise awareness of the dangers of AIDS and its mode of transmission, to raise self-esteem and muster the courage to*

say no to unwanted sexual contact. It is quite another to challenge men's power in the lonely moment of private relations and to negotiate for safer sex. Unequals cannot negotiate" (Baylies, 2000: xii).

It could be difficult for men to accept negotiation and greater mutuality within intimate relations, this necessarily threatens their power to define sexual practice and even their ability to father children and further their line. Relations of intimacy are informed by the same cultural prescriptions and notions of personhood that operate in the larger society to influence the gender division of labour, educational opportunities, the legal system and the gendered structure of employment (Bujra, 2000:7).

Prescriptions of passivity for females and the according of sexual decision making and initiative to men are still repeated, along with a greater tolerance of men's greater sexual mobility, both prior to and after marriage. Interventions in AIDS protection and prevention must expose and challenge those relations of power which drive the epidemic but must also stress the mutuality of interest in their transformation across lines of cleavage. They must promote greater inclusiveness and address those injustices, inequalities and human rights deficit, which fuel the epidemic (Baylies and Bujra, 2000:197).

Intergenerational ties are also discussed, as the research revealed the ambivalence and sometimes the fear and hatred that older people have for the young. They are sometimes blamed for the epidemic. "Far from a solidarity purpose amongst women, there were contradictory currents of jealousy, bitterness expressed by (some) older women towards the young generation, mingled terror and concern, especially when the young people were their sons and daughters" (idem:xiii).

However, in spite of all impediments, women learnt that it is possible to defeat authority and gain power through the development of associations and new networks. They know the necessity of action for changing political processes for them to gain power in decision-making processes at every level.

As social beings, women take meanings, knowledge, values and rules into account as they respond to particular situations. Many women have been able to use and adapt some social rules and turn a disadvantage into an advantage.

In spite of all these impediments, many women have developed autonomy. More and more are distancing themselves from customs and traditions as they become able to think about the new environment in which they live. Tensions arise from the confrontation of old schemes with new ones.

This study provides a space for ordinary women who do not always have the opportunity to express themselves and be listened to. It does not pretend to universality, but it does disclose the capacity of women to engage with an environment that is not always ready to cope with their dynamic agency.

Chapter 1

SETTING THE SCENE

Dar es Salaam, like all big cities, is characterised by complexity, heterogeneity and density. It is a centre of decision making with a high concentration of politicians, managers, administrators and resources. Decisions made in the city may enlarge or reduce the possibilities of development beyond its immediate borders.

The city has approximately three millions inhabitants[1], a figure extrapolated from the most recent census of 1988. Over 70 percent of Dar es Salaam residents are under 30 years of age (68.3 percent of the male population and 76.6 percent of the female population). The population aged 65 years or more represents about 1.4 percent. The number of females is greater in the age group of 5-24 years, most markedly between 15-24 years. From the age of 30 onwards, the number of males is greater, exceeding the number of females by over 20 percent in the age group of 45-59 years.

Table 1: Population growth in Dar es Salaam from 1886 to 2001

Year	Population	Source
1886	5,000	(Kitchener's estimate)
1894	9,000	(Deutsche Kolonial Blatt estimate)
1900	18,000	(Deutsche Kolonial Blatt estimate)
1913	19,000	(Deutsche Kolonial Blatt estimate)
1921	20,000	(Census)
1931	24,000	(Census)
1943	37,000	(Estimated based on hut count)
1948	51,000	(Census)
1951	72,000	(Census)
1957	92,330	(Census)
1988	1, 345,118	(Census)
2001	2, 800,000	(CMOH/DSM- extrapolation)

Source: Leslie, J.A.K., *A Survey of Dar es Salaam*, Oxford University Press, 1963. For years 1886 to 1957.

[1] The Planning Unit of Dar es Salaam region estimates the number of residents at 3 million and a half at night. It seems that this number grows to 5 million during daytime—bringing people from close suburbs into the city for work, trade and to search for job opportunities.

TGNP (The Tanzania Gender Networking Programme),
City Medical Office of Health

The demographic situation of Dar es Salaam is similar to that of many sub-Saharan countries. People move to the city not just because of its resources but also because of imagined or real opportunities.

Rapid urbanisation seems an irreversible trend. In Tanzania, people migrate from rural areas to Dar es Salaam for different reasons, including declining incomes and deteriorating conditions which pushed them out of the countryside. People move to the city to satisfy their need for protection, food, health, communication and job opportunities. Psychological factors such as the need for esteem, respect, the exercise of power and education could also explain the search for a new way of life. For instance, a growing resistance to patriarchal oppression and the desire for improved social services attracts people to the city (TGNP, 1993:43).

Consequences of rapid urbanisation

The urban setting attracts men and women hoping for a better life, but also generates socio-economic inequalities that can be identified spatially and socially. A large portion of the population consists of those whom success has passed by—poor people and poor households[2].

People settle in less favourable city areas and are then exposed to natural hazards and disasters in locations where it is furthermore difficult to provide basic infrastructure such as roads, water and sewage systems. Many settlements are characterised by a lack of basic infrastructure, substandard housing, overcrowding and unhealthy living conditions. Anarchic development has led to the development of peri-urban areas that are undefined and unplanned. They are densely

[2] A study by CARE International (1997) indicates that more than 20 percent of the population lives in a situation of absolute poverty. In the Participatory Poverty Assessment (PPA) (Narayan, 1997: 8) rural people perceived "very poor" as: those who were poor by choice, those who could not even depend on themselves, really low people, stupid fools, people who relied on others, those who were poor but invited it upon themselves, people who relied on luck and others, people who were completely disabled or physically handicapped, and people whom to employ was a threat.

populated with high growth rates. Usually, residence in these areas is not legal.

According to the Dar es Salaam Urban Health Project (DUHP, 1993), 500,000 people live in high mobility, low-income squatter areas. The socio-economic situation of salaried groups has also deteriorated. The Tanzania Gender Networking Programme, TGNP (1993:32), estimated that most men in Tanzania have low incomes and minimal control of productive assets, and therefore have little to "share" with women in their class. The resources available to most men and women are inadequate for a healthy and dignified life.

In the health sector, Dar es Salaam is administered by a number of different healthcare providers ranging from the public to the private, the religious sector and international organisations. Public health providers are managed by the Ministry of Health, the City Council and the local district authority.

The major health problems have been identified as:

- Infectious diseases such as cholera, diarrhoea, malaria, respiratory diseases, tuberculosis, and the pandemic HIV/AIDS, which is the primary cause of death of urban males. HIV/AIDS and maternal mortality are the primary killers of urban females.

- Chronic diseases; increasing because of the higher proportion of older people in the population.

- Transition health problems similar to those of the industrialised world, including road traffic accidents, occupational diseases, diabetes, high blood pressure and psychological problems.

The rapid increase in urban population has also resulted in an inability of the Government to provide basic urban systems. Therefore, considering the difficulties in managing a city of more than three million people, the Government decided in 2000 to decentralise and subdivide the city into three municipalities, the Ilala, Kinondoni and Temeke districts.

Neighbourhoods in Dar es Salaam can be contrasted by occupation, ethnicity and distance from the city centre; and most have residents of varied income levels and social status. The occupational structure of the city[3] includes a high number of people involved in the so-called "informal" sector, skilled manual labour, the unemployed, artisans, traders, office based and a small proportion of professionals. There has been an increase in people involved in the informal sector, both men and women, since the Structural Adjustment Programme.

The government does not regulate this sector even through the informal activities are a substantial and growing part of the national economy and are integrally related to the "formal" sector. Nevertheless, a report by the World Bank (1993) indicated that urban people are about twice as well-off as rural people, even when the difference in rural compared to urban family composition is taken into account. Households living in Dar es Salaam have an estimated per capita expenditure that is approximately 1.5 times higher than other urban areas, and 2.3 times higher than rural areas of Tanzania[4]. But for women, the difference between city and village is less significant, in the sense that both rural and urban women are responsible for generating and administrating their own income (Brand, 2001:302).

The economic crisis and the Structural Adjustment Programme (SAP) had a huge impact on the private and public sector. The incomes of earners in urban areas have been particularly hard hit. There are now more household members contributing to incomes at very low returns compared to earlier periods, when more members may have been in school or retired (Gibbon and Raikes, 1995:72-77). Many households from the low-income areas of Dar es Salaam are under severe stress. Competition to survive economically has become more intense. Most of the population is dependent on the cash economy for its livelihood.

---

[3] See the Adult Mortality Morbidity Project's (AMMP) report, *Policy Implications of Adult Morbidity and Mortality,* 1993:205-210. Occupational categories used by AMMP are the following. For example, skilled manual workers category includes: factory workers, mechanic, plumber, electrician, painter, welder, machine operator, carpenter, dressmaker, etc. The professional workers category encompasses librarian, veterinary, surgeon, clergy, nurse, pharmacist, teacher, radiotherapist, medical assistant, accountants and so on. What is usually called the "informal sector" is inserted in the category not manual - not office worker.

[4] The Participatory Poverty Assessment mentioned that the Human Resources Development study, conducted in 1993, found that income distribution was quite uneven in Tanzania: the average adult equivalent expenditure of the richest quintile was more than six times greater than that of the poorest quintile. Inequalities between rural and urban areas were also considerable: while on an average, rural Tanzanians spent the equivalent of USD 193, their counterparts living in Dar es Salaam spent an average of USD 587 (Narayan, 1997:7).

An increasing number of people in the urban area are unable to find secure jobs.

In response to this situation, a vast array of individual and household strategies has emerged to provide a basic livelihood in the city. These strategies are generally related to the provision of services linked to daily survival.

Development processes have accelerated changes in the social security system, which traditionally protected members from social and economic distress. Urban people have evolved or revived informal security systems such as self-help groups. Tungaraza (1994) quoted that solidarity groups or informal social security networks, which are based on tribal lines and friendships, manifest themselves in many forms. They usually support and solicit contributions from members for events such as illness, death or burial arrangements; acting as charitable associations in securing employment and accommodation for new migrants. Money exchange networks and networks to pool labour, following the principle of reciprocity, are other forms of informal security systems operating in urban areas. Nevertheless, Tungaraza has noted that these groups provide only short-term support to members and in most cases the support is not adequate (ibid). The degree of social differentiation remains great and the population of Dar es Salaam lives in highly variable conditions.

A pluralistic culture

As noted by De Rosnay, (1975:210), the city generally acts as a catalyst to accelerate the development of philosophical and religious ideas, of sciences and technology, and of arts and political concepts. The interrelation between people and the environment is inseparable. People insert themselves into a certain milieu that influences them, just as they influence the milieu through their actions. Numerous changes are visible in Dar es Salaam. These may indicate the passage from a lineage society, characterised by kinship relationships, to a society with a more modern economic style.

Dar es Salaam, as many other African cities, is characterised by its heterogeneity, complexity, inequalities and the emergence of a "modern" society. It is a more open system in which people's behaviours are not foreseeable, and not based solely on the reproduction of the system itself. Flexibility and adaptability replace rigidity and stability. The static vision is slowly moving.

Dar es Salaam offers a multitude of choices. For example, employers can choose between a wide range of specialities and talents; meanwhile employees and consumers have access to more options, jobs, or types of goods or services. It is also a city that fosters communication, as an increasing number of people have greater access to information and technology. The mix of individuals, situations and interests brings changes in social relations and increases the probability of mutual fertilisation and mobility of ideas. In the urban area, confrontation with various groups has affected the perspectives of residents and new migrants on such diverse issues as healthcare, religious practice and gender identity. Associations are made through networks across the city, rather than with those with whom one shares residential space. The activities of women may include greater participation in the paid workforce, taking them away from home during the day.

In general, rural Tanzanians are used to direct and personalised relations. It is a form of encounter that cannot always be found in Dar es Salaam. Nevertheless, in spite of the appearance of indirect relations prevailing in the city, people still incline towards direct relations. Political and economic activities are conducted through family connections, friendship, kinship and personal contacts more than through formal institutions, legal warranties or contracts. It is a kind of manipulation of institutions for personal profit. Daily difficulties force people to turn to direct relations. Most people find difficulty with the non-personification of relationships. For example, people complain about the social distance that is present between them and health staff during consultations at the dispensary (Cloutier, 1996 and Cloutier and Bisanda, 1998).

Women in the city

In Tanzania, as in many African countries, an increasing number of women are moving to the city. Nowadays, they come alone as well as with their spouses. Talking about the 1950s, Coquery-Vidrovitch noted that in Tanzania:

The percentage of independent women (divorced, widowed or others), who moved to Dar es Salaam, rose from 13% in 1950 to 33% twenty years later. Most of them were between 16 and 24 years of age. Only one fourth of the women from 15 and 54 years were considered active (1994: 214).

Most women were searching for economic autonomy through independent activity or salaried work. Access to education apparently facilitated this step. As Geiger (1997) mentioned, by the mid-1950s, there was a tiny minority of Christian-educated women, including women with sufficient educational training to be employed in teaching, hospital work or social services in the city. Indeed, during the colonial period, the city was a place "where African men did or did not belong, depending on colonial labour requirements, and where African women were shadow figures—anomalous creatures inhabiting invisible spaces in a male domain" (Geiger, 1997:22).

Thus in Tanzania, the number of girls who were educated doubled between 1960 and 1970. Thirty percent of educated migrant women came to town in search of work whereas only 4 percent of illiterate women did so. After independence, the rate of rural-urban migration among women increased even more than among men, partly because of the removal of colonial barriers to African women settling in the city (TGNP, 1993:50). Thus, as shown by Campbell (2000:26), women migrated to the city in increasing numbers in search of income, and freedom from the constraints of rural society and traditional marriage.

In 1963, Leslie wrote that:

An independent woman had many advantages in town, both financial and otherwise, and many are loathe giving up this independence for a formal marriage. This independence has raised the status, or at least the bargaining position, of women in town. It cannot be attributed wholly to a disparity between the sexes, for the women are 42% of the whole. But it may be an echo of a formerly greater disparity.

Women's improved access to education enabled them to take advantage of increased employment opportunities in the formal and informal sectors of the urban economy. In the early years urban women were either dependent or had to find employment in prostitution, beer brewing or small trade (Campbell, 2000: 25-26)). Despite widespread urban poverty and poor living conditions, urban marriage/house-holding was well established in Dar es Salaam, irrespective of divorce rates of 30-77 percent in the late 1950s (Leslie, 1963:223). The 1948 census is the first to provide data on the large number of children in town, who constituted 23 percent of the total urban population (Tanganyika, 1953:19 in Campbell, 2000:26)[5]. Marital instability increased as urban women exercised control over their own production and earnings, and hence over their lives. Geiger suggested the following tentative conclusions related to the lives of Dar es Salaam's female population:

> *Generally speaking, the range and flexibility of marital and other sexual relationships in Dar es Salaam appears to have offered all but the youngest adult women more choice and self-control in both sexual and reproductive matters than rural women were likely to experience, a fact deplored by colonial authorities, religious leaders, and some African men. In addition, women in Dar es Salaam had opportunities for earning independent incomes that were largely unavailable in rural areas. For these reasons, unmarried urban women, and even married urban women whose "behaviours" seemed "suspect" were, for all practical purposes, assumed to be prostitutes unless proven otherwise—a factor that had important implications for the women's national mobilizing in the 1950s.*
>
> *There were however stark differences[6] between Muslim or Swahili women and women migrants to the city who lacked*

[5] Tanganyika, African Population of Tanganyika, East African Statistical Department, Geographical and Tribal Studies, 1948, Government printer, Dar es Salaam, 1953.

[6] Leslie suggested that by the 1950s, the desire not to "mix freely" was more an expression of Christian separatism and attitudes towards "coastal women" than a reflection of Muslim-initiated discrimination. Christians (as late as 1957, the latter constituted just 13.7 percent of Dar es Salaam males and 10 percent of females) held themselves apart as they had the feeling of being different (due to a higher level of education, different conceptions of divorce and taboos, and a sense of morality that dictated attitudes and behaviours). Indeed, as mentioned by Geiger (1997:42-44), the Western-educated female population were not among the early nationalist activists and it is related to their triple isolation: by their little number, their religion and their unusual level of education. Campbell quoted that "Islamic influence was considerable in all areas of life e.g. in terms of dress, in the construction of mosques (which grew from 8 in 1880 to 50 by 1970), in music, dance and architecture; and of course in terms of population" (Campbell, 2000:29-30). Leslie (1963:213) estimated that 86 percent of men and 90 percent of women were professing Islam.

education and may or may not have been Christian, and the small minority of educated women, mostly young and Christian. These differences separated women from each other and the educated minority from the nationalist movement (1997:38).

The Tanzania Gender Networking Programme (TGNP) showed there was a sharp rise in female urban migration during the 1970s, which was a period of rapid expansion in education and employment opportunities in urbanised areas. The percentage growth in female urbanisation was 12.6 percent, compared to 3.6 percent for men at the same time. The urbanisation rate dropped in 1980s for both men and women to 1.6 percent and 2 percent respectively, although the women's rate remained higher than the men's (1993:50). Finally, the census of 1988 shows an approximately equal number of men and women living in Dar es Salaam. The region of Dar es Salaam is occupied by 708,149 men and 636,969 women over the age of 25 (DUHP, 1996).

Women's access to work

Much of what Leslie wrote about the availability of work in Dar es Salaam in 1963 is still relevant in 2001. For example, he noted that employment and unemployment were both relative terms:

The ease with which a man can live without working a full month has diluted labour to a significant extent. This ease is due partly to the income derivable from small trade and partly to the willingness of any man to support a relative when he has no income, sometimes for several months. It is so easy to live in town without a regular job or even without a job at all, with the help of relatives, that many stay longer than they should (1963: 5-10).

In April 1957 a new law for a statutory minimum[7] wage came into

[7] Indeed, pay equity is a universal problem that still persists nowadays and almost everywhere. For example, in 1965, in Quebec, in most big bakeries, men were paid CAD 1.50 per hour while women were paid CAD 1.10. In Canada, a National Committee on Pay Equity was founded in 1979. It is a national membership coalition of over 80 organisations, including labour unions, women's and civil rights organisations, religious, professional, educational and legal associations, commissions on women, state and local pay equity coalitions and individual women and men working to eliminate sex-and-race-based wage discrimination and to achieve pay equity (http://www.feminist.com/fairpay/).

force. The minimum laid down for a man was 42 cents an hour if no food, fuel or living quarters were provided—roughly the equivalent of a wage of Tanzanian Shillings 80-85 per month (Leslie, 1963: 125). However, under this law women were allowed a minimum salary of only 32 cents per hour. After Independence in 1962 the Tanzanian State removed this discrimination.

The effect of the minimum wage in raising wages was small. Most of the population had little prospect of advancement to a better-paid job as they lacked education, or technical and professional skills. Tanzanian women were particularly disadvantaged because of their low social level[8]. Few among them were involved in administration, factory work or in the paid workforce. According to Leslie:

> *A wife in town is a hostage to financial misfortune and is not prepared to put up with as much in bad times as a single man. There are, however, many lucrative trades open to women (1963:14).*

Girls were recruited at elementary level for factory work. They were preferred to men because they were seen as hardworking, patient and less problematic[9]. Nevertheless, this employment situation was precarious, and once mechanisation started, men replaced them. Furthermore, laws intended to protect women at work (maternity leave, 1975) had a perverse effect, provoking an immediate halt to women's recruitment. Coquery-Vidrovitch noted that:

> *The Kibo matches factory, which used to employ 90% of women before 1969, reduced its female staff to 30%, then to 20% in 1976, in spite of the doubling of its workforce. The evolution was more radical at the coffee factory in Moshi, where mechanised processes, put in place in 1972, led to the discharge of the entire female staff (800 salaried women).*

---

[8] Leslie estimated that women were among the less educated people in Dar es Salaam. He wrote: "almost half of all males over the age of 6 are entirely without education; their companions, of whom no less than 82% are entirely uneducated, and only 1% educated to beyond Standard 4" (1963:130).

[9] One could note that many private sector employers still have this attitude towards women workers. For instance, when the authorities of the Dar es Salaam City Commission decided to clean the city, they hired women for sweeping the streets. Men were seen as lazy and many in the authorities said that men would spend their time doing nothing. Today, women are seen throughout the city, sweeping at any time of the day or night.

According to Obrist van Eeuwijk:

> *The emphasis on men as wage-earners during the colonial times seems to have reinforced local models of gender hierarchy, rooted in cultural and religious practice (2000:62).*

In Tanzania, the percentage of active women in productive work and in informal activities in 1980 was only 21 percent, compared to 80 percent of men. For example, there were only one hundred women selling foodstuffs compared to 3000 men (Coquery-Vidrovitch, 1994:172). It seems that a woman's identity as a wife was mainly grounded in her responsibilities as a homemaker, and her obligation to depend on her husband (Idem).

The economic crisis of the 1980s brought a change in the economy, which had an effect on gender relations. During the economic crisis, it became increasingly difficult for men to provide for the whole household (Tripp, 1992). In 1976, husbands' salaries constituted approximately 77 percent of the total household income, and in 1988, only 10 percent. This dramatic reversal forced housewives to take up income-generating activities. The proportion of women pursuing such activities rose from 7 percent in 1971 to 66 percent in 1988 (Obrist van Eeuwijk, 2000:62). According to the World Bank's report of 1993:

- *Urban incomes declined between 1969 and 1976. The 1969 Household Budget Survey found an urban per capita income of Tsh 74, 980; while the 1976/77 Household Budget Survey found an urban per capita income of Tsh 23, 890.*

- *Urban incomes increased substantially between 1976 and 1991 and, by the end of the period, urban per capita income had reached Tsh 100, 222.*

According to the 1988 population census, in the whole of Tanzania, some 12.2 million people over 15 years of age were classed as economically active; 53 percent of whom were women. However, only 3 percent of those were employed in the formal sector, compared to 10 percent of the men. In urban areas, some occupations such as administrators, professionals and services have expanded, providing more prestigious and higher-paying work for both women and men.

Nevertheless most women in urban areas work in the clerical, service and small-scale trade. Women represent 39 percent of all service employees, 45 percent of clerks, and 14 percent of administrators and managers. In the formal sector, women are concentrated in traditionally female occupations such as nursing, teaching, and clerical and sales work. They are found at the bottom of the occupational ladder with lower wages and fewer opportunities for on-the-job training and advancement. Women have been denied equal entry into wage employment even in occupations universally recognised as female work. Women are employed for years on a casual or temporary basis, sometimes illegally. Illegal workers are more vulnerable to sexual harassment; men may take advantage of their de facto dominant power to demand sexual services in exchange for a job, a promotion or a positive evaluation of work performance.

The most common informal sector activities engaged in by women in the low-income bracket are home beer manufacturing (brewing) and sale; small trade; food preparation and sale; domestic labour; bar work in local clubs and pubs; and prostitution. Tailoring and fabric manufacture, hair salons, kiosks, and export and consultant businesses expanded in the 1990s, especially for middle and upper income levels (TGNP, 1993).

In the informal as well as in the formal sector, a growing polarisation exists between rich and poor women. Many women are hired as casual workers and others make a minimal living in self-employment. Some women entrepreneurs have been able to invest in successful commercial ventures in hotels, commercial farming, clothes manufacturing and fashion design. However, the working conditions for women engaged in the informal sector remain poor—with long working hours, unsafe and unsanitary conditions, no worker benefits or job security for the wage employed, fluctuating incomes for the self-employed and constant harassment from the city police and other authorities.

Women's access to information and communication is limited by social and cultural norms which militate against their speaking up in public, and by customs which do not favour their travelling or being away from home. Furthermore, their contribution to the economy is undervalued because a great deal of their time and work goes into activities which are not assigned a cash value and therefore are not measured by the statisticians as "economic" activity (UNICEF, 1990:49).

Gender relations and traditions in the urban area

Both women and men are affected by socio-economic processes. Are gender relations reconfigured in the urban setting?

The following story is a good example of current gender relations in Dar es Salaam (2001).

John Mapunda[10] is only 35 years old. He has been working as a computer technician in a private firm for several years. He has been married for eleven years and has two children. His wife is involved in "business" activities; she sells food and other goods. John has been feeling bad for the past couple of days after he beat his wife. He decides to go to church to talk to a counsellor, to tell his story and get some advice.

It so happened that a few weeks ago his wife told him that she had collected the money to pay their children's school fees. As school was starting soon, she wanted to be sure that their places would be confirmed for the coming year. Hearing this, John felt bad because it was the husband's job to provide for such expenses. But as he had not saved the money, he told his wife to give him the money she had saved, so that he could go to the school and pay the fees.

However, he met some friends on the way and went to a bar with them instead. He spent the evening there, drinking and joking with his friends. He came back home late and very tired. A few days later, his wife asked him for the receipt confirming that the school fees had been paid. He was forced to tell her that he never reached the school and that he had no money left. She became angry with him and shouted, saying that she had suffered in order to save the money for the school

[10] Fictional name.

fees and did not know how she would get more money. Then he beat her.

While telling his story and answering the counsellor's questions, he informed him that he was working as a computer specialist, spending more than Tanzanian Shillings[11] 10,000 every day on drinking with his friends. It was not possible for him to have only one or two beers because then he would look stupid in front of them. Oh yes! He felt he was being responsible towards his family, as he was paying for his brothers' education and giving money on a regular basis to his parents. He said it was his wife's job to satisfy the needs of their children and family.

He had beaten her because she shouted at him. As a wife she was supposed to comply with his wishes. She had no right to tell her husband what to do. He had just acted as a man is supposed to do. He was only exercising his rights. When asked by the counsellor why he was living with the woman under such circumstances, he could only answer, "But we are married!"

This story is a good illustration of most Tanzanian men's attitude. It reveals the structure of gender relations through the sexual division of labour, sexual power relations, and the social construction of femininity and masculinity. To a Tanzanian man, strength, prestige and power are the natural characteristics of masculinity. Authority, honour and a position in the family as the main decision maker are among the primary attributes of a real man.

By contrast, Tanzanian society considers femininity to be synonymous with fearfulness, weakness and dependency. Women are seen as supportive, nurturing, acquiescent, subordinate and familial. A woman is perceived as incapable of making a decision; she cannot be a political actor and authority figure. Men and women are thought to have very different traits, temperaments, characters, outlooks, opinions and abilities; even completely different personality structures. Having a binary conception of masculinity and femininity asserts that biology is the order of the game.

[11] Tanzanian Shillings 10,000 is roughly USD 10.

Do the men and women of Dar es Salaam still preserve such ideals, and to what extent does their behaviour today reflect elements of Tanzanian tradition? For John Mapunda and most men in Dar es Salaam, the answer is clear. Tradition still dictates people's behaviour. A woman must obey her husband and undertake the daily duties that have always been assigned to women. This is justified by their biological constitution. Gender roles are clear.

At the same time, John's behaviour also testifies to some changes in gender roles. Ties between spouses are weak and marriage is for no other purpose than to ensure economic security; as men want to benefit from the advantages of the married status, conferred by the social organisation. Finally, John's wife's behaviour also illustrates a new aspect of urban life - women's involvement in economic and productive activities, in order to satisfy their basic needs as well as those of their children.

A review of the literature suggests that Tanzanian gender relations are still characterised by:

- *Power relations*
  These are dominated by the leading position of men in social life, which is based on an ideology of male supremacy. The patriarchal system legitimates the dominance of men and the subordination of women. This ideology is established through the correspondence between a cultural ideal and an institutional framework, which is more collective than individual. A kinship system that classifies and establishes status gives men the authority to organise the lives of women, who then become powerless and subordinated. The authority of men over women leads to the cultural dominance of men in society as a whole. At a global, macro or local/micro level, women are subservient to men. Under patriarchy, men gain honour, prestige and the right to command, while they also acquire material benefits through better salaries, and are more likely to hold state, lineage or clan power. Men's social power, as identified by Connell (1987:107), is made apparent through:

    - Force.
    - The ability to impose a definition of the situation.
    - The possibility to set the terms in which events are understood and issues discussed.

- The capacity to formulate ideals and define morality.
- The power to assert hegemony.

- *Subordination of women*
  Everyday material practices force women to acknowledge the legitimacy of male power and its exercise at the macro and micro level. Men's authority is confirmed by a set of practices that include:

  - Political and cultural exclusion, which means no involvement of women in the decision-making process at any level—government, lineage or family.
  - The depiction of women mainly as mothers, which reproduces the social structure through relationships of exploitation, and constructs femininity as entailing dependence and fearfulness.
  - Legal violence through repudiation, divorce, inheritance and levirate practices.
  - Violence at work and on the streets, manifested though rape and sexual harassment.
  - Economic discrimination (less ownership by women, little control over basic resources, inadequate access to formal work).

- *Sexual division of labour*
  Social obligations and duties are assigned through the sexual division of labour. This is based on the idea that men are leaders and breadwinners; women are assigned to biological and social reproduction. This places a double burden on working women, who usually do not have control over the educational, cultural, political, material and economic resources that would allow them to make more money or have access to decision making and planning.

  The sexual division of labour becomes a social rule, a powerful system of social constraints, supported by different mechanisms. For example, when men and women are trained differentially, discriminatory employment becomes rational from the employer's point of view. Women predominate in unpaid or cheap labour in the household economy, low-paid labour in offices, farms, factories and in self-employment. Generally, men are paid more than women, even when both are doing similar work. The sexual division of labour also involves the design of the work. For example, domestic work is done by women; they rarely benefit from new technology that could make domestic labour less time-consuming or dangerous.

The perpetuation of patriarchy in the workplace helps to maintain the social order at the level of the family and community, without disrupting the structure of power relations. As men occupy posts higher in the hierarchy, they resist any attempts by women to alter their situation. The sexual division of labour is a part of a larger pattern, a gender-structured system of production, consumption and distribution (Connell, 1987:103). Gender divisions are deep-seated features of production itself—central to domestic and industrialised work, central to capitalism and the lineage system.

- *Violence*
  To maintain their dominance, men use violence. This means any type of brutal behaviour directed at women and girls because of their sex.

  Equity Tanzania[12], an NGO dealing with human rights, defined violence against women as:

  > *Any act of gender-based violence that results in, or is likely to result in physical, sexual or psychological harm or suffering to women including threats of such acts as coercion or arbitrary deprivation of liberty, whether occurring in public or private life.*

[12] This comes from an interview that the Director of Equity, Tanzania gave to the Guardian, a Tanzanian daily, on June 8, 2001. She was discussing the Sexual Offences Special Provision Act (SOSPA) that was enacted by the Parliament in 1998 in order to fight violence against women and children in Tanzania. The law resulted from efforts made by the Government to reform the sexual offences law in the country. Such an initiative was prompted by an increase in the number of cases of abuse and violence against children and women. In fact, such legal acts aim to criminalise some acts and conducts regarding sexual offences and gender crimes, with the ultimate goal of enacting national endeavours to protect women and children's rights. For example, a minimum sentence of 30 years has been introduced for rape. Nevertheless, as the Director of the NGO commented, "Three years after its enactment, the law is still not applied effectively. As a result, women and children have continued to be subjected to high levels of sexual and domestic violence."

Men thus use symbolic, physical, sexual, mental and/or psychological violence with the aim of intimidating women or denying them human dignity, sexual self-determination, and physical or mental integrity. They utilise different means such as rape, sexual harassment, domestic assault and murder, and verbal and physical assaults against women. As a consequence, women may live in fear. These behaviours are sustained by an ideology of supremacy that authorises men to exert control over women. Most men feel entirely justified in using violence as an exercise of their rights.

Walby mentioned that:

The system of patriarchy is composed of several interrelated structures. Within each of these structures specific patriarchal practices can be identified which are less deeply sedimented. Structures are emergent properties of practices. Any specific empirical instance will embody the effects, not only of patriarchal structures, but also of capitalism and racism (1996:24-25).

The six structures are:

1. Patriarchal relations in household work: women's household labour is expropriated by their husbands, fathers or cohabiters. The woman receives her maintenance in exchange for her labour.
2. Patriarchal relations in paid work: women are excluded from the better forms of work. This situation segregates them in worse jobs which are deemed less skilled.
3. Patriarchal state: it is also capitalist and racist. It has a systemic bias towards patriarchal interests in its policies and actions.
4. Male violence: it takes individual and diverse forms. Women experience this behaviour, generating fear which has restrictive effects upon the actions of most women. The lack of state intervention is supporting this kind of behaviour.
5. Patriarchal relations in sexuality: men are viewed as the only ones to have a choice in decision as women are seen as sexual objects, be it also for pornography or prostitution.

6. Patriarchal relations in cultural institutions: a set of institutions such as religion, education and media create a representation of women within a patriarchal gaze.

What is changing in the city?

Since the 1980s, the Tanzanian Government and development agencies have taken various initiatives towards ameliorating the situation of women. Nevertheless, gender inequality and women's oppression persists and is experienced in two ways—domestic responsibilities have been redefined, and women are forced to generate income.

Most women thus find themselves in a double bind. As demonstrated by the study of Obrist van Eeuwijk in Dar es Salaam, if a woman does not pursue an income-generating activity, her main constraint is money. But if she is involved in productive work, her main constraint is time and energy. In both cases women are unable to provide proper care in a broad sense, including food provision, cleaning, childcare or care for the sick (2000:181).

Margrethe Silberschmidt (1995) included among social changes, the emergence of new households forms, organised increasingly around a female head of household; a process which is fraught with tensions and negotiations over cohabitation arrangements and obligations (Campbell, Mwami and Ntukula, 1995:224-225). Men seem particularly hard hit by the situation. It leads to changes in both the form and content of the marriage contract. Couples increasingly tend to live together in informal unions.

Many women are left as sole supporters of their families, with men withdrawing from their responsibilities (Mbilinyi, 1994:34-35) and avoiding the claims of children (Creighton and Omari, 1995: 24). In this context, as mentioned by Lugalla (1990) and by most participants in the research, men rely on drinking relationships with other men; with drinking groups often taking precedence over marital relationships and obligations. Sexual bargaining is becoming more instrumental than earlier; men find prostitutes cheaper than "permanent girl friends" (Lugalla, 1990:452-453). As a result women manipulate their various relationships in order to cope. The lack of mutual respect and trust between sexes has serious consequences in the face of the spread of sexually transmitted diseases. Conversely, men with resources are more willing to exploit this situation to their advantage. Here the increase is in cohabitation, as there are signs of men trying to appropriate and control women's sexuality (Creighton and Omari, 1995). Moreover, the reproductive priorities of men will generally prevail over those of women (Omari, 1995).

Women's increased involvement in productive work has positive and negative effects, as described by Koda in 1995. While carrying out fieldwork in Kenya and Tanzania, Raikes (1989:457) noticed that the combination of increasingly heavy workloads and the stress of nurturing and feeding households has contributed to the deterioration in women's health. The quality of life is worsening for many women who have to cope with alcoholism, violence and poverty problems, the high rates of male drunkenness and domestic violence.

Among the positive effects of women's enlarged participation in market-oriented activities, the Tanzania Gender Networking Programme (1993) noted their increased access to independent cash incomes and control over economic resources. As most households and communities cannot survive without women's incomes, this could shift the balance of power in families, and give women greater negotiating strength. The result could be better sharing in decision making and increased control over resources, in spite of continued gender discrimination in the allocation of credit and other productive resources.

Some women have been empowered within their personal and public lives, individually and collectively; partly by acquiring more cash income and economic power, but also by greater exposure to the money economy, urban society and different cultures, which has led to an expanding gender/class consciousness and more networking. Women like these have succeeded in raising the awareness of policy makers in government and donor agencies of their special needs. This has led to women's credit and other support programmes (TGNP, 1993:126).

Among the negative aspects, many men have abdicated their family responsibilities, forcing housewives to take up an income-generating activity and use their income for family needs that men refuse to provide for. As a result, gender and family conflicts have grown. Old forms of marriage and family no longer provide women or men with the kind of economic security and social sustenance they once did. In the workplace, sexual harassment is becoming a significant problem, creating a stressful work environment and threatening women's job opportunities or chances for promotion (TGNP, 1993:127).

CHAPTER 2

THE LABOUR MARKET: WHAT WOMEN AND MEN ARE DOING IN DAR ES SALAAM

A few years ago, Joan[1], the wife of John Mapunda, decided to look for a job. Immediately after her marriage, her husband had made her resign from her work on the grounds that she should stay at home and as a married woman, take care of the house, the children and her husband's relatives. She complained that she was no longer able to help her own parents.

Joan soon realised that she was dependent on her husband for everything, even though his salary could not meet all the needs of their family, let alone her personal needs. She said, "I forced him to allow me to have a job. He accepted my return to work but refused to let me look for an office job. He said it was not safe for a woman to work in any office. He even offered to give me the necessary capital to start my own business."

Joan agrees with her husband's beliefs. In her search for a job she met many different managers. Most of them were men, and many offered her a nice job in exchange for her "beautiful and natural talents." One director even told her that she was losing money by working in an office for a low pay: she had something better to offer. After propositions and the exchange of harsh words in several offices, Joan recognised a pattern. She decided that it would be better for her to look for something in a different environment. The situation reminded her of when she was at school, where she had also refused many offers from teachers. She thought that these "love affairs" in offices and at school were responsible for spreading HIV and AIDS in the young population.
She decided to become independent and started a small business selling food and handicrafts. As she said, "It was the only thing I could do, besides my secretarial job."

[1] Names have been changed to protect identities.

At first her husband was not supportive, claiming that their children's discipline and behaviour were deteriorating because she was neglecting her domestic duties. But he decided to give her the capital for starting an income-generating activity. As Joan was discouraged by the rate of interest levied by credit associations for women, she accepted her husband's offer.

She sold second-hand clothes and did well. Soon she earned enough money to start another business. From then on, she had the full support of her husband. He realised that what she was doing was good for the family as a whole.

Today, Joan is able to send her children to private international schools, and has built a house for her parents. But she also has many more responsibilities. According to her, "If you have money, your problems also increase. Now I have a lot of responsibility towards my family."

She says she really enjoys what she is doing, but there are still many impediments for a woman who wants to be productive in the same way. Women are constantly harassed while at work. Each time she has to renew her business license, the health officers of the municipality visit her and demand bribes or sexually harass her. She continues to work hard because she wants her children to develop skills that give them access to greater opportunities and a good life.

The story of Joan Mapunda shows the numerous socio-cultural and socio-economic constraints on women's promotion. The development of women is dependent not only on improved economic conditions: it requires changes in personal and public life as well. Many social prejudices contribute to the marginalisation of women. These handicaps include the low level of education and educational stereotyping, lack of information, poor social status, lack of experience in political and economic fields, poor self-confidence, an absence of social recognition, a socialisation process that disadvantages girls from birth, and the many constraints on their mobility that prevent them from conducting activities outside the house.

These elements are discussed in this chapter in the light of findings from interviews with men and women in Dar es Salaam. We describe the general characteristics of our sample group, and then cover women's involvement in productive activities and related labour market topics.

The men and women in this study

Sixty-eight women and twenty-two men from different parts of Dar es Salaam participated in semi-structured interviews. A further five interviews were carried out in the village of Tarime, Mara region, with older men aged around 70, to examine more deeply the use of tradition by men to maintain their position of domination in society as a whole[2].

Men who participated in the interviews were not related to the women informants in the study. All participants volunteered to be interviewed.

Table 2: Age of participants

Age (years)	*Women*	*Men*
20-29	16	-
30-39	29	5
40-49	18	8
50-59	4	7
60-69	1	1
70+	-	6
Total	68	27

Life expectancy at birth in Tanzania is 50 years for women and 49 years for men. These numbers come from the most recent population census conducted in 1988. Recent projections done by the Ministry of Health of Tanzania, the World Health Organisation and UNAIDS are more pessimistic, as life expectancy is expected to fall under the influence of the AIDS pandemic.

Of the 16 women in their twenties, 11 attended secondary school (8 up to Form IV, 3 up to Form II). Of the 29 women in their thirties, 13

[2] The interviews were conducted by an assistant researcher who originated from this area. He interviewed some members of his family and a few residents of the village.

went to primary school, 11 to secondary school, 3 obtained a college diploma, and 2 finished university. Of the women in their forties, 1 was illiterate, 6 went to primary school, 10 to secondary school and only 1 had a university degree. It reflects the female share in the general population[3]. As mentioned by Omari and Mbilinyi (2000:296-297), at the primary school level, the enrolment of girls is almost 50 percent. At the secondary level, the enrolment of girls decreases and is less than that of boys. In fact, the presence of girls decreases as we go up the education ladder, from about 50 percent at primary school to about 25 percent at higher secondary level. In technical schools their participation is even lower than this. According to TGNP's report of 1993:

> *There was a steady decline of 2% in the Dar es Salaam Technical College between 1981/82 and 1990/91. Female students are most affected, with a drop of 5% compared to men, with a drop of 0.5%. The female ratio is very low, ranging from 7 per cent in 1981/82 to a low 5 per cent in 1987/88 and 4.5 per cent in 1990/91 (TGNP, 1993:87).*
>
> *The proportion of first year undergraduates at Dar es Salaam and Sokoine University has also remained low, and also decreased. The growth rate has been twice as high for men (5.8%) compared to women (2%). Similar trends occur in post-graduate level at the University of Dar es Salaam (idem).*

Most women were less than 40 years old; only five were over 50. Among them were four who identified themselves as

---

[3] UNESCO's 1998 World Education Report shows that women in Sub-Saharan Africa remain one of the least educated groups in the world. Female illiteracy rates do indeed reach alarming levels in countries like Benin, Burkina Faso, Mali, Gambia, Côte d'Ivoire, Liberia and Niger, all of which have above 70 percent adult female illiteracy rates. Egbo (2000) noticed that while many of the countries have achieved near gender parity at the primary school, the gender gap becomes wider as one moves up the educational hierarchy, since women have even less access to tertiary education, a common prerequisite for participation in social policy formulation within the African context. In spite of numerous literacy campaigns, which in some cases doubled and even quadrupled the enrolment of girls in schools, gender-based inequality persists and women remain substantially less educated than men in the region, especially for reasons related to historical background, a patriarchal and socio-cultural bias, a bias in the type and quality of education, and economic factors. Debates about literacy are dichotomized ; the bulk of the debates centre around the views of those who still believe that literacy can change the lives of women in the region and those who query the efficacy of literacy as a transformative tool, as educational expansions have not done much to improve the status and social conditions of women (Egbo, 2000:4-7, 79-85).

businesswomen, including a woman of 52, who was a lawyer. Twenty men were less than 50 years old. The five older men were from the village of Tarime.

Three of the five women, aged over 50, had attended secondary school. Only one reached Form IV. One woman, born in Dar es Salaam, declared herself to be illiterate. Three had been living in the city for more than 30 years and had moved there for family reasons (to follow their husbands, to help a sister). The youngest resident had been there for 10 years; she too had followed her husband.

Of the men in the sample, it seems that the older ones had few opportunities to attend school. Only one man in his thirties and two in their forties had a university degree. Five men over 50 years had attended primary school while no man over 70 had attended secondary school. They were all retired and had worked as farmers.

Table 3: Religion

Religion	*Women*	*Men*
Christian	37	11
Muslim	31	11
Other	-	-
Total	68	22

Of the women participants, 31 identified themselves as Muslim and 37 as Christian. Men presented an equal number of Muslims and Christians. It could be representative of the general population, which is composed of one third of Christians, one third of Muslims and one third of other religions. However, religion does not seem to be a representative indicator for explaining men's attitudes and behaviours[4]. Across interviews, it became evident that most men, be they Christian or Muslim, all express a similar way of thinking and acting towards women's issues. Men's reference to "tradition" legitimises their situation of authority, domination and violence towards women, which is derived from social prescriptions originating from a patriarchal society. Men informants see women as a group that is placed under their undisputed authority. Most men

[4] The reference to religion is used in case of quotations for illustrating men's similar patterns of thinking.

believe they naturally benefit from legitimate authority in household, which can be absolute according to informants. In fact, men testify about ancestral practices based on natural data, perceived as objective. They negate the social construction of gender relations. Of course, religion reinforces this process but it enters into contradiction with urbanisation, cash economy and the new laws.

However, for women, religion seems to be a more important indicator. Most mention it as an impediment for their emancipation. Men use it as a constant reference to ensure their domination over women.

The majority of informants originate from other areas of Tanzania, and their residence time in Dar es Salaam varies:

Table 4: Residence time in Dar es Salaam

Residence time (years)	*Number of women*	*Number of men*
1-10	6	10
10-20	20	5
20-30	22	3
30-40	6	2
40-50	1	-
Born in Dar es Salaam	13	2
Total	68	22

Most women informants have lived in Dar es Salaam for more than 10 or even 20 years. By contrast close to half the male participants have lived in the city for less than 10 years. While 10 women were born in Dar es Salaam, only 1 man grew up there.

Both men and women were attracted by the prospect of life in the city. They perceived Dar es Salaam as a place offering many opportunities for work. Most commonly, they left the countryside because they could not achieve a decent standard of living there. However, others migrated to the city because they were attracted by a new life and wanted to live independently.

Table 5: Reasons for moving to Dar es Salaam

Reason	*Women*	*Men*
To follow spouse	20	-
Born in Dar es Salaam	13	2
To follow relatives	11	-
For further studies	11	1
To take up a job	5	-
To find employment	5	11
Job transfer	-	5
To live with/help/visit relatives	3	1
For business	-	1
For a medical check-up	-	1
Total	68	22

It appears that the majority of women migrate to the city for family reasons. However, women are also attracted to Dar es Salaam because they believe that the city offers better work opportunities.

By contrast, most men came with the aim of finding employment. This corresponds to the number of men who have lived in the city for less than 10 years. It seems that most arrived alone, without their families.

Table 6: Women and men's social status

Status	*Women*	*Men*
Cohabiting	7	2
Divorced	7	2
Married	37	18
Separated	10	2
Single	-	
Widowed	7	3
Total	68	27

More than half the women and men stated that they were married. Marriage is still perceived as important. What kind of marriages are people talking about? Are they recognised by both families? Is the dowry paid? Answers to these questions are not clear. However, few declared themselves to be cohabiting. This is still seen as an insecure situation for most women, lacking the social recognition that is provided by marriage.

Of the 37 married women:

- 2 said they had been married for over 30 years
- 3 said they had been married for 25-29 years
- 4 for 20-24 years
- 6 for 15-19 years
- 10 for 10-14 years
- 6 for 5-9 years
- 4 for 1-4 years

Separated or divorced men represent 15 percent of the sample; and women represent 20 percent.

When asked, "What is your profession or occupation?" women identified themselves as follows:

- 49 said they were in business[5]
- 5 said they were professionals: 1 lawyer, 1 pharmacist, 1 consultant (sociologist), 2 teachers
- 9 said they were involved in services: 3 hairdressers, 3 tailors, 1 waitress, 1 saleswoman, 1 newspaper agent
- 5 said they were technical staff: 1 accountant, 1 clerk, 1 cook, 2 electrical technicians

It appears that most women (58) worked in the informal sector of the economy. By comparison, only 5 women had a university degree and worked as professionals in different sectors.

In terms of work, men gave the following answers:

- 11 skilled manual: 1 carpenter, 1 electrical technician, 1 driver, 1 watchman, 2 fishermen, 1 soldier, 1 clerk, 3 technicians
- 2 farmers
- 4 professionals: 1 engineer, 1 lawyer, 2 teachers
- 2 traders in the informal sector (not manual and not office workers)
- 1 student
- 7 retired: 5 men from Tarime village and 2 from Dar es Salaam.

[5] The term "business", as usually used by women informants, refers to any kind of activity related to trade and/or exchange, be it in the formal or informal sector of the economy.

The number of men who identified themselves as belonging to the skilled manual category corresponds to the number of men coming to the city to seek employment. They are also involved in the informal sector. Many men are forced to work in the informal sector of the economy, as they do not have the technical skills that would allow them to pursue other types of activities.

In addition to their identification with a specific professions or occupations, most women also said they were housewives[6]. Women working full-time found it hard to estimate time spent in the productive activity. Many women said they were taking more and more time to sell their products[7]. Most of them said they were working (inside and outside home) seven days a week[8]. The number

---

[6] In order to simplify things, terms used by informants are used as is. Indeed, most of them identify themselves as housewives.
There has been a long debate on this. Fougeyrollas-Schwebel (2000:235-241) mentioned that domestic work, domestic production, domestic economy, housework, domestic chores, care...housewife, spouse and mother...all these terms have different conceptual connotations which arouse controversies on the meaning to give to "housework." The mode of domestic production (Delphy, 1974-1998) and "housework" (Chabaud-Rychter et al., 1984) exposed the sexual division of labour prevailing between men and women: paid work is reserved for men and housework for women. However, housework is defined as the set of tasks and care of people that are done in the framework of the family—conjugal house and kinship—free work that is essentially performed by women. The mode of family production under patriarchy organises sexual relations, education of children, domestic services and the production of goods as petty trade affairs. Feminist investigation denounced the invisibility of women's work and it exclusion from the economic sphere, which does not result from the nature of their production. This service relation must be investigated in the set of kinship relations. Housework expresses a multifunctional coordination between the family and other institutions of reproduction. In any case, housework could be reduced to a simple affair, as it implies strong intellectual and emotional dimensions that Monique Haicault (1984) calls the "mental burden" ("*charge mentale*" in French).

[7] Madunagu (2002:173) noted that more and more women, close to 80% in West Africa, combine paid work with trade activity, and are in competition with men in the informal sector of small trade.

[8] Women's time resources are limited, as additional activities have to be combined with and fitted into the normal daily schedule. According to a survey done by Von Holzen on a sample of 463 women of three different areas of Dar es Salaam "employment more or less means a full-time job: 5 to 7 days a week and 7 to 10 or more hours a day. In contrast, women who were involved in small-scale projects were working for 7 days a week but as a part-time job: the daily investment in those jobs varied a lot. More women were occupied for some hours a day only, even when others worked up to 10 or more hours. Some women were doing both: they worked as employees as well running a private business/trade" (1995:17-18). Considering their household obligations, women were asked how much time they spent on shopping, cooking, fetching water, cleaning and washing. The majority of women were doing those duties themselves. They needed 2 to 3 hours a day for cooking and washing/cleaning. For shopping they needed less time: 30 minutes to 1 hour a day. The majority of interviewed women had to fetch water, which was taking the majority 30 minutes to 2 hours a day. A large number of the interviewed women (88 per cent) found time to rest about 2 to 3 hours a day, only 30 women stated that they didn't have time to rest. In general, women went to sleep around 9 or 10 p.m. and got up early between 5 and 7 a.m.

of hours spent at work each day indicates the double burden common to all working women. Many said that they rose very early in the morning and went to bed very late because there was a lot to be done: cooking, fetching water and wood or charcoal, washing, cleaning, shopping, taking care of children and/or parents and sick people, sometimes gardening and feeding animals. Few of the informants said they hired a house girl. Household tasks were often shared with, or became the responsibility of, the younger girls of the house. No woman mentioned receiving help from her husband, even when he was unemployed. Men do not seem concerned with domestic chores.

Married women gave the occupation of their husbands as:

Table 7: Husband's occupation

Category	*Number*
Business	11
Professionals (engineers, doctors)	6
Manual workers	6
Traders	5
Drivers (short and long distance)	4
Civil servants	2
Soldiers/police officers	2
Unemployed	1
Total	37

Of the informants, close to 30 per cent of the women had completed primary school. The number is almost the same for women who had completed secondary and high school. However, only two of them had a university degree, despite the fact that five had completed college level education.

Table 8: Education level

Education level	*Women*	*Men*
Illiterate	2	1
Primary school	21	11
Secondary school	22	4
High school	2	2
College	5	2
University degree	2	4
Adult education	14	3
Total	68	27

It is difficult to know whether women who have completed secondary education have been able to use their knowledge to develop further activities that could be congruent to their training. Even if women informants have more education than most women in the city, it does not necessarily mean that they have easier access to jobs or productive activities.

According to the Statistics Bureau (1992:44), only 27 percent of those on the middle or higher level of the occupational ladder are women. Most of these are working as nurses, midwives, teachers or clerks.

Women in Dar es Salaam are increasingly excluded from the formal sector of the economy. In recent years they have become more active in the production field, because the urban environment creates the constant need for cash and their husband's income alone cannot cope with the high cost of living. In view of most women's low level of education and difficult access to the formal sector, it is not easy for them to enter the modern sector of the economy. They are usually excluded from the public sector, civil service and the private sector of the formal economy, as they do not possess any specific professional or technical training. Most of the women informants had to enter the informal sector of the economy because it does not require specific professional qualifications or skills: they can reproduce knowledge acquired through normal socialisation processes.

Women's involvement in productive activities

Most of the women interviewed identified themselves as "businesswomen." In reality this is a very broad term. Women use it to indicate activities that are initiated by one woman alone, using her own capital that brings in sufficient profit or revenue to allow the activities to continue. It is very rare to see a woman engaged in only one activity at a time. Multiplying their money-producing activities is a key strategy for most women in Dar es Salaam. For example, one very successful 42-year-old Christian woman said:

I started teaching (typing, secretarial duties and office practice) in 1992 at Chang'ombe[9] Catholic Training Centre. I am also self-employed with the following businesses:

1) *Two commuter buses (daladala[10]) from which I earn Tanzanian Shillings 60,000 per day*
2) *One hair dressing salon that gives me Tanzanian Shillings 30,000 per day*
3) *One retail shop that provides Tanzanian Shillings 20,000 per day*
4) *One café with Tanzanian Shillings 30,000 per day*
5) *One class of a secretarial course with 25 students. Each student pays Tanzanian Shillings 5,000 per month as tuition.*

I can earn close to Tanzanian Shillings 150,000 a day. Working is very advantageous for me since I started the other businesses. I started selling dolls that I got from the Catholic Church and my starting capital grew from Tanzanian Shillings 10,000 to 50,000. I tried to sell second-hand clothes and also food. Later on, I had a tender to supply 100 chickens to the Silent Inn Club in Mwenge ward. My business grew rapidly and then I got another contract to supply chicken noodles to the New Africa Hotel and the Sheraton. As a result, I bought a new car, a BMW, and I initiated other businesses. Now, I can send my daughter to Nairobi for further education, as well as build a new house for my father.

At first my husband did not support me and he was so hard on me, claiming that our children's discipline and behaviour would deteriorate because I was doing something else instead of being at home all the time. Now, I have full support from my husband because he realises that what I am doing is good for our family's development.

This example is a rather special case, since most women do not earn so much money.

In general, women's production activities are more concentrated in activities and skills that they have been allowed to develop since

[9] The name of one ward of the Temeke municipality.
[10] A Kiswahili word to designate public buses.

childhood, and are related to the social roles to which they have been assigned. Thus most of them concentrate their efforts on food production and preparation. They invest in food handicraft and are *Mama Ntilie*[11], snack producers, or supply hotels and restaurants on a regular basis. They produce candies, ice cream, fruit juices and other food products. Some women own a grocery store or retail shop while others have opened a café, bar or restaurant. Most of these are "informal" activities, and few, if any, had a license from the City Council.

Other women own "poultry farms", raise pigs or goats, or sell dairy products such as milk on a daily basis. Many women work as dressmakers, as clothing is seen as a necessity. Eight of the informants own a hair salon. Some "businesswomen" invested in a local handicraft production called *makonde* carvings. Others became retail saleswomen for handicraft products in the city and others were successfully involved in the import and export of handicraft.

Many informants work as saleswomen, for example selling fabrics such as *kangas*, *vitenge*[12] or cereals, Nestlé products, charcoal, kerosene, women's garments, *mitumba*[13] or handicrafts. The majority of women sell local products, produced by intermediaries or bought from women producers who are not allowed to go out to sell their wares. They resell flour, charcoal, wood and many other things in small quantities.

The lack of diversification and the growing number of women offering the same products to the same places and at the same time has slowed down sales. The chicken industry is a good example of limits to the improvement and development of activities. Women all buy the small chickens at the same time. They are highly dependent on Interchick, which is the only producer in the region of Dar es Salaam. If the company stops production, the women must stop too.

---

[11] *Mama Ntilie* is a Kiswahili word for women who prepare and sell food on the roadside or in special cafeterias. They can be found near building sites or any place where there are workers.

[12] *Kanga* is a Kiswahili word for a piece of cloth on which a proverb is written. Women collect them, often as the only property that they can sell in 'bad days'.

Vitenge is a Kiswahili word for printed cotton fabrics locally manufactured and imported from other neighbouring countries like Congo and even from as far as, Senegal, Mali, etc. It is also known as *'pagne'* in Francophone African countries.

[13] *Mitumba*, a Kiswahili word that refers to used clothes from abroad. This is a flourishing business in the city.

Furthermore, they all try to sell their chickens or eggs at the same time, as they do not have access to storage facilities, which minimises profit. Women very often lack space, money or water, obliging them to limit their production. Sometimes, their neighbours or staff steal from them, which is only noticed when it's time to sell; the final number of chickens may be quite different from the number bought a few months before.

Only three women stated they were involved in the import-export business. One sold gemstones abroad; the second traded cereals from Tanzania to other countries, and the third imported goods from Nairobi to Dar es Salaam, via Zanzibar.

Few women could be categorised as professionals. Only three fit into this category due to their training: one was a pharmacist, another a lawyer and the third was a sociologist. Others defined themselves as belonging to a specific professional category although they did not have the training for the activities they perform. For example, one woman said:

> *I have my own pharmacy, which my husband opened for me. Earlier, I had a grocery store and I was also selling beer. Then my capital grew and I got enough money to open a pharmacy. My husband added some money to what I had to help me build a place for the pharmacy. The earnings per day are from Tanzanian Shillings 10,000 to Tanzanian Shillings 18,000. We sell Panadol[14] in large quantities.*
>
> *I do not have any professional training related to medicine but my husband is a medical doctor. So he teaches me how to give medicine to patients. I also know how to perform injections.*
>
> *We employ a pharmacist in my pharmacy and I supervise and help if it is necessary.*

Few of the informants said they were negotiating their professional services in accordance with their training. For instance, only one

[14] The brand name of a popular painkiller serving the same functions as aspirin.

teacher uses her skills to earn more money, by giving classes after official work hours.

Some women tried to invest in more lucrative activities such as embroidery or handicraft. Unfortunately, most do not succeed, because people perceive these goods as luxury items and few can afford to pay for these commodities.

Origin of capital and means of production

Starting capital comes from diverse sources. Cash originates from employment, self-employment or is provided by the husband, a relative, a credit association or *upatu* [15]or other saving groups. Indeed, Tungaraza (1994) noted that most of petty-businesswomen in urban areas practice an informal social security support system and they got their capital for their business through *upatu* in order to safeguard themselves against the loss of acquired standards of living. Some women said they received money on the occasion of their wedding. Twelve women said they received the money directly from their husband; sometimes the money was borrowed, and the woman had to reimburse the husband or relative.

Thirteen women mentioned that they saved money from their personal salary, i.e. they tried to multiply their activities to make more revenue. Nine others said that they earned money by developing small-scale activities and made enough money to invest in more productive domains. Three women used money from retrenchment benefits and one from resignation benefits. Only one woman said she obtained money through PRIDE and SERO[16]. Most

---

[15]The term refers to small credit groups or money exchange, which are based on faith and reciprocity. Members agree among themselves to contribute a fixed amount of money every week or month so that each member is assured a lump sum of money within a week or a month for buying essentials. A study conducted by Tungaraza (1994) in Manzese ward (one of the most populated and poor wards of Dar es Salaam) has shown that 89 percent of the urban dwellers participate in money exchange support system. At the moment of the survey, 85 percent of the poor people were covered by informal social security systems, compared to 15 percent who were covered by modern social security systems in urban areas. This kind of money exchange system has proven to be inadequate to provide the full protection of structural and conventional social security to the poor, but only minimizes the existing hardships. As far as contributions are based on faith and there is no act to defend or control members who are unfaithful to the system, some members become problematic to others (Kilonzo, 1994:14).

[16] PRIDE and SERO are two NGOs specialising in credit for women.

women found the interest rates charged by credit associations too high and preferred to initiate their own social or saving groups.

In spite of their lack of skills, women demonstrate a remarkable ability to overcome constraints. A 39-year-old woman said:

> *I am a nurse by profession but I resigned in 1988 after seeing that the salary was not enough to fulfil my needs. I started a business. I began by taking orders of snacks such as samosas, chips and doughnuts for stores and primary and secondary schools. My starting capital was Tanzanian Shillings 1,000 and it grew to 300,000; it helped me start another business selling sunflower oil. I was taking sunflower seeds from Arusha and sending them to Moshi for pressing. In 1988, my capital grew to Tanzanian Shillings 500,000 and I decided to open a pharmacy in Moshi. After one year, I followed my husband to Dar es Salaam and left my drug store to my sister-in-law. I go frequently to Moshi to watch the evolution of my business and I come back to Dar es Salaam to take care of my new business, which is in mitumba (used clothes).*

Women use common, low technology means of production, i.e. their own kitchen utensils: pots, mortars, pans, plastic basins, trays and strainers. All food is prepared at home on a small kerosene cooker. Working conditions are frequently poor and may be hazardous both to their health and to their children's wellbeing. Producing their goods by low technological means is also more time-consuming.

Performance of production activities

Women stated that "getting a market" was particularly problematic. One 39-year-old Christian woman explained her difficulties. She said:

> *I have been performing these activities since 1993. I started by decorating framed pictures with cross-stitching. I sell these pictures for Tanzanian Shillings 70,000 per picture, and it takes me approximately two weeks to make it.*

The picture has a high price because the frame alone costs Tanzanian Shillings 18,000 to 20,000. And I have to add the price of the cross-stitching materials such as thread, the border, time and skills. The picture is not easy to make. That's why I sell them at that price. But I do not have a market and I sell randomly.

In my poultry farm, I also have 600 broilers. I sell them at Tanzanian Shillings 1,500 per broiler when they weigh 1 to 1.5 kg; this is for retail. For wholesale, I sell them for Tanzanian Shillings 1,200 to 1,300. For a chicken to grow takes 6 to 7 weeks.

If I had a market, I could sell them for 2,500 per broiler. Another problem is that the Interchick Company destroys our market by taking orders to supply chicken, instead of producing chicks and chick food. For example, Best Bite Fast Food gets chickens from Interchick Company; so Best Bite Fast Food does not bother with local tenders/orders. My suggestion is that the Interchick Company should not interfere with the local market. It should concentrate on producing chicks and chick food.

I sell 50, 20, to 2 chickens a day, not at a fixed price. My suggestion is that poultry farmers should start an association or a group, which will help us fight for a market and to fix prices of products. Take the example of our fellow cattle breeders. They have an association that helps them set the price of milk throughout Dar es Salaam, and they also have a wider market compared to the poultry farmers.

I have been performing these activities for seven years but have not had great success. What I mean is that I am stationary, I cannot move forward. For example, the Palm Beach Hotel gave me a tender for broilers and they told me to feed my chickens for a longer period because they wanted them to get a higher weight. After seven weeks they were ready and I went there to sell them. They told me, "sorry, we got chickens from another tender." Since then I have felt discouraged with this business because it is only a part-time activity, as I am teacher on a full-time basis. So I have lost a lot of money because instead of selling my chickens for Tanzanian Shillings 2,000 to 2,500, I sold them for 1,200, 1,300 or 1,500 shillings. I lost money because I put a lot of effort into feeding them correctly.

I experienced the problem of market. If you are not known, nobody is going to give you an order. A well-known person will always get the order.

Women testify to other difficulties encountered by the majority of the population. For example, the accumulation of capital is a big constraint. Women's profits are sometimes very low, despite the efforts they put in. As shown by Nadia Von Holzen (1995) many factors contribute to this, such as lack of innovation in income-generating activities, which originates in the lack of education, professional skills and knowledge of women. The weak buying power of customers is related to the economic crisis in the urban environment. The high rate of unemployment leads to a lack of cash to buy essential commodities. People migrate to the city with the hope of finding work. Very often, they remain unemployed or work on a very irregular basis.

Civil servants are not paid regularly; there has been considerable retrenchment in the public services. Money circulates very slowly and women, as small producers, suffer the consequences of this situation. The weak buying power of customers means that the time needed to sell goods is longer, which reduces the amount of time women have to be at home with their children. For those who prepare fresh food, such as cakes, *chapatis* (pancakes) or fried fish, failure to sell the product often means being unable to continue the activity. Too many women are using petty trade as their major activity, so that competition is very high. But most of the informants said they lacked the professional skills to develop new channels. Those who perform better are the ones who take more risks by travelling abroad, doing import-export, or exploit specialised activities such as exporting gemstones to Europe.

Nevertheless, many women said they saw the benefits of their activities. Achievement means being able to help their friends and relatives, afford a better life and buy a good house or car. One 41-year-old Muslim woman said:

I am a businesswomen and I have been engaged in these activities since 1986 with a starting capital of Tanzanian Shillings 200,000. At first, I went to Kigoma, taking vitenge (cloth) and sold them to women for Tanzanian Shillings 25,000 per three pieces.

After that my capital grew and I went to Uganda to trade in women's garments and shoes. Then I went to Kinshasa to buy various items for ladies and men, and sold them. I made a lot of profit from this business.

When I was back in Tanzania I got a friend, a woman who is used to travelling to Bangkok, Thailand. She told me that this business was good and that I could make a lot of profit if I was willing to travel there. I went to Bangkok with a capital of Tanzanian Shillings 4,000,000 to cover the accommodation, fare and goods that I bought there.

Now, I return there because after selling those goods (garments for ladies, men and children, perfumes, shoes and all types of cosmetics) my earnings reached Tanzanian Shillings 6,000,000. So, the profit was Tanzanian Shillings 2,000,000. I go there every two months, that's six times a year.

I see the benefits of doing business, as I have been able to build a house, buy a car, and help my relatives, without any problem.

My friend introduces me to clients in Kariakoo[17] *where I go to sell at wholesale or retail prices.*

Women working in isolation: modern and traditional associations

There has been a proliferation of multiple types of organisations and groups. The disengagement of the State through implementation of the Structural Adjustment Programme, and the reduction of State intervention in health and education services, forced women to make use of the new openings for nongovernmental organisations (NGOs) and many other associations concerned with legal reforms, human

[17] Kariakoo is an important ward of Ilala municipality and is located in the centre of the city. It is the centre of affairs, the main market area of Dar es Salaam.

rights, women's condition and credit. The economic crisis and concomitant pressures on women obliged them to secure new sources of income and welfare relief through collective activities at the community level, such as the implementation of neighbourhood groups organised around work activities or social welfare needs, or savings clubs. Tripp (1996: 288) has argued that the implementation of these organisations was part of a conscious strategy by women to transform their everyday circumstances.

Most participants are reluctant to join official organisations, contradicting the assertion of Tripp that "women creatively formed new types or organisations to meet new needs; sometimes combining older models of organisation with newer models of proceduralism" (1996:287).

Some informants said they preferred to initiate groups based on family, tribal or religious affiliation. These are perceived as more helpful in the event of misfortunes such as death or illness. Most commonly, small saving groups called *upatu* are initiated. These are especially favoured to finance special events, and are usually formed between the members of the same family (brothers, sisters, parents) or with members of the extended family such as in-laws. A fixed amount of money has to be paid each week or month. As most women work in isolation, the creation of such networks provides a moral as well as financial support to increase their buying power. The question is whether these informal associations will benefit to women in a longer term. Will they lead to more viable structures such as co-operatives, or do they only represent transient means of survival?

Table 9: Association membership

Membership	*Age of informant (years)*				
	20s	30s	40s	50s	60s
Not a member of any association	13	11	9	2	1
Member of professional association	-	3	2	1	-
Member of credit association such as PRIDE, SERO	-	6	1	-	-
Member of CCM/UWT	1	5	3	-	-
Member of parents' association	-	-	1	-	-
Member of tribal association	-	1	2	-	-
Member of *upatu*, ward or religious association	1	6	6	-	-

The reasons given by women for not joining any official associations include:

- Lack of faith in the leadership
- Problems with favouritism
- Leaders are liars who exploit the membership fees of others
- Lack of time to participate
- Lack of information on types of associations

Informal savings associations such as *upatu* are slightly more popular because they are based on mutual trust. Women tend to stay away from official credit sources, preferring to group through a family or religious basis, thus retarding their integration into broader social movements.

Many women mentioned that although official credit associations are supposed to help them start production activities, they felt that such associations are not really helpful as too many conditions are imposed and most of the rules are detrimental to their development. Credits are not given easily, and interest rates are too high, so that women feel exploited and see no benefit in membership. For some women, their husbands vetoed their joining.

While many women informants recognised the potential of a group for sharing experiences and ideas, giving and receiving support and external professional advice, they were still reluctant to develop new ties with others and were suspicious of official organisations or associations. They associate them with women from the elite who have a greater ability to use the benefits for their own purposes. They feel they are not part of the same game.

This does not mean that informants did not try to find out more about these organisations. To an extent, they have inserted themselves into the few available interstices of development organisations and explored possibilities that could allow them to perform better in their activities. For the moment, however, it seems that the majority prefer to become members of informal associations that are perceived as being closer to them.

What women do with their benefits: organising housework and childcare

Most of interviewed women said they were making more money than their husbands. Some of them thought they were earning almost the same salary as their husbands. However, salaried men avoided telling their wives the exact amount of their wages. Thus, most informants were ignorant of the exact amount their husband earned, but estimated it from his lifestyle.

According to the women's answers, most of them, 40 women out of 68 (close to two thirds), shoulder all responsibilities for the maintenance of the family. This means that they take care of the children, pay their school fees, buy food and clothes and provide for all the basic needs of every member of the family and other residents in the house. Women also have to pay for healthcare and any household equipment. Most women help their parents and relatives, and pay for school fees and other necessities for relatives' children, as they and other people coming from rural areas are also seen as members of the extended family.

The history of a 34-year-old woman, who identifies herself as an electrical technician by profession, is instructive. She has developed many other income-generating activities and is involved in businesses such as poultry farming, goat rearing, tailoring and retail. She said:

> *I have a lot of responsibilities since my salary is not enough to fulfil our needs. I had to do other activities that could provide me with more money. In my family I have a lot of dependants who are in fact relatives. They need school fees, food, clothes and all necessities of life. I also have to take care of my parents.*
>
> *I am responsible for the children's education, because a man is like a child. He has to be pushed to make things go smoothly. If you do not work hard, your children are going to be illiterate and your husband will spend all the money of the family with other women and will come home drunk. A house is in the hands of a woman. Nothing will get done if you leave it in the hands of a man.*

I have five relatives who are dependent on us. All of them are still studying and we are the only ones to pay for school fees. The first boy is studying at Cats computer school. The second boy is at the Future World Vocational Training Centre, Ilala. The third one has finished a driving school course at VETA[18] *and is now looking for a job. The fourth one is a girl, studying domestic sciences and tailoring, and the last one is working at my sister's hairdressing salon preparing to be independent. I'm happy taking care of these relatives because I believe one day they will be able to fulfil their own needs and then help me. And they will have a good life with their children. So in one way or another I help society too.*

For the time being they help me in terms of advice because they are grown up enough to know what is good and bad. And they are very supportive when I am not around. In Africa, the extended family is an inevitable thing!

Another 42-year-old woman identifies herself as a businesswoman and housewife. She sells food such as *chapatis*[19] and *maandazi*[20], and also charcoal, and got her starting capital of only Tanzanian Shillings 2,000 from her child. She said:

It's me who takes all the responsibilities for the house because my husband has a small salary. He is working at night as a watchman. He is like a minor supporter, and it is me who generally provides money for anything necessary in the house.

I've learned something: when a husband knows you have money he won't contribute to anything. His daily refrain will be, "I have no money." Just like that!

It's me who gives advice to my husband and he always agrees with me when I suggest something. I am not so stupid that I ask him when I want something. What I do is buy things, and afterwards I report to him. Just to confirm that I already

[18] VETA is a professional training centre located in Temeke district. It is funded by Danida.
[19] *Chapatis* are a kind of pancake sold almost everywhere in the streets and shops of the city.
[20] A kind of cake.

bought something. He does not complain because he knows that I have money.

Treating a man like a fragile egg is not a habit of mine!

Even if women pay for all family requirements, it does not automatically bring respect from their husbands. Most women perceive it as normal if the men want to control everything, including the profits from their wives' activities. Only one 36-year-old woman who sold food and was married to an unemployed man said:

We live without a problem as I am the only one in the house who earns money and my husband respects me, as I also respect him. I am the only one who earns money because my husband is not working. He was made redundant. I am responsible for all the things that are necessary in the house, and also for my children's education. I am like a husband and my husband is like a wife, because he cannot help me with anything. He is like my child.

Few of the women interviewed said they shared money or decision making with their husbands. They gave the following reasons:

- Most men earn less money than their wives. So in some cases, women have gained power in the decision-making process. They only inform their husband after making a decision.
- Due to prevalent polygamy, a woman is often alone and has to earn her own money.
- Men's irresponsibility about family needs, and lack of interest in pooling money with their wives.
- Women are ignorant of the exact salary of their husbands.
- Jealousy and the husband's attitude of domination.
- A lack of trust between spouses, and the absence of common interests or aims.

Most women are responsible for members of the extended family as well as their immediate family members.

Table 10: Number of relatives for whom women were responsible

Number of relatives or residents	*Number of women*
0	6
1	19
2	11
3	7
4	6
5	7
6	7
7	-
8+	2

Extra members of the family include stepchildren, grandchildren, nephews or nieces, housekeepers and frequent visitors who stayed long enough to be considered regular members of the household.

There is controversy on the issue of supporting relatives from the husband's family. Most women perceived it as an additional burden but said that they had to tolerate this situation because it is a social obligation. Moreover, the uncertainty of life means that nobody knows when he or she will need help from somebody else. Only one 30-year-old woman involved in the import business complained:

> *I have been divorced since 1998 and have three children. My husband was working in his own garage. Our relationship was not good as he brought a lot of his relatives at home for me to take care of.*
>
> *Even worse, my parents-in-law were living in the same house. I could not tolerate that. We could not develop because the family was too big. We used a lot of money in feeding them, taking care of them, etc.*
>
> *I was doing my business as I told you. I was going to Zanzibar taking some items for sale. One day, I came back from a journey to find that my things had been stolen by my husband's young brothers as they had nothing to do, just eating and lounging around at home. I told my husband to find them a place to live and he refused. He said they were his relatives and he had no place to send them. He said, "I have to live with*

them as I am their elder brother and my parents are too old to live alone. If you cannot tolerate this situation, it is better for you to leave the house." I decided to get a divorce because I was not benefiting in any way from him.

Now, I live alone with my children. I educate them, pay for their clothes and all their needs. My husband left the children to me and he is not helping me in any way. I am the one to send them to school, because my husband does not have enough money to send them to an international school. That's why I took them with me. I know they will suffer if they stay illiterate.

When we divorced, we divided the property and now I buy other things with my own money. I will never allow him to take the children back because he does not take care of them. The children themselves do not love their dad and are big enough to know what is good and bad.

My life is good now because I have been able to buy a plot in Mbezi and have already started building a house for my children and myself. After that, I have a plan to buy my own car. For me, the divorce was the solution to my problems. When we lived together we were stagnating, just feeding his relatives. Now, I can pay school fees for my children, and buy those clothes as well as my personal things.

But most women still consider that taking care of their husband's relatives is a normal affair. For example, a 41-year-old businesswoman, travelling abroad to bring goods into the country, said she is earning enough money to have a good life and help her relatives as well:

I live with six relatives because I have enough money. There is no problem in catering for them. As you know, an African family is an extended one. So you cannot avoid that. Also, I have to live with other people because in life you never know who will come to help you, if not your relatives or your children. Life is like a lottery.

Women's bargaining power in the decision-making process

Divorced, separated or single women have more power in the decision-making process than others. They can make decisions for themselves and their children according to their capacity to pay.

Most women were separated or divorced because of male attitudes. Many had been beaten, abused or robbed. As an example, here is the story of a 43-year-old businesswoman working as a secretary, who also owns a hairdressing salon and a boutique specialising in garments, shoes and beauty products.

> *I was married in 1973. My husband is in business. He has a cafe. He has little money compared to me. In fact, he did not have enough money to satisfy the family needs. He felt inferior to me because most of the family responsibilities were on me. So we decided to separate.*
>
> *It has been a year since we were separated. We were married for about 25 years with a lot of problems. He used to beat me all the time. When he had money, he would go out to drink beer and then come back home making a lot of noise and abusing me for no reason. Really, he was not helping the children and me. He stole money from my handbag when he had no more money. We separated because of that situation in the house. It was a shame to have children and to show them this situation. I left my husband's house, which he had inherited from his father, and moved with my children to another house. My husband does not take any responsibility for the children and does nothing to help them survive.*
>
> *Now, all the responsibilities are on me. I have seven children and four other relatives. I have to pay for their school fees, buy food and clothes, and pay a house rent of Tanzanian Shillings 650,000 per year. My parents also depend on me because they are too old and cannot work anymore; I treat them like my children.*

I am building a house at Mbagala[21]. I live peacefully with my children. One thing I have discovered is that my daughters love me more than their brothers, who continue to visit their father.

Another story comes from a 48-year-old female tailor:

I am divorced, with four children. I was married twice. My first marriage lasted for five years and I had two babies. Then, the second marriage lasted for ten years and I had another two children. My ex-husband is a car dealer; he takes cars from Dubai and sells them here.

My first husband abandoned me and went to Arabian countries, and the divorce followed later. Life was difficult and miserable because my husband was rich, and I was not able to stay alone.

Life with my second husband was very good; he was also very rich. But the problem was that he did not allow me to work. He wanted me to stay at home but I preferred to work because I could have my own money and be proud of it. Your husband does not always give you money for what you want. Finally, I forced him to open my tailoring shop.

Another problem with him was that he liked small girls and concubines too much. I found him with different women many times. One day, I caught him red-handed with a woman. He climbed into his car and me into mine. We chased each other up to Mnazi Moja and he stopped there and so did I. I broke his car windows and lights and we separated for a while. Worse, he later had an affair with my sister. After that I asked for a divorce and he agreed.

Now I am living alone with a housekeeper, but without a husband. Since we divorced I am operating my business nicely and I have been able to build two houses and buy two cars. I did not take anything from my ex-husband's house. I decided to divorce him because I feared catching HIV from him, as he was like a prostitute.

[21] A ward of Temeke municipality.

Many married women said they feared HIV/AIDS because they could not refuse to have sexual intercourse with their husbands. Nor could they suggest using condoms. One 38-year-old Christian woman said that:

> *Earlier, I had very little money compared with my husband, and that was the reason for my humiliation. He thought even if he was doing bad things to me I wouldn't leave him because of my dependency in almost all things. But it reached a point where I was fed up with his behaviour. I thought that if he had an affair in my house with a house-girl, what about outside? Maybe he has a lot of concubines. I cared about my health and asked myself, "Why should I catch diseases for no reason? It is better to leave him. What is money, anyway! I can find my own, nobody is born with it."*

Married women have more problems in the decision-making process. Most of them earn more money than their husbands but still do not have the authority to spend it as they wish. Some mentioned that they had to share decisions with their husbands on how to spend their own earnings. Very often, they cannot benefit from their own money. A 41-year-old woman, who identified herself as a businesswoman and housewife, said:

> *Another problem is that my husband wants to control my money and I cannot take any decisions concerning the earnings from my business, my hairdressing salon. Furthermore, he does not appreciate what I am doing. For example, paying for school fees for children or buying them school requirements. What I am doing is nothing to him and he does not acknowledge his responsibilities.*
>
> Sometimes, I am overloaded with all my responsibilities. He can produce full-time in his job, while I have a lot of responsibilities both in the house and in my hairdressing salon. As for buying things for the house—we have to discuss that first so as to reach a conclusion. What I buy are those small, cheap things. He gives me financial support when I need it. Somehow, I have freedom for my things but not total freedom.

Many married women also find it difficult to support their husband's families but said they had no power in these matters. A 41-year-old woman said:

> *There are frequent visitors to my house. I can't throw them out. Some come to start a new life, others come to visit and they stay for one month, one year.*

Another 36-year-old woman said:

> *I live with three relatives of my husband. One is my mother-in-law, and two others are brothers-in-law. It is very difficult to live with them, especially my mother-in-law. She tells lies to her son. I put up with these difficulties because I do not have any other alternative. I put some cotton in my ears, to avoid hearing anything. If I could find a place to send this mama and her sons, I would be very happy. I would like to send them somewhere but there is no place because my husband is the elder son, as well as the first born in his family. Everyone looks up to him.*

Women said that supporting their husband's relatives became a burden that sometimes took all the family's resources, to the detriment of their own children.

Perception of women earning more money than men

Out of 22 men, 15 believed it was wrong for women to earn more than their husbands. They all felt that men should not be economically dependent on women. Most of them said:

Women would not respect their husbands any more.
They would want to have more power and influence in the decision-making process.
They would refuse to conform to their traditional gender role and division of labour.
They would spend the money on trivial things.

Some said that women "will give cold love to their husband." As money is power, the one who has money will want to speak on behalf of the other. Problems will arise if men have no say in the decision-making process or are challenged by women who develop a "superiority complex." It could lead to separation or divorce. Some compared this situation to women coming from rich families.

For a man, earning more money than his wife helps in "maintaining family ties." One 56-year-old Muslim man, working as carpenter, said:

> *Many marriages where a woman is earning more money than her husband end up in divorce, unless a man decides to be dominated by a woman. I believe in marriages where men are earning more money than their wives.*
>
> *I have already said that men are heads of the household. Now do you think that a head who has less influence on the family can continue being the head? Obviously, his responsibilities as the head will be taken over. My friend, let me tell you that money is always power; the one that has the money will also have the power. Because men are superior to women, let men earn more money—as much as they can, and more than women. This will help bring gender balance to the family.*
>
> *There are some families where the children do not respect the men because they always get gifts or clothes from their mothers. It means that the father is looked upon as a stranger in the house.*
>
> *Therefore, for the power balance in the family, let men earn more money than their women. Any money earned in the family should be used for the family's development.*

Most men believed that if women earned more than men, they would spend the money on themselves, and that they were only interested in buying trivial things.

Some men said that this situation has become more common, as women now have better education than before. The solution, suggested by informants, is that everybody should know their spouse's income. One 40-year-old Christian man, working as a civil servant, said:

> *Women should not forget that they have some obligations to fulfil that are related to their gender role. Many conflicts develop in the family because of role conflicts, which are usually caused by women who demand too much freedom from their husband, such as sharing their responsibilities.*

Among the seven men who were more positive about this situation, most said it depends on the communication ties that already exist in a family and between spouses. Good relations could guarantee harmony. It is the spouses' business to decide together about the use of their incomes. Some mentioned that men are afraid of losing control over their wives if they cannot decide on important issues for the family. As a 57-year-old Christian man said:

> *It depends on the relationship between spouses. I also believe in cultural significance. There are some spouses, coming from different ethnic groups, who do well even if the wife earns more money than the husband. I know of one man who has a broken leg. His wife is earning more than four times what he is earning but you can't see any difference in their relationship. They are living well together. They are coming from Morogoro*[22].
>
> *I have another example of two spouses. The husband is coming from Morogoro and the wife is from Moshi*[23]. *The wife is earning a lot of money because of her business and her husband is just a Government employee with a small salary. In fact if you see that family, you cannot tell who the husband is and who the wife is. She humiliates the man very much. She can humiliate him even in front of guests; it is very strange in our tradition.*

[22] A town in the north-eastern part of Tanzania.

[23] A town located in the Kilimanjaro area, in the northern part of Tanzania.

It appears that men fear losing their dominant role over women because of the associated loss of power in the family and of respect from their wives.

Only one 60-year-old Christian retired man disagreed with the general point of view of informants. He said:

> *I think the problem here is the interpretation of gender relations; of who is supposed to get the money. I think women are the ones. Because when men get money, they drink and they go back home with empty pockets.*
>
> *Therefore, I don't see any problem when women earn more money than men. What is prevailing among men is just a fear of losing their traditional role of determining everything in the family. What I think is, if it is well arranged, everything will work out and nobody will complain.*
>
> *Problems arise when men and women are not open with each other. Everybody is trying to hide what he or she earns. Every single coin earned in the family should be used to develop the welfare of the family.*

In general, men have difficulty accepting women performing different productive activities. They only mention the negative effects of this new phenomenon. In reality, when accusing women of behaving differently, they are describing their own behaviour. Most informants said that money should be pooled in the family, that the salary of spouses should be known by each other, that every coin should be spent on family needs. But in real life, what is happening? Are men really committed to their family, children and wives? Are they themselves doing what they ask of their wives? In fact, most men recognise that the urban economy and the existing competition that prevails in the city puts pressure on them. They have more and more difficulties in fulfilling their social and family obligations. They do not have enough money to respect the terms of the contract.

Division between paid and unpaid work

Tanzanian society allocates specific types of work to women and to men. This firstly allocates work according to sex, and secondly encourages segregation by placing constraints in practice: for instance, skills are acquired according to gender.

Tanzanian society thus virtually excludes women from opportunities for the accumulation of wealth on a scale usable as capital, or from career paths that would lead to control of significant capital. In addition, solidarity between men is actualised through daily practices.

In the labour market, there is a high degree of segregation between women and men. It is achieved through specific mechanisms, such as a socialisation process that denies girls education and professional skills and training. Over the long term, it has resulted in a technical division of labour, favouring men. For example, Mbilinyi (1991) recognised that gender discrimination in education and gender stereotyping in education are among the factors that constrain women's participation in education, particularly in institutes of higher learning. National statistics indicate that most girls do not study beyond primary school. They marry very young, and parents do not see the importance of investing in a person who is going to work for another family. Since education determines one's access to positions of influence, most men occupy higher posts in the hierarchy than women. Consequently, women are denied power, influence and good salaries.

As boys and girls are trained differently, discriminatory employment becomes rational from the employer's point of view. The sexual division of labour is transformed into a technical division of labour. The best-trained person for a given job will get it, and most of the time men are better trained than women. Skill development and training are two of the mechanisms by which the sexual division of labour becomes a powerful system of social constraint.

The sexual division of labour also involves the design of work. Who gets access to appropriate technology? What about household work, and what do women use to help them to accomplish daily duties? In the city, we can see men using expensive four-wheel drive cars and mobile phones. What about their wives at home? Do they have access to water or any modern conveniences for cooking or other household tasks? It is not surprising that women rarely own any modern domestic technology, since men are not interested in it. In the case of women from the elite class, they usually transfer these obligations to servants or younger relatives from rural areas.

In Dar es Salaam homes, the division of domestic labour is not equally shared between spouses. As has been demonstrated in surveys performed in Nigeria (Fapohunda and Fapohunda, 1976; Oppong, 1987), Tanzania (Obrist van Eeuwijk, 2000) and other African countries, women claim that their husbands still do nothing in the house. Taking the example of Oppong, we can summarize the sexual division of labour in Dar es Salaam as follows:

- The management of financial resources indicates that, generally, spouses do not pool in their incomes or have a joint bank account, and rarely own common assets. Women fear potential polygamy, the irresponsibility of their husbands towards the family, and inheritance procedures.
- The spouses do the financial provision for household needs jointly, usually with little or no help from kin. Women's contribution to household economy has more than doubled since 1971 (Koda, 1995:146).
- Domestic chores are the wife's responsibility, without the husband's participation, but with help from kin, mostly girls[24]. Indeed, examples of men stepping to assume household responsibilities are few and scattered, as it came out in the study done in twenty-three countries (Narayan et al, 2000:115). Isolated incidents of men sharing some of the "female" responsibilities include when the wife is unwell, away visiting relatives, attending to other social obligations, or when work keeps her away from the home for long periods (Bangladesh, Brazil, Indonesia, Malawi and Zambia). Casual work done by women doesn't seem to merit additional help from husbands.

- The rearing of children is done by the wife, without help from the husband, but with help from kin, generally girls.

[24] Lecarme-Frassy (2000:148) noted in the case of Senegal, that women's economic independence requires the free labour force provided by young girls of the extended family. It also favours the reproduction of the social relation of subordination from the elder to the youngest girl. It allows elder women to face motherhood, maintenance of the domestic space, all services needed by other residents and to finalise all merchant activities.

The "political economy of masculinity" reflects the dominant definition of men's interests, and it justifies their retention of power. Housework and childcare are not seen as suitable occupations for men. This is an extraordinarily deep-seated notion. Since men have more control over the division of labour than women, their collective choice is not to do childcare. The structured pattern of masculinity strengthens men's solidarity and is a strong cultural and economic force.

Nevertheless, there are some attempts to reverse it. The creation of new posts at parliamentary level shows the willingness of leaders of the Government to integrate women and allow them to participate actively at the national level. Women are at a disadvantage in a masculine institution, dominated by men who reproduce prejudices against women and block their access to higher posts. This indicates that the sexual division of labour is still a practical obstacle.

Tanzanian society structures men in the logic of accumulation. For centuries men have been favoured in accumulating prestige and wealth through various processes. All economic benefits are concentrated in one direction, economic losses in another. Benefits and costs are not equally distributed between the sexes. The present organisation of work depends on the persistence of patriarchal relations, which reproduce the unpaid family labour of wives and children (Mbilinyi, 1991). Women's work remains unrecognised in the national statistics.

Conclusion: Organic organisation of work or segregation?

This chapter has shown that city life forces women to develop income-generating activities. Women cannot be idle if they want to survive and satisfy the needs of family members, while their husbands have difficulty finding employment in the city. For many women their earnings are vital to their own and their families' well-being. The welfare of children is connected with their mother's ability to earn an independent income. Moreover, it provides some women independence and self-determination.

We have seen that most women working outside the home are involved in the informal sector of the economy, and have initiated small-scale businesses. Salaried women occupy the lowest positions in the formal sector, as semi-skilled or unskilled employees. Women face many problems while starting productive activities, including the lack of investment capacity and markets. Furthermore, competition between similar activities conducted by many women, lack of time, limited financial resources and the social isolation of women are huge impediments to the development of new activities and trends.

The sexual division of labour discriminates against women and acts as a constraint on daily practice. Even in the city, the social rule is that women are responsible for household tasks. Men are still viewed as the heads of the household even if an increasing number of women are *de facto* heads. The increased workload does not bring about a corresponding increase in the rights and privileges of women. Indeed, the number of women-headed households is difficult to evaluate, as they do not benefit from *de jure* recognition, as they are still confronting a cultural and political blindness. Many women informants recognize that they would like to live with a "helpful husband": which means having the capacity to develop real cooperation, negotiation, communication, common understanding and involvement in the decision-making process for family matters. However, nowadays, many women prefer to stay single, or be separated or divorced, as they can be independent, live according to their aspirations and offer a better life to their children[25]. This is also proven in research findings in other African countries. For example, Krieger (1998) found that the children of women entrepreneurs in Cameroon were significantly taller and heavier for their age than those of primary producers. Indeed, there was a positive association between income-generating activities of women entrepreneurs, household food supplies, and child growth. These results indicate the need for policy analysis and recommendations, to investigate women's entrepreneurship, rather than to subsume such activity under the general heading of household or petty trade. It is also demonstrated in the case of education. As Pilon (1996) reports, results from different surveys done by the World Bank in Côte d'Ivoire and Ghana, and census or demographic surveys conducted

[25] The World Bank report (1993:31) has findings from Sender and Smith (1990) concerning inequalities in the family. The authors noted that when surveying "several households contained women and children without shoes, or any adequate clothing, while the father/husband had a watch, several sweaters, pairs of shoes, and a coat."

in Mali and Togo, demonstrated that more children from female-headed households are sent to school than otherwise. Female headed-households invest more in their children's well-being than men do; be it in terms of time, money or affective support.

Most women have to initiate small-scale business activities. Women do not have access to the new technology that could help them perform more efficiently, and are thus confined to traditionally feminine types of work. Rutashobya (1995) has demonstrated that the historical legacy of inadequate education, social prejudices and the lack of legal rights, all handicap women in business, as does their prevailing socialisation. The issue of the subordination of women remains to be resolved. "Despite their changing role in both family and society, gender stereotypes and prejudices are still found in all spheres. In fact, women are overburdened and doubly oppressed." (idem).

Under economic pressure women may organise themselves, for instance initiating *upatu,* which could be seen as an informal route to financial capitalisation or as a strategy for reinforcing female identity (Amougou, 1998:167-169). Men perceive these organisations as subversive because they open up space for feminine communication, and could become a real outlet for women in Tanzanian.

Despite these difficulties, women can acquire power in the decision-making process. As they gain money through their production activities, some become responsible for almost all family matters. Even if located in the informal sector of the economy, some women have been able to perform in such a way that they are able to accumulate goods and free themselves from unequal relations. Women learn that they are no longer obliged to tolerate situations that are detrimental for them at every level.

Whether or not they achieve the level of power that "Nana Benz" (Cordonnier, 1991) obtained in Togo or the women "bosses and fishermen" of Dakar (Le Cour Grandmaison, 1979), they discover that financial independence can help them live as they wish, and reject imposed rules that keep them segregated from power and responsibility. As summarised by one nurse informant:

> *I dislike depending on my husband for anything. I always want to have my own things because these men are not trustful.*

The sexual division of labour is deeply rooted in the social organisation. Benefits, opportunities and costs are not equally distributed between the sexes in Tanzanian society, and this motivates the active demarcation and exclusion, practised by many groups of men. This is the subject of the next chapter.

CHAPTER 3

WOMEN'S AND MEN'S INDIVIDUAL TRAJECTORIES: HOW ARE POWER RELATIONS EXERCISED?

Joan Mapunda feels the new laws in Tanzania are favourable to women; but they seem to be more theoretical than practical. For example, a few months ago her neighbour was raped when she was coming home from work. She decided to lodge a complaint, but was asked to bring a witness! "How can you bring a witness when you have been raped at night in a deserted street?" asked Joan. "It is the same for many other things. Years ago the Tanzanian Government signed an international convention on the elimination of all forms of discrimination against women. We have not seen any results so far. What has the Government done to improve women's lives? Almost all women here are ignorant of their rights. If it is like this in Dar es Salaam, can you imagine what is happening with women in rural areas?"

Few women can own land or property, or have access to further studies. She said the tendency to denigrate women still exists. "I personally have the habit of proving to people that I can do anything, regardless of the fact that I am a woman. The Government of Tanzania preaches on this and that, but what they say and what they do are two different things. For example, the aid and loans given do not target the right people. The Tanzanian Chamber of Commerce gave loans to Mama *Ntilie* for improving their working conditions. Where did the loans go? It goes into the pockets of people working in those offices, and their friends."

According to Joan, society in general, and men in particular, do not recognise the work done by women. "Women are still behind. Most women have very miserable lives. We are poor in all sectors—development, education, and finance—and even when we make an effort, we get no help. Some laws today are more favourable to us, and to an extent they do help women. But the problem is corruption."

For Joan the ancestral tradition is bad because it sees women as slaves. To have women do all the work is thought by men to be the natural state of affairs. "It is difficult to change people's minds and remove all the false ideas. For example, if a girl decides to study, people will complain 'why is this woman studying for so long instead of being married?'" This shows that society itself contributes to women's poor performance in school, because they see a woman as someone who will only get married and not have the option to do something else.

This chapter is an introduction to sexual power relations. Various institutions hinder women's development, favouring men over women.

The Tanzanian State introduced "positive action" to enhance the status of women. Many laws have been changed to provide better opportunities for women. However, women's comments suggest that the discourse of the Government does not reflect the reality, where laws are poorly and rarely implemented.

The family and marriage are further impediments to women's autonomy. Women complain about men's behaviour. They exercise power and authority in the decision-making process, denying women any influence. Men justify this by appealing to so-called tradition[1]. Even women do not always recognise the value of their own work.

Nevertheless, changes are appearing. Older women prefer that their daughters develop skills towards independence. Marriage, even if

[1] According to men informants, "tradition" refers to a code of moral values, attitudes, behaviours and practices (for example, the code of modesty) that women have to respect to be in conformity with "African culture." As observed by Geisler (2000:57)) for the case of South Africa, the intricacies of claims as to what is "tradition" and what is not, or which tradition is useful and which obsolete, are complex and contradictory. Tanzania is not a singular case where disputation about tradition is and has been happening. Tradition has never been static, and it has been an important arena for social and political struggles as it is still "a crucial ingredient in cultural nationalism" and remains an important arena of contestation in modern African states. It has largely been the prerogative of men, who have used it to ensure their control over women and to circumscribe the scope of women's action. "Tradition" and "custom" are therefore often seen as the linchpin of African women's subordinated status and the single most important obstacle to their emancipation. However, African women have sometimes appeared as the custodians of tradition and thus the agents of their own subordination.

still almost mandatory, is no longer seen as the sole priority. Most women informants know they have to challenge old social customs that hinder their possibilities or choices for becoming more independent. However, many are still reluctant to join new types of associations or groups that are not based on family or tribe ties. They have been too isolated to challenge the patriarchal system in a deeper way.

Is the Tanzanian Government practising "positive action"?

The Government of Tanzania, like many other African countries, has reformed its laws. These reforms include employment opportunities and conditions of work. It also ratified many international conventions, such as the International Labour Convention, including Convention 111 on Discrimination in Employment, and the International Convention on the Elimination of all Forms of Discrimination against Women (CEDAW) in December 1979 (which entered into force in September 1981). This top-down approach supposes that the national laws and legislations within the country are changed or instituted as necessary to conform to the principles of the convention. In addition, in ratifying a convention, a State agrees to international monitoring and reporting on its compliance (Women Moving Human Rights Centre Stage, 1999). What has really been implemented in the country?

Before the 1980s, much of the organised activity of women was performed by the Union of Women of Tanzania (UWT). The Tanzanian national party, TANU, created the women's wing of the dominant political party. The thrust of the women's wing was to solicit support for the male-dominated parties. The UWT has played a very significant role in mobilising mass support for the party. UWT was involved in income-generation activities, cooperatives, handicrafts, animal husbandry, efforts to improve women's and children's healthcare, and popular education promotion. Tripp noted that its activities were not only controlled by CCM but that its plans had to coincide with the government's five-year development plans and the design of ministries and parastatals (Tripp, 1996: 289).

The women's wing compromised women's rights to equal participation in the management of society by accepting the "positive action" introduced by the Government, which ensured the participation of some women in Parliament and in the party organs. The allocation of special seats to women only ensured the maintenance of the *status quo* in the male-dominated decision-making organs (Mannathoko, 1992:75).

During the 1990s there was vibrant growth in the women's movement, promoting women's leadership, rights and participation in the country's political life. Women rapidly discovered that none of the parties fully addressed women's concerns and that women were excluded from the multiparty context. Women created the Union of Eastern Africa Women's Parliament in March 1996 at Moshi, Tanzania. The women's movement and associations conceptualised democratisation as a bottom-up process, connecting notions of family democracy to national democracy issues. It included women's rights to the ownership of land, reproductive rights, the right to be heard and acknowledged, the right to respect and equal partnership (Tripp, 1996:298). Numerous networks of women's groups, such as the Tanzania Gender Networking Programme (TGNP), emerged in the 1980s and 1990s to coordinate activities around legal reforms and policies affecting women's education, health and work opportunities. Moreover, many NGOs and local groups became prominent. "It gave to the women's movement a voice outside of party interests and for the first time gave them the potential to challenge not only the *status quo* but, in particular, the politics of sectarianism and patronage" (Tripp, 1996:289).

Throughout the 1980s and 1990s, Tanzanian women initiated numerous groups. Examples given by Gaidzanwa (1992:81-82) include:

- The opening of various legal clinics.
- The Tanzanian Media Women's Association (TAMWA), which was one of the first national organisations involved in research and popular education. This organisation has challenged the official media's stereotyped images of women and general invisibility in the media. It tries to deconstruct the negative images of women and to provide them with an alternative medium called *Sauti ya Siti.* The emphasis in TAMWA's publishing work has been on media images aimed at achieving positive portrayal of women in the media and

permitting the voices of the voiceless to be heard (Alloo, 1995:311).

- The Tanzania Paukwa Theatre Group attempted to use popular theatre to sensitise the public on gender inequalities.
- The Women and Education Group has challenged educational stereotyping in the curriculum. Its research has facilitated some changes, for instance encouraging the re-writing of material from a gender-sensitive perspective.

Effects of "positive action" on women's lives

The *Gender Profile of Tanzania*, which was developed by the Tanzania Gender Networking Programme (TGNP) in 1993, is still a good illustration of women's situation in the country. The book delineates the persistence of gender inequality and women's oppression, in spite of the many positive steps that have been taken by the Government and other development agencies to change the situation.

According to the document, since 1985 the Government, donors, NGOs, communities and individuals have adopted different strategies to empower women. In general terms, there was the creation of the Women-in-Development focal point headed by the Ministry of Community Development, Women's Affairs, and Children. Credit guidelines have been prepared, as access to human and other resources has been recognised as important for women's development. Donor agencies, as well as many NGOs, supported and funded women's groups to carry out research, consultancies, education curricula, communication and networking activities and to support productive, trade and educational activities at the grassroots level. Enough suggests that not enough time has been devoted to consciousness-raising and action, while women's groups are still extremely dependent on donors. Many NGOs initiated gender groups but they do not appear to serve the needs of members. More often, they represent powerful elite at the local level. The really poor are often marginalised or excluded from grassroots organisations. The needs of sustainability have also not been given adequate attention.

From a political, legal and organisational point of view, women do not fully participate in, or control access to, political power at any level. Little has been done to remove patriarchal gender relations in all sectors of society. No affirmative action has been taken to increase women's power in the household, extended family or clan. Women themselves have not emphasised the creation of pressure groups to advocate change in the cultural values and practices that support patriarchal social relations in the law, economy and society in general.

Is the public sector advantageous for women?

Equality between the sexes is still compromised by the lack of information on women's economic activities and the pervasiveness of sexist stereotypes. The lack of information about women is reflected in the absence of statistics that differentiate by sex. Women remain invisible in macro-economic planning exercises. They are not involved on an equal basis with men either as decision-makers or as foci of concern, and are treated as peripheral and marginal. This is true not only of Tanzania but of many other African countries as well, as noted by Oppong (1987: 3). Direct discrimination is based on the fact that a man is seen as the head of the household and that a wife is not an independent agent.

Most women are involved in the informal sector of the economy. A large proportion of women do not earn wages because they are unemployed. Many more women than men have low incomes. Statistics on income are, however, difficult to obtain. It is clear that men control most wealth, as they occupy the most strategic posts in all spheres of the society. Economic segregation between men and women still exists.

Women in Tanzania: generous discourse but poor practice

When asked what has been done for women in Tanzania most women informants demonstrated a high level of discontent. Of the 67 women who were interviewed, 13 had a more or less positive attitude to improvements in women's lives. The other 55 women said that in practice almost nothing had been done for women in Tanzania, even though there were crucial needs to be met.

There is a large gap between those in high-level posts such as members of Parliament, ministers, and women working in prestigious institutions, and women at the grassroots level. Women emphasised the lack of unity; the interests of women from different classes are different. Some women mentioned that the right people are not targeted. For instance, loans are given to leaders' wives, Members of Parliament, their friends and relatives, or are reserved for women in high level posts.

However, some informants recognised that things had improved compared to the situation years ago. For example, there are new associations and NGOs that at least consider the issue of women and development, or are concerned about equity. And laws that are more favourable to women have been passed.

Some participants also mentioned that more women are eager to be active, and that an increasing number of girls want to be independent and achieve something by and for them. In many cases, marriage is no longer seen as the priority; it is felt that it should come after girls and young women have completed their studies. Many think that women are more "awakened than before." Girls' access to primary school is greater than before; sometimes widows inherit from their husbands and some women can get divorces. One 39-year-old Muslim woman, a mother of two children, who had studied up till Standard VII and was working as a businesswoman, said:

> *At least there are a few things done, compared to those days. Now women can start organisations to fight for their rights like TAMWA*[2]*. There are a lot of local women's groups, which we see on TV. This shows how many women have taken a step forward in their development.*

Nevertheless, the majority of participants said that old beliefs hinder changes, so they occur slowly.

---

[2] The Tanzania Media Women's Association (TAMWA) has its seeds in 1979, with a group of women who had just finished journalism school and were beginning work in various mass media institutions. They decided to produce radio programmes, as the manner in which women's issues were covered was unsatisfactory. In 1987, the formal association was registered. Among various activities, the association produced various media programme (radio, TV, magazine, seminars), developed a research and documentation unit, together with a reference library for material on women, as various needs related to information and education emerged. The center provides legal literacy, counselling, and fights court cases involving violence against women. It also provides paralegal training, an exposure to and training in information technology, and some training in NGO management to members of up-country women's organisations, who then return to establish community-based centres in rural Tanzania (Alloo, 1995).

Favouritism, class dominance, inequality and lack of solidarity are among the most frequent *leitmotivs* with women informants. They mention that being a member of the dominant political party was the best way to get benefits for improving their lives. This is confirmed by most participants, who insist on the huge demarcation line existing between women from different social classes. A 42-year-old businesswoman and a 43-year-old woman working as secretary said:

> *To some extent the work done by Tanzanian Women Association is good but their work is biased towards a few members, such as those at ministerial levels and members of the Parliament. Other people who benefit are the wives of ministers and women in other institutions who have money. Their work is not good compared to other countries like Uganda or Kenya. These women above forget their fellow women in rural areas, housewives and those having low incomes. Solidarity among women is very important.*

> *There is a big gap between those in higher posts, for example women who are members of the Parliament, or ministers, or working in higher institutions. They do not think of women occupying lower posts. In other words, they are not united in order to fight their common interests and rights. Women are not united because they differ in terms of social classes. Those in the middle class do not share the same interests as women from lower classes.*

Access to loans and to information about women's rights is denied to the majority. Women are ignorant of their rights even if they are members of UWT or CCM. Women also mentioned the lack of commitment of leaders "who are not working with humanity." Corruption is seen as the main problem and "even though there is a Warioba Commission, corruption is still rampant". A 52-year-old illiterate woman said, "UWT is rotten. It is full of corrupt and untruthful leaders, who forget that this association is for all people." Many informants mentioned the need for women to fight tradition as "women are poor in all sectors such as development, education, and finance." As a 23-year-old woman said:

> *Things done for women are hindered by some bad beliefs, which we have inherited from our ancestors. And those*

beliefs are in our blood, in the mindset of people. It will take a long time to change them. The dream of being equal with men is impossible. I doubt it will be possible to change people's mindset.

Informants focused their complaints on laws and women's associations.

Laws: women recognise that most laws have been voted on and reformed. However, many laws are not applied or implemented. They don't seem to be designed to be enacted. They are not as favourable as they could be, because women are not taken seriously; they are still oppressed and humiliated and their rights inadequately respected.

Many informants said that justice is also affected by corruption. People with money are in a better position to defeat laws than those without. Civil servants or managers were perceived as favouring a few people while the majority suffers. The chair of the national women's organisation, also working as a ten-cell leader, said there was still a major problem with favouritism, particularly with respect to the laws on inheritance, rape and sexual harassment.

Women's associations: few participants were members of official associations. Most women do not trust them, and they do not feel they are equal there, if they are from a lower class. Women do not have any confidence in UWT, which is perceived as a political organisation of CCM. Several informants claimed that even prominent members of this organisation were under the domination of their husbands once they were out of the public eye. The widening gap between women from the upper and lower classes was also mentioned. Here, one informant claimed, "It is so much fun to say women are oppressed while others are enjoying the national cake in Tanzania."[3] Some said that using poor women from lower classes was a foolproof way to get more money from international organisations or bilateral aid agencies.

---

[3] An instance: In 1994, a director of an international organisation proposed to women members of a national organisation to collaborate with them to develop a programme for legal literacy that would reach out to women from the lower classes. She offered to pay them USD 300 per day. The Tanzanian women refused, arguing they were receiving USD 500 per day from the World Bank (personal communication).

Many women said they were fearful of reporting to some organisation, and a 36-year-old Christian woman working as a businesswoman said:

> *Nothing is done for women in Tanzania. Laws are there but they are not run with justice because of corruption. Also, Tanzanian women are fearful. For instance, when there is a problem of inheritance between a woman and her in-laws, she will be afraid to report it to organisations that deal with widows or women's rights in general, like TAMWA or SUWATA. Women are afraid of being bewitched by their husband's relatives. So, women are ready to lose their rights and those of their children too.*

To improve the situation, informants suggested that:

- Official mechanisms should be created to encourage women to speak in public. This is perceived as a major factor in improving women's situation.

- Community participation in the decision-making process should involve women, and ways of allowing them to express their views and needs should be developed and encouraged. This would facilitate the development of solidarity with women of rural areas.

- Old traditions and beliefs that are detrimental to women's development should be rejected. The Government's responsibility should be to inform women about their rights relating to marriage, inheritance, rape and sexual harassment. All types of information media and means should be used such as seminars, courses or workshops.

- Laws should be amended updated and applied correctly. Corruption should be stopped because it obstructs all levels of intervention in all sectors. The Government should eliminate segregation between women from the middle and lower classes. Furthermore, it should abolish favouritism towards leaders' wives who are members of the Union of Women in Tanzania, through a fundamental reform of this official association.

- Women should initiate business groups that should be officially recognised. Practically, loan restrictions and interest rates should be reduced to facilitate access to new resources for poorer women.

- Women should be encouraged to respect themselves and not tolerate sexual harassment.

- Education for girls should be encouraged and supported, for example by reducing school fees and building more schools.

- A widows' association should be established to provide more support to widows and abandoned women.

Informants said that women have to work very hard to become independent. They have to join groups to get loans and aid. Many recognise the importance of being involved in associations for developing better support institutions. The reformation of associations such as UWT is thus seen as vital, because it is perceived as being profoundly corrupt and favouring leaders' wives. Women said it would be important to find leaders genuinely committed to developing equality between women and men.

One 46-year-old Christian woman working as a businesswoman, who is the mother of two children, said:

> *I hate this habit of saying please do this for us or do that for us. If we preach equality we have to do what men do. My business is dominated by men but I managed and I am successful compared to a lot of men. In order to enhance or change women's lives, we have to join groups to do things collectively.*

Two informants however categorically contradicted the view of the majority. They said that each woman has to work hard and do something by herself. They were aware that more and more women were trying to organise themselves or initiate groups, to enhance their production or develop more activities. However, they do not support this way of doing things. They believe only in self-initiative and efforts; women really have to resist old customs, and struggle for more autonomy.

Many said, "A woman is a human being, not a tool for production, as viewed by the majority of men." This affirmation testified to the need for social recognition of women's work. A 41-year-old Christian woman working as a businesswoman said:

> *Nobody will do things for us. Therefore women themselves must make efforts. They have to investigate what their fellow women do and try to start their own activities. I've noticed that many women can't make anything by themselves, because they simply cannot do it. They are used to being under a certain someone or a man.*
>
> *I do not see it like this. I have never seen direct results for women. We have to struggle to get them. They, the Government and others, cannot bring everything to our door. So you have to fight; and learn where it is possible to get help, or get information by speculation or from your friends. Do not wait for everything to be brought to you.*

Even when women were conscious of their exploitation and of being dominated, most of them, especially the poorer ones, said that they had no alternative. "Women have too many responsibilities, too many children and no opportunities for study."

Do women know the value of their work?

To the question "Do you think Tanzanian women see the importance of the work they perform?" informants said the following:

Women's answers	Number of informants
Women see the importance but men and society hinder their development.	35
Women see the importance but they have no other alternatives.	15
Women see the importance and they fight for their rights.	6
Women lack unity and solidarity.	5
Women need encouragement to fight for their rights.	2

Women are less afraid than before.	2
Women see the importance of their work but refuse to do something.	1
Women do not see the importance of it because they are used to being exploited.	1
Women's views are taken into consideration.	1
Total	68

There is almost a consensus that men hinder women's development. Women's exploitation is seen as having gone on for too long. One woman mentioned that men have changed how they exploit women. She said that nowadays most men prefer a woman who is working. They do not want "goat keepers" any more; they "want to exploit us; they have been exploiting us indirectly for many years, but now they have changed their tactics by exploiting us directly."

Many participants said men have to be educated to change their behaviour and attitudes. Women mentioned that it was a question of value. As a 26-year-old Christian woman working as a businesswoman said:

> *Now, women see the importance of the work they are performing, especially those in the big cities and towns. They are few, and the majority is not yet prepared to accept it. If the women in towns and cities could unite forces for a women's revolution, it would influence those in rural areas and they would be able to fight their common enemy, i.e. men. They would also contribute to reducing women's oppression, exploitation and humiliation. The first thing is to live independently of men. If this could be done, men would respect us.*

Another 23-year-old Muslim woman, who also works as businesswoman, said of women's life in general:

> *A Tanzanian woman sees the importance of her work, but men and society in general do not appreciate what women are doing. Society as a whole does not value these women. Take the example of a woman who is going to look for a job. She will be asked to have a love affair with that employer in*

order to get the job. Otherwise she will be sacked from the office, even though she is qualified. In schools too there are a lot of beautiful girls. That is enough reason to be pestered by teachers. If you refuse them, they hate you and start to lower the girls' grades. We women see the importance of the work we are performing; that is why we struggle and put more effort into our work, but society does not appreciate it.

Nevertheless, in spite of all impediments, women today have been able to enter new fields of activities. One 37-year-old Christian woman said:

Women even do jobs that were done by men before. For example, they do tasks related to construction, mechanics; they are pilots and drivers of large vehicles. But men see all these activities as nothing; they do not appreciate what women do. They are always saying, "Why is a woman doing all these things instead of staying home, cooking and cleaning?" They think women are incapable of doing "men's activities", as they call them. Also, when a woman decides to study, people complain and many men ask, "Why is this woman studying for so long, instead of getting married?" This shows that society itself contributes to women's poor performance in school. Society sees women as people to be married only, and not people who do anything else.

Tradition and old beliefs contribute to hinder development. One 41-year-old Muslim woman said, "It is inherited from our ancestors, to see a woman as a slave. Everything she does before people's eyes is nothing."

Improving the lives of young girls: what more can be done?

Many women recognise that girls' access to education is better than before. Girls can benefit from education, at least until primary school, and can pursue further studies. They can perform jobs that were previously exclusive to men. Nowadays "people increasingly see the contribution of daughters to the family." However, "girls' opportunities could be greater if people's minds were more open."

Many women thus claimed that although the Government declared it was in favour of increasing the number of girls in secondary schools and institutes of higher education, this involvement is more of a theoretical exercise than a reality, and has not been fully implemented. There are too many barriers to girls' education, such as early pregnancy, parental attitudes and traditional beliefs. Girls still lag behind boys and the pursuit of their education is not seen as a priority by many parents. Many parents still have a tendency to marry off their daughters early. It is detrimental for them because then they cannot pursue further studies. Society as a whole fails to recognise the importance of women and their work, and the need for equal rights of women and men. The Government should, therefore, be pushing for gender-related policies and revised laws. For example, people should be educated about the importance of women's education. One woman said, "Boys are still socially recognised—have prestige, respect and are given what they want in society, simply because they are married and have paid a dowry."

Boys still have more opportunities than girls, even if some mentioned that their possibilities were reduced because of the current social and economic scenario. Usually, boys are more likely to have secondary education or government sponsorship for higher education. One woman said, "We have to change this habit of favouring boys. Equal rights must be given to girls and boys." This habit comes from the custom of seeing boys as the future head of the family.

Some women also said that education in general was deteriorating in Tanzania. One woman said, "Today teachers want to have love affairs with students. Students are also badly behaved. Furthermore, the level of education is low and most teachers teach ignorance." The same woman suggested raising the standards for students to pass exams; and also wanted the sexual harassment of girls to be stopped. "Women should refuse to participate by reporting all cases of sexual harassment."

Many think that girls are freer than before, but said they use this freedom badly; they prefer an easy life to working at their studies. It is the same for boys, who tend to seek out an easy life and succumb to drug addiction. Many women said that both sexes look for "luxury things, instead of studying and making an effort." Nowadays, it is harder for parents to have authority over their children. Many refuse to be directed by their parents. That is why it's important to create a good environment to motivate youth for further studies.

Suggestions for enhancing and facilitating change focused on the following points:

- To educate the society about equal rights for boys and girls
- To abolish beliefs and traditions that are detrimental to women's rights, and to implement positive discrimination for women
- To provide information on improving the condition of women
- To put leaders' discourses into practice
- To revise laws that do not help emancipate women
- To stop corruption
- To stop sexual harassment, through special programmes and punishment

What do women wish for the lives of their children?

Education is seen as an investment. Most of them want both girls and boys to achieve a high level of education, at whatever cost, and obtain a good job. They hope their children will get a good job, "not only for the sake of it, but to get insight into running their lives," and also so that they can help their parents when they are older.

Women also want a better life for their daughters in particular. Education is seen as the first priority and a way for girls to counter discrimination and abuse. According to them, education opens doors to emancipation, independence and responsibility. It gives women wider choices and better life options. Indeed, older women believe that education would help their daughters understand their social, political and material world.

Emancipation is achieved though the possibility of getting a good job that allows a woman to develop her capacities, and to find her own fields of interests. Harmful traditions must be removed in order for girls to have equality. One 41-year-old woman working as a businesswoman says:

> *I want my daughters to study hard and get a job later; then marriage will follow. I have three daughters. The decision of marrying them in our Haya*[4] *tribe is like destroying a daughter's future. This custom of taking children to* "unyago[5]" *is outdated. You take permission from the school in order to do that, but you know that their fellow students are continuing with their lessons. This system is retarding the girls' development at school. We have to abandon this behaviour as quickly as possible. Leave daughters free to choose what they like, and this will benefit their lives. Parents should not decide for their children.*

Independence empowers girls in the decision-making process. They should not be obliged to marry against their will, but should be able to choose their own future. Equally, they should not to be spoiled by too "easy" a life.

Most women want their daughters to complete their studies and "not run off to get married before they can depend on themselves." Independence from men is viewed as the first priority for young women "because nowadays men are too irresponsible."

One 34-year-old Christian woman, mother of three children and living with five relatives, who is working as an electrical technician and also has a business, said:

> *I want my children to get as much education as possible. What I invest in my children is education. This will be their only inheritance, not wealth. Therefore, education is first and other things come later as a bonus.*
>
> *I don't have a daughter of my own, but I live with my brother-in-law's child. This girl was living in the village and*

---

[4] A tribe from Kigoma region, Tanzania.

[5] This word means initiation.

doing nothing. My brother-in-law wanted to marry her off because he had no money to pay for her studies; she was very young, about fifteen years old. This decision pained me a lot and I suggested letting the girl come with me to Dar es Salaam, where I would find her a school, even a domestic sciences school. Because what I believe is, if someone has an education, even a small one, they will have the knowledge to do a wider spectrum of things than those who are illiterate. This will reduce the dependency of women.

He agreed, and now I live with her and she is studying needlework and domestic sciences. I wish all daughters could have their own earnings and not be dependent on their husbands. When they get married they believe that their husbands will give them everything. It is not true.

Responsibility for girls and young women's own lives means they know their rights, and so are not oppressed, exploited and abused. It also means the ability to make choices and be able to support the choices they make.

Informants mentioned some other, more practical points for improving girls' lives, such as:

- Discourage religious discrimination
- Favour access to loans for women
- Educate youth on the importance of education and on the need for good behaviour
- Teach English as an official language at school
- Raise school standards
- Abolish taxes for NGOs that help people

Family and individual objectives

Informants were asked what they have been able to achieve according to their desires and life objectives, what were the major constraints, and what helped them achieve what they had planned. The following are the major constraints.

Constraints	*Number*
Marriage arrangements made by the family/discouraged by parents/relatives	18
Lack of money in the family	14
Failed crucial exams	8
Found a job before finishing studies	4
Became pregnant before finishing studies	4
No specific desire for a profession/family problems	4
Encouraged to develop informal work	3
Not selected by a specific school	1
Total	56

Many women informants said that they did not achieve what they wanted because of their parents' attitudes. Most of them did not have enough money to pay for school. However, many parents also did not perceive any advantage in sending a girl to school. In many tribes, it is still more valued to acquire cows or a bride price than to pay school fees for a girl who will leave the house and work for another family. One 38-year-old Christian woman working as a businesswoman, selling *dagga* (small fishes) from Mwanza and Lake Tanganyika at the fish market, explained the situation of young girls:

> *My parents were peasants. I come from Mara region. My father owns about 60 cows and a large number of goats and sheep. We were 5 children in my family and I am the third-born.*
>
> *I have primary level education. My parents were not able to send me to school because I was a girl. They were looking for wealth and wanted to receive a lot of cattle from my husband. They did not allow me to continue to secondary school level because they had already found me a husband.*

After finishing my primary level I got married. I was so young! I had a lot of problems with my first delivery since we, Mara people, practice circumcision, and also because of my tender age. When I think about those things, I do think that men are very bad people, and that they do not have any humanity.

I did not achieve what I wanted because of my parents, particularly my father, who wanted me to get married because they would get financial benefits from the marriage. They got a lot of cows as the bride price.

Another 42-year-old Muslim businesswomen working as a newspaper agent confirmed this:

My parents were peasants and there were six children in the family. I am the third-born. My parents just know how to write and read.

After completing primary school, I stayed at home because my parents didn't have enough money to pay for my school fees. They sent me to be circumcised and be taught "unyago" *while I was waiting for a husband. I stayed home for a very long time, helping my parents till I got married.*

I wanted to become a teacher as many other girls of my age were going to teaching college. After one year they were coming back and working.

I did not get what I wanted because my parents were just peasants, having only enough money for daily needs, not for studies.

Some of the women who did not pursue further studies said it was due to their family's situation. Some were not supported by anyone; others came from a family that experienced problems and had been given less encouragement to pursue their studies. For example, a 27-year-old woman, who is now a businesswoman, despite the fact that she wanted to become a nurse, told her story:

I was born in Dar es Salaam in 1973. My parents are from Dar. They divorced in 1979, and we lived with our father and stepmother. My dad was working at his garage, which enabled us to live and study. We were eight children, but only six survived. I am the first-born in our family. My dad studied up to Form IV, while my mum had primary education.

I studied at Kinondoni Primary School from Standard 1 to VII. Then I joined Lugalo Secondary School, a private school, from Form 1 to II. But I did not finish my secondary education as I decided to leave school, because of my relationship with my boyfriend. We were going out, listening to music. I did not see the importance of going to school. I thought I was wasting my time there.

Now I regret it, because I see that it was ignorance and laziness. It was childish behaviour. I wish I could finish my Form IV education. However, the environment I lived in also affected my ability to pursue my studies. After my mum got divorced, we lived with our father and stepmother; it affected us a lot. There was nobody forcing us to do anything; dad alone could not do it.

Also, we didn't communicate much with our dad, even though we had problems. Our stepmother stopped us from being close to him or talking to him about what we wanted. So, we had nobody to fall back upon; we were just waiting to grow up and weren't thinking about anything else.

That's how it is—if you live in a good environment, in a family that has children who like to study or parents who are literate, automatically you will like it too. Even if you do not want to go to school, you will go because you will be forced to go.

A mother is like a pillar of strength in the house, and when she is absent, nothing can be done. That is what happened to us while we were living with our father and stepmother. A lot of stepmothers have "bad hearts" towards their stepchildren. They do not like to see them developing, and they discourage their husbands from taking care of them. As a result, the children get very little care, which makes them unsure about the right thing to do.

This leads to bad habits, such as drinking alcohol, in order to numb their feelings. That's what happened to me when I decided to leave school for no reason at all—not because they had no money to educate me. Maybe if my mother had been there, I mean if she had been living with my father, I could have finished school. There was no one to help us morally and we did not get any advice from relatives or friends, because we did not even try to say what we were experiencing with our stepmother.

Family problems can act as impediments to making choices for the future. Another example comes from a 42-year-old woman, now working in business:

My parents were peasants and my father studied up to Standard IV. My mother was a housewife. My dad had two wives. They had three children each. I am the only child of my dad. My mother married another man and had three more children, then another man, with whom she has two children. My dad also married his third wife and had four children with her. So my father had ten children.

I studied at Saranda Primary School from Standard I to IV, then at Itigi Primary School from Standard V to VII. I was not able to continue because of my stepmother, my father's first wife. She used to beat me so badly. The other children were given food after coming back from school, but I had to cook my food. One day she beat me so much because I refused to cook "ugali" *that she injured me near my eye. I was very young and could not cook a lot of* ugali. *So my father shifted me to another wife's place, where life was also very difficult. My brain was so mixed up at that time because of the treatment I got. I had no professional direction.*

Nevertheless, a small number of informants succeeded in achieving their goals. Out of 68 participants, 12 women managed to beat the odds.

- Of these, seven were directly encouraged and supported by a woman: the mother, an aunt or a stepmother. A 45-year-old Christian woman, working as a teacher and businesswoman, said:

  My mother seemed to have more influence on me than my father, because he was travelling a lot. Most of the time, I was alone with her at home. She told me to study hard, so as to have my own life in the future.

  I paid nothing in terms of school fees as the Government paid for us. We were just told to make a contribution of Tanzanian Shillings 25 at primary school, 250 at secondary school and 180 for boarding school.

- Four were helped by a man who paid for further studies: a father, brother, or an uncle.

- One said she was self-motivated to pursue her studies, as she really wanted to become an accountant. However, her parents also encouraged her. This 37-year-old Christian woman said:

  Definitely, my parents influenced me. We grew up in church surroundings, meeting different people. My parents always talked about women who were successful, and wanted us to be like them.

  My father was a Reverend in the Lutheran church, and my mother was a housewife. We are three in the family, and there were two girls. We were so happy and our parents always encouraged us to be a family wherever we went. We were encouraged in religious terms to be innocent, patient and tolerate things.

Another 41-year-old Christian woman, working as an accountant and having her own business, said:

> *After my studies, I was selected to go to the teaching college, but I didn't respond because it was not my plan. I did not like teaching. Then I cleared the interviews for East African Railways in 1978 and got a job there. I got married in 1982. I*

was working and my husband appreciated my work. He did not have any problems with it.

My professional aim was to be a nurse, but my father discouraged me. He told me that nursing was not a good job, and it was risky because I would be playing with disease all the time and might get infected. In this way, my desire died. I had no alternative after my father discouraged me from nursing, and because I did not want to be a teacher as the Government had chosen for me, I decided to become a clerk. My parents helped me in terms of school fees and pocket money.

One woman learnt to read and write in adult education courses, as part of the national policy. This 52-year-old Zaramo[6] woman explained how she finally succeeded:

*After my first menstrual period, I was locked inside the house for one year, waiting for a husband. Then I got married and left my family. I was only 12. I was not able to study because in our Zaramo tradition, when a girl gets her menstrual period, her parents stop her from studying and lock her inside, to be initiated "*mwali.*" Nobody is allowed to see you except your relatives and any man who is expecting to marry you.*

If your periods start and you have never attended school, then you will never attend it. If you are not lucky with men, you will stay inside, maybe for five years, until you find one.

They do this because parents are afraid the girl will become a prostitute if she goes out. When you are inside, they teach you a lot of things including how to take care of a husband, a family and the house. What's worse, they also teach you how to perform sexual intercourse, and parents fear that a girl, once outside, will want to have sex to know how good it is.

That's why I did not study until after my marriage. My aim was to know how to read and write so as to get rid of my ignorance. In our day, President Julius Nyerere insisted that people who didn't have a primary education should study at adult

[6] One among the 120 tribes of Tanzania.

education centres, in order to fight disease, ignorance and poverty.

The Government provided free adult education, and so the President helped us become literate. Now I know how to read and write. I can read a magazine without any problem; I can even write a letter.

Some informants said they had no personal objective or professional aims. Indeed, in many circumstances, the Government or other agencies determined people's professions. One 39-year-old Christian woman, who is now working as a teacher, said:

In those days there were no employment problems. We were selected directly from schools for teaching college, police training, A levels, or direct employment. The posts were determined by how we scored in our Form IV examinations. I was chosen to go to the teaching college at Kireruu-Iringa. That's why I had no professional goals; wherever they placed us, we had to go.

Lack of information and communication also blocks young women from making choices about their future life. One 52-year-old Muslim woman, also working as a businesswoman, said:

After completing Standard Seven, I stayed home to help my parents. Then I got married.

Professionally, I was always interested in going to town to work. I thought that being a teacher or a nurse were the only occupations for a woman. As I was a village woman, I did not really know what was going on in the real world. I thought being in town was something; being in town meant you had succeeded in life.

I was influenced by my mother, who was always talking about life in town as being easier and better than life in the village. She also talked about married life, and how to take care of a husband, to like his relatives, to respect him. So I dreamt of being married and going to town in search for a job.

The major constraints for young girls wanting to pursue further studies are at the:

Macro level: State and lineage organisation, national policies related to education, legal issues, marriage, social services, introduction of cost-sharing for education and health services, and the social construction of femininity.

Micro level: Socio-environmental elements, such as family support and organisation. Many parents still make arrangements for their children's lives. Characterised by the predominance of the community over the individual, there is still a lack of interest and of motivation, as many parents do not perceive the importance of education for girls because boys are seen as the future "head of the household." Financial, psychological and informational constraints are among the major impediments.

In summary, the family is still based on the father's uncontested authority, which is viewed as the pillar of traditional familial organisation. The family is seen as an institution that guarantees social order, the father being representative of State authority.

Clear social roles in the institution of marriage[7]

In Dar es Salaam, marriage[8] is still perceived as an important institution for all, both men and women, fulfilling essential functions

---

[7] Oheneba-Sakyi (1999) noted from her study done in Ghana that it may no longer be appropriate to see marriage arrangements as fitting idealistically mutually exclusive cells such as "arranged marriage," or "entirely chosen by partner/herself," nor can we independently classify such marriages as customary, ordinance, church, or consensual, since there are dynamic processes that usually overlap. Marriage arrangements in African societies are complex, and attempting to put them into certain pre-determined modes may leave the respondent with no choice other than to say what the researcher wants to hear. Even living arrangements of couples often change in response to the varying demands of the larger extended family or the couple itself (1999:183).

[8] In her dissertation submitted in 2000 for partial fulfilment of the requirements of the Degree of Bachelor of Arts (Sociology) at the University of Dar es Salaam, Tabu Haule found that for most Tanzanians, unity in the family is seen as essential to the child's health as families are required to perform four basic tasks: reproduction, regulation of sexual relations, economic cooperation, and the care and socialisation of children. Divorce is seen as a shameful event, leading to a lack of social support for the children of divorced spouses in terms of education, security and health provision. One immediate effect of divorce is to create female-headed families without adequate financial support. In her survey, she discovered that 70% of interviewed children lived with their mothers after their parents' divorce and all reported tremendous changes in their quality of life. In comparison, those living with their fathers reported no significant change in social support.

for the whole society. Most find that it confers prestige, honour, social recognition and legitimisation, and generally facilitates life. Divorce is perceived as a severe disturbance that jeopardises the family. As stated by Leslie:

> *The marriage being between two families, both sets of in-laws have an interest in its survival and will bring their influence to bear and give their assistance in settling quarrels before these get to the stage of "grounds for divorce" (1963: 224).*

Different social roles clearly identify who is doing what and on what basis. They define the identity of each person, which enables the transmission of social memory. By integrating their roles, individuals internalise the specific knowledge that is linked to it, while making the institutional order livelier through role identity (Kaufmann, 2001:194). Individuals continue to define the situation while internalising the social memory that is included in the social role. The marriage institution allows men to express their authority over women concretely, as they define themselves as the leader and the main decision maker.

Marriage is good for men

Most men informants said that marriage was very important to them. The following reasons were given:

- It is God's command.
- It provides respect and prestige in the community.
- It is the way to have children and new generations.
- It is a means to fulfil sexual and biological needs.
- It is a way to avoid STIs and AIDS.
- It is a framework for developing mutual help and support.

Marriage is perceived as an "institution established by God." Muslim men claimed that, "The Holy Book said that it is not good for a man to be alone," while Christians said, "It is a command for a man not to be alone, it is God's plan, commandment or order."

Socially speaking, marriage "gives respect and prestige in the community." A 42-year-old Muslim man said, "Marriage is symbolising that a man has reached a certain stage in society. Married men are respected in society and they can also influence decisions in the community. An unmarried man of a certain age is seen as a hooligan." It seems that a married man gains respect in society and that people do not trust unmarried men. To get a wife is seen as a sign of maturity. It is "a symbol of manhood."

Some others also perceive marriage as a way of raising a family "in which children bring happiness and enjoy parental care." Parents must be responsible for their children and take care of them. One 41-year-old Christian man mentioned, "To have children outside marriage is not recommended in any African tradition."

Marriage is seen as a way to fulfil sexual needs, and avoid AIDS and sexually transmitted diseases. It is a preventive measure in the current context of the spread of STIs and AIDS. Some informants said that they were afraid to have many partners. One 46-year-old Christian man said:

> *Even biologically it is very clear that human beings need someone for their intimacy. Morally, we are not permitted to commit adultery, and biologically and socially, there is a threat of sexually transmitted diseases. To be free from diseases and respect God's command, marriage is very important.*

Marriage facilitates mutual economic help, cooperation and support between spouses. It is a way of sharing daily life and family responsibilities. One 76-year-old Christian man said, "To have many wives permits an increase in the labour force of the family."

Most men expect the following qualities from their wife:

- To be a good mother by taking care of the children and reporting to the husband about them.
- To respect the husband, his relatives and friends. This means taking into consideration, and conforming to, decisions taken by them.
- To have good manners, which means being obedient, humble, sober and polite; to have wisdom, and not be greedy.

- To be a hard worker, honest and transparent; a reference to social roles that delineate a clear sexual division of labour.
- To be a co-partner in the family's development, for example "to give constructive advice on the development of the family" and to handle family affairs effectively—including child care, homemaking and all household duties. One 43-year-old Muslim man working as a teacher said that a woman must "feel obliged to contribute to family affairs in all aspects."
- To love her husband, which means that a woman must conform to all her husband's desires.

Respect is the most common quality expected by informants. Men want their wives to acknowledge that they are the "head of the family" from the beginning, and that they have the power in the decision-making process for all matters related to family affairs. As stated by a 41-year-old male Christian engineer:

> *It is quite different when we talk about respect and fear. She has to be free to express her feelings and exercise freedom. But what she expresses and exercises must not go beyond the "boundaries." She has to realise that she has a certain limit she can't go beyond, for instance when it comes to the case of decision making in the family. On decision making, the man has to take responsibility.*

One man mentioned "to communicate very calmly and to be informed of the situation of the family and of children." In general, few men see communication as a way of strengthening family ties. Only one man mentioned that sharing common interests could be good for spouses.

Most male informants declared they were married. Many of them experienced several marriages[9]. Some were married under family pressure, others while they were still young, through family arrangements. The most common reasons given by men for

[9] It is difficult to evaluate the type of marriage that men said they were involved in. Do they refer to formal marriage, with the full consent of parents and guardians and the sanction of the religious body concerned? It seems that two persons living together are married, with or without religious rite or tribal custom.

separation or divorce were adultery, infertility of the woman, financial differences between the families, interference by the woman's family, and independence of the woman. The woman proving to be incapable of providing for all the family's necessities was also an important cause of divorce. The presence of a woman's relatives in the house is perceived as a lack of respect for the husband and his relatives. Differences in income or religion, and lack of common interests, were also seen as impediments to a good life between spouses.

Most men return their wives to their parents' house once they decide to get a separation or divorce. It is an official way of abandoning their responsibilities onto their parents-in-law, as a way of starting a new life. One man said, "I brought her back to her parents' place in Dodoma to force her to change her behaviour."

Rarely do men pay their ex-wife and children any maintenance[10]. Many justifications are given for this, which can be summarised as:

Their mother refused to obey me and was treating me like a house-boy[11]*; I do not have to feel responsible for them any more. She did not respect me. They can manage and I do not care any more about them.*

Men perceive themselves as being more influential than women in family affairs. All informants agreed that they are and have to be the "head of the family." For most of them this means:

- To be the wage earner for the family
- To take responsibility for family affairs
- To fulfil every family member's essential needs
- To have the final say in all family matters

---

[10]The situation is also not exclusive to Tanzania. For example, in the province of Quebec, Canada, in 1994, 55 per cent of parents who were legally obliged to pay alimonies were not doing it. In December 1995, the Government of Quebec adopted a law facilitating the automatic collection of alimonies to solve this problem of bad debts. Indeed, alimonies are directly collected by the ministry of Revenue-Income Tax, and are subsequently paid to the beneficiary. (www.educaloi.qc.ca/LVD_loi/B_Dossiers/index.php3?no=4)

[11] Hired male help.

The head of the family has direct and indirect control over all matters concerning the family. He is a decision maker, who establishes the rules and regulations to be followed in the family circle "even without consulting anybody else." He is the official speaker at all social events and acquires authority as "the president of the nation." A 32-year-old Christian man working as a carpenter said:

A father must supervise his family and be sure that everything is maintained. A family works like any other organisation, which needs leadership and hierarchy. As the head, I am responsible for making the final decisions for my family.

Most men justify this attitude by religion and tradition. Some mentioned that it is the way to do things if everyone wants things to work normally. One 46-year-old Christian man working at TANESCO[12] said:

> *If you go to a community you will see that there is always somebody who is responsible for running the community. There is no meeting without a chairperson. In the family, there are some family matters, which demand a spokesperson. As a husband, I feel responsible for all family affairs. A husband as the head of the family is also biblical. It is stated clearly in the Bible that men are the heads of the household and should be respected by women. The same is also emphasised by our African traditions. Wives are subjects to their husbands.*

When men talk about mutual help, they mean that they are the ones to decide and plan. Afterwards, women have to accomplish all their duties, as already delineated by social rules and structure. It is under an ideology of cooperation that men can dominate, oppress and humiliate all women of their society.

The decision-making process illustrates how structural features in society lead to perceptions, which command particular behaviour and determine actions. Clear social roles determine who does what, ignoring principles of democracy. Social or religious sanctions are powerful deterrents against motivating people to adopt new behaviour patterns.

---

[12] The Tanzanian Electricity Company.

However, besides men who take refuge in tradition to justify their right to dominance, some recognise that tradition should be abolished in certain circumstances, for instance in the decision for marriage. Many think that it is a personal affair that should be in the hands of the partners themselves. The influence of parents and relatives from the extended family should be limited. According to many participants, much of the problems that married couples encounter are due to interference from relatives and parents who want to extend their control to other aspects of their children's married life. Marriage is no longer seen as a being confined to a tribe or a clan, and extended family members should act as advisors only.

One 42-year-old Muslim man mentioned that he had never paid the dowry and that his parents were not involved in his decision to cohabit. He said that he preferred this way of doing things because he felt freer. In town, this attitude is becoming more common.

Despite the importance of allowing the partners to decide on their marriage, some participants recognised that "there are more and more divorces nowadays because people do not take time to know each other." One 57-year-old Christian man working as a watchman said:

> *I still strongly believe that parents have to decide on the marriage. In my experience, there is a big difference between marriages in our day and the current ones. The rate of divorce and separation has been growing. I think it is because of the wrong choices of our children, whether boys or girls.*
>
> *You know earlier, before a couple got engaged, the parents of both sides had to sit together and analyse various issues related to the expected wedding. They went to the extent of checking if there were any chronic diseases in the family, and the general traits of the two families, such as infertility, were analysed effectively.*
>
> *What is happening today is the contrary. A young boy meets a young girl at school, and after six months, they go introduce themselves to the parents. In those six months they have been staying together just like a husband and wife. To meet the*

parents is just a matter of procedure. They have taken the decision and nobody can convince them otherwise.

I still believe that parents have a big role to play as far as marriage is concerned. What I think is that parents can allow their children to express their views and accommodate those views when decisions are made.

However, in spite of these comments the majority of men were more in favour of free choice. It seems that tradition is only used when it serves men's purposes.

Domestic authority and its contestation

Domestic authority is obtained through marriage. Most women are afraid of their husbands and take a non-confrontational attitude. They feel they have to respect their husband's authority, and "they tolerate the situation because of their children." They are even told by their parents that "this is how life is in marriage," so they have to put up with it.

Women who feel uncomfortable in married life, frequently mentioned lack of communication and mutual support, or the way that men treat them like slaves. One woman said, "Respect is there, depending on how you treat your husband. You have to do things in order to prevent him from going to see other concubines. You know, a man is like a baby. Sometimes, he does not know what he is doing."

Thus, women said they were afraid of being abandoned and this is why they respected most rules and husband's attitudes. Even those women who earn more money than their husband are afraid of being left alone. Moreover, working outside the home is still poorly perceived, even if many informants admitted that it was an economic necessity.

It is difficult for women to be alone. They experience pressure from their parents and family, and are made to feel they are being selfish, or are forcing their children to live without a father. They are accused of not respecting God's principles, of being too proud or refusing to forgive a husband, and of being responsible for any trouble within married life.

Some women cannot tolerate this kind of life anymore. That's why some informants decided to separate or are now divorced. They'd rather live alone with their children and other relatives, than share a so-called common life. Eight women identified themselves as separated and six as divorced. Separated or divorced women gave the following reasons for living alone:

- Lack of responsibility: the husband was not taking care of them or the children
- Abandonment: the husband did not return home for many years
- Dependence of the husband
- The woman did not see the benefits of her work, because of the burden of her husband's relatives and the impossibility of "developing themselves"
- The husband did not allow his wife to work, but she wanted to be financially independent
- The husband was a womaniser, having relationships with young girls, house-girls, and many other women
- The husband's jealousy
- Pressure or hostility from relatives, not from the same tribe
- The husband's aggression

Violence against women is institutionalised through family, marriage, religion and State. Statistics about domestic violence in Tanzania are not available. But if we consider the number of newspaper articles that are written on this issue, we can assume domestic violence is very common. Women are afraid to report these cases to the police or to go to the hospital. They know in advance that they will be the losers.

It is the same for rape. How can the number of rapes be estimated? Most rapes are not reported to the police. Insecurity on the streets of Dar es Salaam is great for most women and it is reported as an important impediment to women living in popular wards (CARE, 1997). Street intimidation is common. Sexual regulation and surveillance is done in practice through the imposition of a code of modesty, the need for women to ask the husband's permission to go out or perform any activity, women's seclusion ("a woman is like a flower"), the lack of authorisation for women to speak in public or to other men outside the home or family environment, and through various body signals such as reverences, forbidding women from looking men directly in the eye, and so on.

A divorce story: as told by Hamisi[13], a 41-year-old engineer, and a Christian who has lived in Dar es Salaam for 12 years

I have been married for 10 years. I remember well, we got married in June 1978. At first, it was a very good experience. But, I don't know what happened some years later.

By then, I was a teacher in a secondary school, and my duty station was in the southern part of the country. My wife was a banker by then, here in Dar es Salaam. When we got married, we went to live in the south of Tanzania.

The problems started in 1988, when I decided to join the University of Dar es Salaam for further education. After my first semester, I went back home for vacation. That is when I started to notice changes on the part of my wife. She was always complaining that I was irresponsible about family affairs, that she was spending her whole salary on the family without getting any help from me.

After vacation, I went to the college to continue with my studies. At that time, we had only one child, a daughter. After some weeks I got the message that my wife had been transferred from the south to Dar es Salaam. I didn't know this before, and in fact, it shocked me.

I went to see her and found that it was true. Although she knew that I was a student and I was receiving an allowance to support me in my studies, she demanded some portion of whatever I was getting to support the family. Whatever I did brought no changes in our relationship. She was complaining that what I was giving was not enough. After realising that the situation was becoming worse, I decided to consult my friends and relatives to resolve our conflict.

The situation disturbed me to the extent that I decided to postpone my studies for one year, just to solve the problems. All my efforts were in vain. She did not change and she insisted that what she was demanding was right.

[13] Fictional name.

After that, we decided to separate for a time, to give everyone a chance to reconsider the situation in depth. After three years, nothing substantial was realised. She took the further step of not allowing me to visit my daughter at her home, even if I gave my daughter a present, she didn't accept it. That situation made me angry.

When I was in the fourth year of my studies, I decided to divorce her and it was the end of our marriage. I believe that our differences in income lead to the breakdown of our marriage. If I had been earning more than she was, I could have salvaged the situation.

Another divorce story: told by Mohamed, a 45-year-old lawyer, and a Muslim living in Dar es Salaam for six years

Actually, I can say that we are separated. You know, with us Muslims, it is not as easy to divorce as you might think. For us it is a long process. Divorce is the last resort after all other efforts have failed. These include consulting the parents of both sides, and also friends and religious leaders. But I can tell you that to be separated for a while is very easy, and afterwards you abandon the relationship. I think it is easy to get a separation because our tradition and our religion are not very strict in terms of wedding vows. Our religion and tradition allow a person to have more than one wife. Therefore, it is very easy to get a separation today and tomorrow to have another wife.

I also think that it is difficult to divorce in our tradition because it costs a lot, particularly for the husband. You know, when you divorce a wife, everything you have earned together has to be divided equally between the two spouses. Many men do not want this. They get a separation and keep in contact with their wives, just to show that there is still some relationship existing.

We decided to separate after we failed to settle some problems, which still exist in the family. I am a Muslim and we have a tradition to keep. Unfortunately, my wife is Christian. All the years we were together as husband and wife, I have tried, together with my relatives, to convince her to change her religion, but all efforts failed.

I am the first-born in my family and I think I need to be an example to my young brothers and sisters. When we got married, at the beginning we agreed to keep some Islamic principles. She used to cover her head and put on our traditional dress, the *"baibui"* all the time. She sometimes used to fast during the Holy Ramadan. My relatives were at least happy with those changes. But, as time went on, things started to change. She stopped covering her head any more and she started to wear trousers. For some years, we tried to solve these differences, but in vain.

I was not happy at all with the situation and as a last resort we separated for a period of time, just to see if any change could be achieved. We separated in 1997. Indeed, because my religion gives me permission to marry more than one wife, I decided to marry the woman I am now living with.

Marriage is very important to me because I need somebody in my life to help me in all aspects of life. You know, I am a social being and there are some social needs which I have in life; things like love, affection and encouragement, helping each other in life. Marriage is also important because, as a human being, I have biological needs, which have to be met by the opposite sex. With the existing diseases, it is better to have a wife to avoid diseases.

Conclusion: Women creating the city

This chapter has shown that institutions such as the family and marriage still structure the lives of individuals and the community. Personal life objectives are very often difficult to achieve, as too many people have the authority to decide for others. Koda (2000) demonstrated that tensions between parents and children are based on misunderstandings and the lack of dialogue between the two groups.

The marginalisation of children and youth in the decision-making process has had drastic effects on the manner in which their needs, interests and aspirations are addressed. In relation to marriage, Foster (1995:102) wrote, "The expectation everywhere in Tanzania is that all or nearly all should marry." The elders' authority remains considerable in marriage "especially since kin will have to be relied upon to provide bride-wealth." However, ideals do not always correspond to reality, because irregular forms of marriage occur. For instance, individual choice is positively reported and it is becoming increasingly popular nowadays. Many other changes are also noticeable as greater awareness of the outside world develops.

Nevertheless, marriage in Tanzania can still be perceived as operating in the interests of male objectives. The dominant Tanzanian gender model is hierarchical and defines masculinity in terms of leadership and household provision, which are regarded as the main attributes of male identity. Even various social policies assume women's dependence on men and the State apparatus reinforces it through family and marriage institutions.

The use of force and violence seem at the basis of gender relations. Men need authority and seek prestige and domination; it is connected to a relationship of command and control, and reciprocally, to obedience and submission. Women's respect of men is perceived as mandatory, as men's authority is completed by women's submission and obedience.

The State influences the daily life of women and men through laws that directly affect people's lives and choices. The lineage structure reinforces the State apparatus through the reproduction of the *habitus*. Thus the public-private separation in the debate over state versus women's control over fertility is artificial. This is clear in the Tanzanian context, where corporate relationships and kinship groups are still relatively cohesive and have significant importance in the formulation of public policies.

The power structure is an object of practice as well as a condition. In Tanzania, multiple components at the core of the power structure of gender are clear:

- *State political level:* Men control the planning and executive machinery of the central State; they have absolute control of the political leadership and they make decisions on all topics. Women face exclusion from party politics and the public sphere. Political parties barely address women's concerns, in a continuation of the historic exclusion from formal politics, despite the fact that women contributed actively to the liberation struggles in various African countries (Gaidzanwa, 1992; Geiger, 1997). There is a tendency for male-dominated organisation to show a progressive profile to the donor community, while in actual practice sidelining gender in mainstream activities (Meena, 1992: 23).

- *Political and religious milieu:* Tripp (1996) mentioned that there is an uneasy relationship between the women's movement and the multiparty movements, showing how women's increased activism has not readily been incorporated into the reform movement. It is difficult for women to open up spaces for greater political participation, guaranteeing human rights, enhancing government accountability and institutionalising political pluralism and political liberalisation. Their participation is not taken account of in political reform, as access has been curtailed by discriminatory educational opportunities, limited economic opportunities and the resources necessary to run for office, time constraints due to domestic responsibilities, religious and cultural proscriptions on women's involvement in public life, and lack of access to bids for political power (Mba, 1989; Chazan, 1989:189-192; Parpart, 1988: 216-218 in Tripp, 1996:295).

  The religious milieu also blocks women's involvement in decision-making spheres, as it places too many proscriptions on women's behaviour. Religious groups may also encourage women's subordination by arguing that their place is in the home and they should be responsible for domestic tasks. The religious milieu reinforces the patriarchal ideology.

- *Working milieu:* In Tanzania, the Government promulgated laws, giving equal access to work for men and women. Nevertheless, these laws are not applied in a way that genuinely ensures women's equal participation in work. Access to work is still male-biased, and women do not have equal power in decision making at all levels. Sexual segregation of some kind is still apparent in the labour forces. Moreover, a lack of information on women's economic and other activities still exists, as do sexist stereotypes. Women's economic activities are seen as low status, even if their contribution ensures the survival of many households and families.

- *Lineage and family milieu, and kinship relations:* These legitimize power and authority for men. All social organization functions in this way. Culture and social organization takes precedence over individual autonomy. For instance, marriage is seen as the core of existence and life; it is a duty, an obligation towards the community, a life rhythm that obliges everybody to participate in it. Abbott (2001:494) reported the words of an Anglican priest, John Mbiti, who declared that in Africa, an unmarried person is a malediction for the community, a rebel who challenges the law. An unmarried person is not only an abnormal individual, but a sub-human person. In practice, marriage is generally detrimental for women, as can be illustrated by the dowry issue. Many women are still dependent on their families; their father or other male relatives take decisions concerning them directly. Moreover, the interactions between spouses show how a husband can exert power over his wife to enforce behaviour, actions and even beliefs that she would not otherwise have had. There is no democracy at the household level; patriarchy and the seniority of age influence social relations.

Power relations are supported by women's subordination. As Christina Obbo demonstrated in the case of Uganda, and Obrist van Eeuwijk in the case of Tanzania, women have developed an attitude of non-confrontation with their husbands. In total:

- Women are socialised to confinement in the home, and to being responsible for domestic tasks.

- Women are not used to expressing their views, as they are not authorised to talk in public.

- Women are afraid to "fight for their rights." They believe that it is impossible; they still believe that they will be empowered through discussion with their male counterparts.

- Women do not negotiate or are afraid of negotiating with their husbands, for example over childcare and rearing or household duties. Their strategy is to share those activities with other women of the house or relatives.

Why do women act like this? They face too many constraints. They do not actively consent to be dominated, but the strength of constraints forces them to act in conformity with authority. Men use force and violence as a means to ensure their authority over women and to obtain what they want from them. Violence is expressed through different means and can be physical, mental or psychological. Men can beat their wives, insult them, repudiate them unilaterally, deprive them of their children or of access to material and financial resources, and even rape or murder them. Men continue to believe it is their absolute right.

Many laws related to marriage, discrimination against women, access to work and education have been amended in Tanzania over recent decades. The question is, are they changing minds and behaviour? As noted by many women informants, new laws do not change attitudes of prejudice and discrimination nor deliver justice. In many cases a gulf exists between legal achievements and the actual status of women. Protective legislation may not necessarily be respected.

Various institutions were established in the 1970s and 1980s to promote the participation of women in employment and development, creating awareness of the condition of women in society. Nevertheless, the forces perpetuating discrimination against women and inequality in the sexual division of labour and responsibilities, as well as introducing new forms of inequalities are increasingly recognised as complex and pervasive. Ancient cultural values and social practices, as well as women's greater burden of household work, subsistence labour, and childbearing and childrearing, were noted as factors perpetuating women's subordinate position in social systems. This is true, not just in Tanzania, but in many other sub-Saharan countries, as observed by Oppong:

> *Continuity with the past is clearly discernible. Traditional Tanzanian institutions persist despite change. According to informants, the old initiation ceremonies are still carried out. There is even a revival of old forms of beliefs and practices. What was noted by Swantz in the 1970s is still alive today. For example, even in Dar es Salaam, girls in certain groups are still secluded during the puberty rites, from the time of puberty until the day of their marriage (Oppong, 1987:157-160*).

Nevertheless, changes are taking place in accordance with the new urban life conditions and environment. New gender relations are emerging. Women are learning that old ways of patriarchy no longer work since they cannot be guaranteed land, jobs or remittances from migrant husbands (Gaidzanwa, idem:123-124). Similarly, men who do not have jobs and resources are unable to exercise their gender roles as fathers and patriarchs in the household.

Women earning more money than their husbands are not taken seriously as the head of the household, because their work is perceived as part-time or casual. Nevertheless, urban life, as manifested in political and religious organisations, cultural production, and the environment of neighbourhood networks, has benefited from and sometimes pivoted around the contribution of women. The development of urban communities depends on women's contribution in central ways: through their political involvement, religious activism and economic organisation. Women's daily efforts to enhance their own communities have been major forces in creating the city (Sheldon, 1996:22).

CHAPTER 4

DAILY EXPERIENCES OF FEMININITY AND MASCULINITY

Joan Mapunda, like many other women living in Dar es Salaam, finds that her responsibilities are increasing. She says, "If you leave it to your husband, the children will not go to school. I have to be very strict, so my children get an education."

Though Joan is earning enough money from her productive activities to support the whole family, through time, she has discovered that "when a husband knows you have money, he won't contribute anything. His daily refrain will be, 'I have no money!'" She says that her husband no longer acts like a "good man" who supports his family, is responsible for the wellbeing of all its members, and takes all decisions. She feels a man must be strong enough to confront life's hardships. For some time this has not been the case for her, as her husband is always going out to drink with his friends and coming back late. He spends more money on beer than on his children's studies. She is afraid of getting AIDS or another sexually transmitted disease, but she can't say anything to him as he is the head of the family.

Joan is not the only woman in this situation. Some of her friends have told her that they too feel overburdened with family responsibilities. They also have to support many relatives or other dependants who need school fees, clothes, food and other necessities. Joan said, "If we do not work hard, our children will be illiterate, as our husbands spend time with other women and come home drunk. A home *is* due to a woman; nothing will be done if we leave it to a man."

Many men have children outside their marriage, and very often they try to impose them on their wives. In spite of their behaviour, most men are jealous when their own wives are concerned. Very often, as Joan says, "My husband is jealous when I talk to other men. He thinks that every man whom I talk to is my boyfriend."

Joan finds that her life is tough because her husband does not help her with anything. He shows more responsibility to his parents and relatives than to his own children. Her mother-in-law is now putting pressure on her son to divorce Joan because they do not belong to the same tribe.

Her husband does not provide for all the family's needs, as he prefers to spend money on himself. When he comes home drunk, he wants his wife to cook him a meal and sometimes he quarrels with her all night. Discussion and communication with him is impossible; he feels that his wife cannot tell him anything because he is the "head of the family."

Joan would like to cooperate with her husband in order to "develop" themselves and their children. She would like to have an easier life, and sometimes dreams of being seated in a nice restaurant, eating chicken in a good sauce with cashew nuts…but she knows that it may never happen!

In the urban environment, both women and men are confronted with changes. They try to adapt their behaviour to the new situation as they develop new social and gender relations. Joan testifies to the necessity for women to be innovative in spite of their lack of facilities. Confronted with a new environment, she has to develop behaviours that are not always in accordance with tradition. The difficulties of daily life in a time of economic crisis and uncertainty put more responsibilities on women, without improving their conditions. Marriage is no longer seen as security. All these factors put enormous pressure on women, even as they create new needs.

Femininity and masculinity as perceived by men and women

It is generally accepted in Tanzania that women and men have different traits, temperaments, characters, outlooks, opinions and abilities, and even whole personality structures. One set of traits defines masculinity and another set femininity. This unitary model of sexual character is a familiar part of sexual ideology (Connell, 1995:167) and influences social roles inasmuch as female and male roles are clearly defined. For example, it is believed that women's sexual nature prepares them for mothering and the care of others, while men are seen as proactive in the public sphere. The unitary concept means that biology determines feminine and masculine characters.

What do men in Dar es Salaam say about femininity?

All male informants were asked about the criteria for good female behaviour, and the attitudes of a good wife or ideal woman. They were also asked if it was suitable for a woman to work outside the home. Most men responded like this 59-year-old Muslim man, working as a security officer, who said, "Women are inferior beings and they need constant encouragement."

According to the majority of participants a woman should be polite, responsible, and tireless in family matters. She should take care of children, clean the house, and prepare food. She must be a hard worker and prove it "by waking up early in the morning before her husband." She should love and respect her husband and his relatives, as she should fear God. She must be tolerant, a good communicator, and very clever. A woman must wear decent clothes and have orderly manners. Furthermore, she must know how to handle a house; "this is why initiation ceremonies are important, because they teach how to manage a family." If employed or working outside home a woman should never forget that she has responsibilities to fulfil after normal working hours. Domestic chores are intrinsically linked to women's roles, duties and obligations. The same 59-year-old Muslim man said:

> *A good woman is like a mirror in the family. As a mirror she has to be honest, diligent and polite. She must demonstrate good relations with her husband and other members of the family through respect and general behaviour. A good wife should be a good teacher in the house. She should know exactly how to take care of the family and be well trained in all household chores. She should know how to welcome visitors, how to handle family matters, particularly when it comes to*

> *issues concerning in-laws. Many families have troubles because of their in-laws. Sometimes, they want to control the affairs of the family. If a wife is not wise, she might end up frustrated at the end of the day.*
>
> *A good wife should be God-fearing. You know, to fear God is the beginning of wisdom. Therefore, for a family to prosper, God should be put first.*

The ideal woman is seen as a person who does not forget her responsibilities as a woman. She has to respect men in general and should not ask too much of a man. She is submissive and loyal to her spouse and parents. The community respects this kind of woman.

How do men perceive a woman working outside home? Most informants think it is a bad state of affairs, but it is accepted because of the economic realities of life. Essentially, a woman's role is to be confined to the home and to perform all home-related activities. Many men said that Islam prohibits a woman to work outside the home. One 37-year-old Muslim man said:

> *Some men allow their wife to work outside the home. However, the first work and duty of a woman is to fulfil the household's needs. To work outside the home is seen as a "threat" to male dominance, because if a woman works and the man does not, then the woman can dominate him. If both are employed, the social division of labour between the spouses may not be respected. A woman should not work outside the home.*

A young man working as a night guard said, "When they work outside, they cannot fulfil their household activities and they do not respect their husband. The family loses something."

It is also considered bad because in some cases "it is not good to have a house-girl at home, as the man can ask for conjugal rights." Thus, it is the role of a woman to wait for her husband at home and to greet him when he comes back.

In today's situation some men recognise that work outside the home is *good* for a woman and her family. A woman can assist the development of the family through her financial contribution and by pooling money with her husband. It is perceived as a good thing "if there is good communication in the family circle." Still, many men are afraid of losing their power, because a woman working outside the home could have more influence in the decision-making process. One 41-year-old Christian man said:

> *For me there is nothing wrong with a woman working outside home. It has many advantages. For instance, if both the spouses are working, it will help them run family affairs better. Spouses should be transparent with and trust each other.*
>
> *Their relationship should not be measured by how much one is contributing to the family. In fact, if you undertake research to find out why so many marriages fail, you will find that one of the factors is income. This becomes worse when women earn more than men. They decide to take on the responsibilities of men, especially when it comes to sensitive issues.*
>
> *Let women work outside the home, but this should not be taken as a warrant for them to dictate terms and influence all decisions in the family. Their role should remain the same as if they were not working.*

Another Christian man, aged 57, working as a watchman, expressed his reluctance to let his wife work outside the home. However, he mentioned both positive and negative aspects of women working. He said:

> *Sometimes, it is good and sometimes it is not good. It depends on the culture. Women who work outside the home pretend to be equal to men. I don't think this is a good practice. I will give the example of one of my friends. This man is retired from work, but his wife is still working in a United Nations organisation, represented in our country. This woman has started a poultry-keeping project and has assigned her husband the task of collecting eggs all day—in the morning, afternoon and evening. When she comes home from work she demands all the eggs. I think this is mistreatment.*

On the other hand, women working outside the home are good for the development of the family. If the two can use the income to develop their family, then this is something very good.

Working outside the home places a double burden on women, as recognised by the majority of men informants. According to them, women should not "use this work as an excuse for not performing household duties as a woman should, like taking care of children, cooking and maintaining the general cleanliness of the house."

Table 11: Activities suitable for women, according to men

Activities suitable for women	*Number of men's answers*
Cooking	22
All domestic activities	22
Taking care of children	22
Gardening	1
Teaching	9
Nursing	3
Community development work	1
Depends on their qualifications	5
All activities can be done by women	5
Only domestic activities/no others	2
Work outside the home prohibited	1
According to woman's desire	1

When asked what activities were suitable for women, all male informants included domestic activities. Other jobs such as teaching and nursing were seen as being more acceptable for women, because they are associated with the feminine aspects of the personality. Men do not feel obliged to do housework because it is not paid. Moreover, it is a task socially assigned to women. How can an unemployed man do housework when his wife is responsible for it, even if she is also earning money for the family?

Respect: a social obligation for whom?

There was a general consensus that women, whether illiterate or with a university degree, should respect all men in general. The male respondents justified this assertion on structural and religious grounds.

Respect is a gender assignation for women because men take on responsibility in the family and in society in general. Women must be confined to household activities and other light duties, because men were created first, then women. African tradition puts men in a position of dominance. It is women's duty to respect men, and this is reinforced by initiation ceremonies and religion. "Since the beginning, women have been subordinated to men and they are just helpers to men. A woman must respect all men because she does not know which one will become her husband," said a 41-year-old pub supervisor.

A 45-year-old Christian man working as a lawyer, with a university diploma, also said:

> *In general women have to respect all men, regardless of whether they are their husbands or not.*
>
> *This has always been there. Respect for men has become one of the gender roles, or I can say that respect has gone beyond a gender role to be a sex characteristic of women. It is important to say here that gender roles vary from society to society, while sex roles are always the same in all societies, because they are biologically determined. I can see respect as biologically determined in African traditions because, wherever you go, the same thing exists for women.*
>
> *The tradition of women respecting men comes from other traditional practices and religious teachings. It is a normal thing for our tradition to assign different roles to boys and girls. Most of the roles assigned to girls have something to do with requiring girls to pay respect to boys. Girls have to cook for example, and then girls give the food to the boys first. Girls have to clean the table and utensils. All these elements reinforce the whole idea of paying respect to men.*

Girls take this experience through their life, as part of their specifically designed role. Many girls nowadays do not go through initiation rituals, but they grow up hearing that one of their roles is to respect men. They are taught this during their childhood.

Thus, the fact that women must respect all men is stipulated in initiation ceremonies and accepted by the whole community. It is expressed through gender roles and division of labour.

Roles that are socially recognised, legitimised and imposed, are seen as worthy of respect. Femininity and masculinity are socially created through the performance of different roles and tasks. A 41-year-old Christian man working as an engineer said:

Spouses must trust each other. Everything must be clear to everyone, as each must know the income earned. They must respect each other and all decisions must be agreed upon before any action is taken.

There must also be separation of powers in the household and roles should be clearly stated. In the household, there must be someone who has the final say when it comes to decision making on matters pertaining to the welfare of the family. In this case, the husband has to stand and speak.

Mutual respect, trustworthiness and transparency are the key to family development and maintaining good relations between spouses.

The need to respect gender roles as assigned and developed by society seems important to most informants. A 43-year-old Muslim man, working as a teacher, summarised what many other men said:

Good relations between spouses should reflect mutual understanding and respect. Everyone in the family should be respected and their contribution to the family acknowledged.

However, this does not mean that gender roles should be ignored. The husband should remain the husband and the wife remains the wife. When it comes to gender assignment, everyone should take their responsibilities seriously. For instance, household duties like cooking, fetching water and taking care of the children should be carried out by women while men should remain with their responsibilities, unless the two spouses agree to help each other under certain circumstances, which will not change the social division of labour according to genders.

Women's respect for all men should be a natural process, free of material considerations. One 56-year-old Muslim man working as a carpenter said:

> *What I know is that all men deserve respect from all women. This should be done regardless of the status and position of either men or women.*
>
> *Some men are respected because they have a good job and more money, and have a good life in general. And some women, because of their status and position, demand respect from men. They tend to consider their material things as something very important. Because of that, they show disrespect to men by reducing them to nothing.*
>
> *My position is that, even if a woman earns more money, respect for men is here to stay. Money or other material goods should not be exchanged for respect.*
>
> *This tradition has been there for a very long time, and it has penetrated very deep into our African culture. In every society there are some traditions, which should be maintained, regardless of time. Respect is one of them. This is always begun during childhood, when grandparents teach such values to their grandsons and granddaughters. Children grow up knowing exactly what they are supposed to do and how they are supposed to behave according to their genders.*
>
> *Teenage boys are taken to initiation ceremonies where they are instructed in the social values they are supposed to know. They are taken far away from their homes, preferably to forests where they camp. Men are instructed on how they are*

supposed to behave as heroes in society. They eat flesh, fresh blood and some roots, which are thought to make them powerful and strong, to protect their people against any threat. In some cases, in order to be recognised as heroes, they have to fight a lion or a leopard. To kill a lion or a leopard adds to the status of a young warrior. On these occasions, food caught is mixed with a wide variety of herbs and cooked together.

Women are taught how to be good wives who can handle their families effectively. In some traditions, women are prepared to take on household activities. The main responsibility is to bear children and take care of the family. Since their husbands are warriors, women have to look after their families.

For a woman to respect all men, irrespective of age, is seen as a must. A 37-year-old Christian man, studying for his master's degree at the University of Dar as Salaam, added, "Even a baby boy of two months deserves respect from women." Women have to manifest respect explicitly on different occasions, such as at funerals, where they must genuflect before the men, eat after them and so on. Women are perceived as "subjects of men" because they are "made inferior to men." "Usually, men give the dowry, initiate the relationship and decide on everything. It stems from tradition and from body morphology," said a 59-year-old Muslim man.

When asked about the origin of women's respect for all men, all participants turned to tradition to justify it. But when asked to explain this tradition or its origin no one was able to do so. This was not related to age or place of origin: men of all ages share the same way of thinking and are ignorant of the origin of this so-called tradition.

Traditional beliefs and men's attitudes

When questioned about the origin of the tradition, most of the participants said:

- It was revealed in Holy Books and religions, and is "a command given by the Creator of the universe."

- It is passed on from generation to generation and children grow up knowing it.
- It is associated with tribal initiation rites.
- It is a natural practice, since African attitudes are more favourable to boys.

For many men, "It comes from African tradition and it is here to stay. It is a good tradition because it demarcates what is to be done in the community, and by whom." This "tradition" maintains discipline in society. However, some expressed fear that "this tradition is losing its impact under the influence of external cultures, and this will have a negative impact on family relationships," as one 37-year-old Muslim businessman claimed. Another 49-year-old Muslim farmer added:

> *I learned such traditions from folklore told by my grandparents when I was very young. Such tradition is emphasised during initiation ceremonies when both men and women are gathered together to be instructed on the family roles they are supposed to fulfil during their adulthood.*
>
> *Not only that, but in many African societies a baby boy is more valued than a baby girl. This is very clearly shown when dealing with issues such as inheritance and family support in general.*

In the interviews many women said that men are the cause for their underdevelopment and that men humiliate women. Men were asked to comment on this statement. Half of them agreed with it, while the other half disagreed.

Men that agreed with this statement gave the following reasons:

- *Sex segregation:* From birth, sons are usually given priority whereas girls are not taken into consideration. Girls are confined to the home to accomplish household duties. They cannot develop any skills and do not benefit from resources. Women have no influence in the decision-making process. One 43-year-old Muslim man said, "Because of customs and traditions, some of the freedom and rights of women have been taken by men. That is why they can humiliate them."

Some traditions specifically oppress women and not men. For example, Muslim men do not allow their wives to venture outdoors.

- *Lack of access to education:* Girls are deprived of knowledge and access to school. Because of their poor education, they cannot benefit from good job opportunities.

- *Early marriages:* Girls are placed under the authority of their husbands, and are ignorant of their rights. Very often, men beat their wives because they see them only as objects. They are also deprived of rights to inheritance.

- *No access to productive activities:* This happens when a man denies a woman the right to engage in productive activities. Many men oppress their girlfriends or wives. Some informants gave the example of women in Zanzibar or Pemba; they are not allowed to undertake any activity outside the home.

One 45-year-old Muslim man said:

> *Many societies are reluctant to change and still consider women as weak, passive and emotional whereas men are seen as strong, dynamic and active. This is why it is seen as normal for boys to be offered science subjects at school, while girls remain with subjects such as home economics. Such situations retard women's development. In most families, boys are favoured in terms of education while girls are obliged to perform household activities, and afterwards they do not have time to study or relax. It is the same thing in the Church and community. In that way, what women are saying is true.*

Nevertheless, some claimed that nowadays it was easier for girls to get an education and to have greater choice than it was before. Some men said that a single woman would have more opportunities to choose what she wants to do, while in comparison, a married woman should respect her husband's advice.

Men that disagreed with the statement that men were the cause for women's underdevelopment, gave the following reasons:

- *Women's irrationality:* Women are not able to make good choices. They are "very weak in taking decisions" and "when they have money they use it for themselves on futile and stupid things." "They mismanage the money given by their husband or boyfriends," said many informants.

- *A high level of dependence:* Women need assistance and their development depends on men. It is usually the husband or the boyfriend's initiative that starts any productive activity. In general, women tend to be passive and expect everything from men.

- *Women's inferiority complex:* Women naturally feel inferior to men because they know they are not strong enough to do many things. They always need to consult a man. It is only "when things go wrong that they blame men." Women are too hesitant to take decisions and this is why men are so much involved in the decision-making process.

- *Lack of solidarity between women:* Women do not fight enough for their development and their rights. They should work towards a better position in society. Women are isolated but are afraid to join women's groups.

- *Customs and tradition that favour men:* Men consider that tradition indicates the appropriate behaviours for both women and men. It is a code of reference for all members of society; they must perform according to the sex roles. Men are natural leaders who have to take responsibility for the wellbeing of family members and for all family affairs. Women are naturally obedient and must conform to these prescriptions. Most men consider that the tradition indicates clear social roles to everyone and clarifies people's identity. It also facilitates the transmission of knowledge.

- *Women's misbehaviour:* According to informants, women who make such statements are those who do not follow social rules. They do not respect their social role and they violate social regulations. What they call humiliation is the result of their misbehaviour. Most men see urban women as aggressive and independent-minded, with a tendency to become manipulative and immoral by refusing to act in conformity with tradition. One 56-year-old Muslim man working as a carpenter said:

> *I am not convinced, and I will never be convinced, that men are responsible for women's underdevelopment and humiliation. What is nowadays defined as humiliation and underdevelopment of women is an attempt by women to go against what they are supposed to do in society. They are demanding employment outside the home like men and many things that they are claiming to be their right. What I believe is that women are not particularly humiliated when men simply try to exercise their authority. It is even written in the Holy Book that women should respect their husbands. Men are the heads of the household. My view is that what is called underdevelopment and humiliation of women is nothing other than the violation of social rules and regulations, which confer roles according to one's gender. It is heard of a lot nowadays because of the interference of western culture in our culture. Some women are getting money from abroad that they use to destroy our cultural values.*

When asked what they were doing in practice to improve the lives of their daughters and sons, men answered as follows:

Separated or divorced men: When the children are living with their mother, most fathers "do nothing" and do not feel responsible for them. Children's wellbeing and needs are seen as being the responsibility of their mother. One even said, "I do not feel obliged to do something, even if the children ask me."

Married men living with their children: Most of these try to send their children to school if they have enough money. Men still encourage their sons to study technical subjects. Girls are still assigned to tailoring or primary education, or in better cases they are encouraged to become a nurse or teacher. Only one man said that he encouraged his daughter to become an engineer as he was.

Men who have young children want to send them to school. Only one man, working as a lawyer, said that he had opened a bank account to safeguard the future of his children. Another one built a house to rent out and save money to pay the school fees of his children.

Family problems, such as multiple marriages or a large number of children, prevent parents from sending all their children to school. Most of them are confronted with daily expenses and cash expenses that are perceived as too high.

When asked what they felt responsible for as a son, husband or father, all men informants answered as follows:

Table 11: Men's responsibilities according to social status

Responsibility	*Son*	*Husband*	*Father*
To respect his parents	X		
To obey his parents' rules	X		
To assist his parents in various activities	X		
To support his parents	X		
To get education towards a good job	X		
To respond to parents without hesitation	X		
To love his wife		X	
To do the best for his family		X	
To be responsible for wife and children		X	
To have a good wife and family		X	
To take control of family affairs/be spokesman		X	
To fulfil his wife's needs		X	
To be the head of the family			X
To be the family lawmaker			X
To initiate all decisions			X
To fulfil all the family's requirements			X
To encourage children's education			X
To help children develop good behaviour			X

As sons, most participants said they felt responsible for respecting their parents, and listening to the social values they learned from them.

As husbands, men's responsibilities are to take all decisions related to family matters and to satisfy all the needs of the family members.

Only one man said that good communication with his wife could be advantageous for the family as a whole.

As fathers, men see themselves as making all arrangements for their children and initiating all decisions related to their children and their future.

Daily relations and changes

One important area of daily relations is money. Most women who participated in the study said they did not know their husband's exact salary. They could only estimate it by their husband's lifestyle. By contrast, men seem to take their wife's salary for granted; most of them seize it and decide by themselves what to do with it. Most women who are earning more money than their husbands still cannot decide by themselves how to spend their money. Forty married women declared that their husbands had the final say in decisions related to household expenses. Women earn money but they are not allowed to spend it according to their needs or desires. Some said that they could buy small things without asking their husband, but few said that they were "co-operating" in the decision-making process.

Most men want to have many children but fewer have the capacity to support them. Nowadays, in urban settlements, women have to work outside the home. It is a necessity, as men barely earn their own livelihoods. By using the money earned by their wives for their own selfish purposes, they show that there are no common aims in married life. Men want to benefit from all its advantages without respecting their social role as provider and supporter.

For example, Amina[1] who was working as a secretary in an NGO only discovered after her separation what the value of her salary was. Earlier, her husband used all the money to go out and drink; she did not have enough money to eat properly every day, she was always badly dressed, and was beaten. She never had money available and was obliged to borrow. She was so astonished to discover how much

[1] The name has been changed to protect the identity of the informant.

she was earning. Today she has enough to build a house and has many other plans for her future.

In Tanzania the social status of women is low, as indicated by the very high degree of marital insecurity for women. This situation is made worse by numerous health problems, such as the high blood pressure that women attribute to poor communication with their husbands, and sexually transmitted infections (STIs) including HIV/AIDS, which are associated with men's carelessness and promiscuity. Women have no power in the decision-making process, even for things related to their own sex lives. They cannot refuse to have sexual relations with their husband because they risk being beaten or disowned. Men profit from their recognised and legitimated position of domination, but they do not respect the obligations that are linked to it.

A 41-year-old Christian woman, who defines herself as a housewife and businesswoman, with four children and one relative at home, summarised the situation between spouses as:

> *The decision of the children's education falls on me. My husband does not have enough time to take care of them. He has a full-time job and the children fear him. He has no soft words for the children, especially for the boys. When my children come back from school, I listen to their problems, take care of things before they go back, i.e. pay the school fees, social requirements, and see to uniforms and pocket money.*
>
> *My husband also tends to neglect my parents and relatives. He does not take care of them in any way and makes no contribution towards their wellbeing. But for his parents and relatives, everything is a right! They get everything from my husband. He fears making them unhappy.*
>
> *Another problem is that he wants to control my money from my hairdressing salon.*
> *Moreover, he does not appreciate what I'm doing, for example paying the school fees. What I am doing is nothing to him and he does not realise that it is his responsibility instead of mine.*

Sometimes, I am overloaded with responsibilities compared to him. He uses his time properly and he is able to work on a full-time basis, unlike me. I have a lot of responsibilities in the house.

Most of the things I do are decided by me, but if my husband says "No" it means no. I have no say after that.

As for buying things—we have to discuss this first, so as to reach an agreement. I normally buy small things that don't cost much.

He gives me financial support when I need it. In some ways I have freedom for my things, but not total freedom. I live a very hard life but I have to tolerate it because I want my children to have a better one. I know the problems of living with a stepmother.

I used to pray to God to take my husband first. But if God takes me first, my children will have a lot of problems because my husband's relatives and parents are looking at my husband's wealth. My mother-in-law has no love for my children. I am trying to prepare them for a good life before I die. I always pray.

In Dar es Salaam, as in many other African countries, one can observe a growing number of single-parent families as a result of AIDS, migration, divorce or other reasons. A new phenomenon, called *"maternité polyandre"* (polyandrous motherhood), is growing. It means a mother with children from different men, who has co-parental ties with more than one father of her children. Thus, as described by Vangroenweghe, the classical ties of intergenerational and lineage inter-dependence are restored by a lateral connection. In most cases, the men do not really want to recognise these children officially or to support them financially. However, men exercise their power over these women through sexuality and pregnancy. Very often, men promise marriage to the pregnant woman who decides to keep the baby based on this promise; subsequently, the men disappear and do not recognise the children socially or officially.

Women are left to care for these children alone or with the support of their own family.

The urban elite is officially monogamous but there is a growing tendency towards polygamy, presented in a new form of *nyumba ndogo,* which literally means *small house* (mistress or second family), in the Kiswahili language. This represents the modern form of polygamy. A number of women in this kind of arrangement gain some degree of social respect because they are regarded as "married." Moreover, because these women normally reside in different areas of the city, they feel that they benefit from more freedom and independence.

Young people and women have much greater access to money in an urban environment. Consequently, they are less dependent on their husbands or their parents when it comes to issues such as dowry. They feel more independent. Some changes are seen as a generational conflict. Young people want to make their own choices and express themselves. The notion of respect for one's elders, which was once mandatory, is now changing. In the city, some children beat their parents or refuse to obey or live in conformity with their parents' rules[2]. As Koda writes, "The violation of democratic rights of children within the household also contributed to the increased number of street children" (2000:255) and the increased number of early pregnancies or single-parent households, as young people learn to control their sexuality and exercise their democratic rights.

Dislocation of family ties is intensifying, and a growing number of women are heads of the family. A report by DUHP in 1993 noted that, within the loose classification of low-income people, there are approximately 200,000 households headed by women. Moreover, a growing number of children are abandoned and survive on the streets, trying, as shown in the case of children in Kenya, to produce or reproduce a certain community (Rodriguez-Torres, 2000: 327). They do not benefit from any social services, education or information, and are at high risk.

---

[2] Personal communication from Father Loire who initiated help groups in Dar es Salaam.

The arrangement of marriage is also showing some change. The rules of marriage depend on the type of marriage that is recognised: religious, civil or traditional. These three forms are all officially recognised in Tanzania. They have precise rules that are not always observed. For example, the Tanzanian law on marriage does not allow the marriage of girls under the age of 15 years[3]. Yet the number of young girls married under this age remains significant. A small bribe to the civil servant in charge is enough. Parents and relatives still have a say in marriage issues, in terms of the choice of husband and when the marriage should take place. Such arranged marriages involve some exchange of resources between the two families. This is the main reason why parents refuse to take back a daughter if she wants to walk out of her marriage. The exchange of resources prevents any turning back.

However, we can observe a growing number of inter-ethnic marriages that are decided by the individuals themselves and not arranged by their parents. Nowadays, a lot of people recognise that marriage is a personal affair that should be decided by the people involved. One must say that this kind of situation can backfire on married couples. They are isolated from the extended family if things go wrong because they refused to follow the advice of their elders.

There is a small but growing number of young women who refuse to get married. They all say that they want to stay single because men's attitudes are not favourable to women's emancipation. This attitude is related to higher levels of education that help younger women be financially independent.

---

[3] The Penal Code, Chapter 16 of the Revised Laws of Tanzania, as amended by the Sexual Offences Special Provision Act 1998, specified and raised the age of marriage for girls and boys. It went from the age of 12 to 15 years for girls, and to "the apparent age of eighteen years" for boys. This law clearly defined that any person married to a girl under the age of fifteen years shall not have the right to "carnal knowledge" with or without the girl's consent. The person is guilty of an offence and is liable to imprisonment for ten years. Nevertheless, these kinds of marriage are still frequent. Are husbands involved in child marriages patient enough to control their sexual urges and wait until their infant wives are old enough to participate fully in sexual intercourse without any fear of physical injury? (The Guardian, 24 October 2001). Students from Mpwapwa District in their speech at a graduation held at Mpwapwa Teacher's College said that stern measures should be taken against parents who force their children into marriages in order to get dowry, instead of taking them to school. "They said some parents deliberately stopped their girl children from attending school, saying they cannot pay their school fees, hence denying them their basic rights." (The Guardian, 24 October 2001).

Some changes are related to the mode of communication between spouses. In families where communication and negotiation exist, a man will not impose his will against his wife's wishes. As a 25-year-old woman from Jangwani said:

> *It depends on the cooperation inside the house. A father who is always drunk knows nothing about his children. As long as he has money, even if you tell him the children are sick he will say, "Now what do you want me to do?" So, it depends on how you live. If you cooperate, both of you will take the child to the hospital. If my husband is at home, we both take the child to hospital. I don't feel good going alone. If he is around, we go together to the hospital. In other homes it is different. Other women do not like to walk with their husbands. They feel shy (laughter from other women in the focus group discussion).*

Women's interaction with husband, parents and relatives

How do women perceive their life with their husbands? What kind of relations do they develop? What about love?

Lack of democracy between spouses and the absence of assistance from the partner are among the most serious and frequent complaints of women. Generally, men believe that women have to respect their authority and live in conformity with their decisions. Women often say, "The sweetness of marriage is on the day of the ceremony. It is a very sweet day with a lot of happiness. Thereafter you will see the bitterness of it."

Lack of communication is a constant theme; women perceive it as a lack of affection. They feel abandoned, neglected and ignored by their husbands who still perceive themselves as the masters of the house.

Most women feel that men oppress them and hinder their development. Women question traditional attitudes. Some informants said they preferred to live alone, forgetting all relationships, because men are too conservative and abuse their position. Most women cannot even seek refuge in their own family; once they are married, they cannot come back. They will be buried in their husband's home.

The cost of dowry forces women to stay in their husband's house. Their in-laws, meanwhile, look at them as strangers profiting from the resources of their husbands.

Many women have to endure the mental and physical violence of their partners. On their part, men do not perceive their wives' heavy responsibilities. Women work from early morning to late at night to ensure all the family's needs are met. These conjugal problems very often provoke social and familial rupture. The increasing number of women as heads of households, the number of abandoned children and the neglect of old people, all testify to the new social problems expressed by women. The "family" is changing and may no longer function as before.

When asked how their parents, relatives and friends perceive them and the way they were running their lives, women's answers were mixed. Some responses were positive and others seemed more negative.

Among the positive answers, married women said that parents and relatives admire them and some "see me as a woman with development."[4] Women working outside the home are often seen as good examples for the family. Some relatives or friends ask for advice because they find that the active woman is a model for other members of the family. As a 39-year-old Christian businesswoman said:

> *My mother is very happy about the way I run my business. I help her even though she has money. She has her own business in Moshi, a shop for hardware equipment. But she feels good that I can help her and also because she sees the fruit of her child's work. My relatives admire the way I run my activities and they come for advice, even money to start their own business. Nowadays, everyone in the family has their own activities. There is no problem between us.*

Women helping other members of the family admitted that the admiration of relatives is proportional to the help or assistance they

---

[4] A woman with development means a person who likes a high level of material development, i.e. a lot of money and other things. It also means a person who is not dependent on anyone, who has the capacity to initiate different activities and is successful in her activities.

provide them. Indeed, it would be seen as lacking respect for traditions and customs if a person who earned a lot of money and lived well refused to help her parents and relatives. It guarantees security and respect amongst one's relations. The habit of taking care of all members of the extended family is perpetuated. This makes it difficult for active women to keep the profits of their work for themselves alone. As a 36-year-old Muslim woman with four children and living with six other relatives, working as a businesswoman, said:

> *My mother has already passed away. My father pities me because I am the only one who takes on all the responsibilities. I take care of him, and my sisters and other relatives. My father told me to work hard to make sure that my parents and relatives are looked after. He did not think that there would be a day when I could help them. He only thought of his son. Now, he is wondering how the world has changed.*

These working women mentioned that jealousy was also a part of the game. A 27-year-old Christian woman with two children, working as a hairdresser, said:

> *My parents say nothing about the way I run my life. They are just happy that I help them once I get money.*
>
> *I am the only daughter who is married in the family, and my fellow relatives have children out of the marriage. They all say bad words to me.*
>
> *I do not have a good relationship with my relatives. They always say that my father loves only me and favours me in many things. That is the only reason for them to hate me.*

In the case of widows, most informants said that their relatives feel sorry for them because they have many responsibilities, and are in charge of their children and other relatives. However, the majority receive no help from others. Some receive support from their relatives in times of major difficulty, while others can only afford to pray for them.

In daily life, widows have to fight for their rights and can barely earn a living for their children and other relatives. One 46-year-old Muslim woman with six children and two other relatives to look after, working as businesswoman selling kerosene, with a tailor shop and selling snacks to hotels, declared:

> *My parents and stepmother feel sorry for me because they depend on me for everything. They are not working and they live with me in the same compound. I wish I could find them something to do instead of staying home waiting for me.*
>
> *I try to develop a close relationship with my parents because I do not want them to feel sad because they are dependent on me. I want them to be happy and their happiness will help me to succeed in my business. I am trying very hard to comfort them.*
>
> *As for my relative—we help each other in difficult times. We have developed a loving relationship.*

Other widows said that relationships with their relatives were mostly "cold" and polite. Many women have been cheated of their right to inheritance by their husband's relatives. Children are nowadays considered to be burdens, especially by those who are in charge of the children of dead relatives. These behaviours could be a result of urban life, in which children are not always seen as an asset in terms of increased labour. But how is it possible to relate this attitude to the still predominant desire for many children?

Some families still perpetuate or encourage the old custom of levirate. Nevertheless, many women now reject this tradition and say they are afraid of getting AIDS or other STI.

Separated and divorced women are perceived as having too many responsibilities. People feel sorry for them because they "broke" their marriage ties and have to live alone, without the support or protection of a man. "Nowadays, everybody carries their own burden; life is so difficult that everybody has to suffer on their own. People have to shoulder their own responsibilities, regardless of whether they have money or not."

As divorce becomes more and more common, many parents regret having organised their daughter's marriage. Some admit that their daughter suffered a lot in the marriage because of the irresponsibility of the husband. Despite this, most parents encourage a daughter to stay in a bad marriage and to tolerate her husband's behaviour; "it is just normal married life."

Others have a more open mind. Nowadays, some parents recognise that married men may profit from their wives without sharing common responsibilities. One woman was advised by her mother, "Work is the only husband I want to have now. You know, these men are like dogs because they have no humanity at all. They can leave you at traffic lights wondering where to go."

Most women receive moral support from their parents or relatives, but very few among them receive financial or material protection. Generally, women who are involved in production activities are the ones who provide financial and material support to their parents and relatives. This is why many women turn to NGOs or international organisations, which support women's income-generating activities. Nevertheless, there are exceptions. One woman said that her parents and relatives think she has too many responsibilities, and they support her financially and morally. This person is alone with four children and also houses five other relatives.

Do women receive help from their relatives or friends?

Few women said they were receiving material or financial support from their relatives or friends. They are generally viewed as the ones able to help, and not the ones to be helped. One 49-year-old Christian woman with seven children of her own and responsible for six other relatives, who works as a businesswoman travelling between Nairobi and Dar es Salaam, said:

> *I do get help from my relatives but not always. My friends give me more help than my relatives. For instance, this idea of going to London came from a woman friend. She advised me and promised to pay for my ticket to London if I failed to get money. She is always shuttling between London and Dar es Salaam.*

Some informants associated the term "friends" with membership of an association, and said they were members of neighbourhood or tribal associations or cooperatives. The aim of these associations is to support people in case of special events such as marriage, death or illness.

Some said that they did not have friends. They avoided being too close to people because they feared others and were afraid of gossip. One 35-year-old woman said, "I do not have friends because I avoid them. Sometimes friends are not good and they might spread gossip. Finally you will end with quarrels." Another 31-year-old Christian woman who works as a pharmacist mentioned something similar:

> *I do not have friends to chat with because they are very bad people and they make you and your husband quarrel. They are very good at spreading gossip. I avoid them.*

Many other informants share this suspicion. A 24-year-old woman working as a shopkeeper says, "I do not have friends because I cannot trust them. I do not like them because they may hinder my progress." A 21-year old Muslim woman said, "I do not like to have friends, especially women."

Many women mentioned that their husband refused to let them have friends. For example, one 36-year old Muslim woman with four children and three dependants said, "I don't have friends in my neighbourhood. My husband refuses to let me visit strangers. At first, they visited me. My husband did not like it, so they get tired of me because I never went to see them."

To summarise:

- Most women do not receive financial help from their relatives.
- Nevertheless, most consider it normal to provide financial and material assistance to their relatives and parents.
- Some would appreciate receiving help from parents and relatives, but receive only moral support and advice.

- Some mentioned that in real need, they would receive more help from their friends than from their relatives.

- The suspicion of others illustrates the level of competition in the urban area.

Despite the bleak picture given by informants here, it also seems that things are changing in the city. Without generalising, there are indications of a developing solidarity network between friends in urban areas. It is very difficult to survive without this kind of network. Friends help to find employment, a place to live, and a social or work group. This is a new development compared to rural customs. In the case of illness, for example, people consult their neighbours, borrow money or seek advice. They do not rely on relatives.

Thus greater links develop between people who are no longer dependent on only the kin or clan relations. This does not mean that kin relations are abolished. In towns, people reproduce the structures of the social organisation based on village segments of lineage. Solidarity between towns and villages still exists because the ideology of social relationships stays the same. People define themselves through belonging to a consanguineous group of three or four generations. The control of elders is still persistent and is shown through matrimonial strategies, recognition of status, and the importance of sex and age in social institutions. Nevertheless, this is undermined by new urban behaviour patterns. The struggle between the so-called "tradition" and "modernity" leads to practices that are not always clear or moral.

Perceptions of work colleagues, relatives and friends

Some see these women as persons who have fought to succeed. Relatives, colleagues or friends feel that these women can do a lot "without education" or without having many resources initially.

One 34-year-old Christian woman said that women should work together to reinforce their efforts and to encourage others to perform different and new things. Co-operation is seen as a way of encouraging more women to be proactive. It is also viewed as a way to break isolation and to bring more opportunities to women. She said:

> *In our compound there are a lot of activities done by women. What I am suggesting to my fellow women is to join us and invite certain leaders of the Government to come and see our activities. We could take photos so as to be seen and heard in the media. Such things would help us to be known and might open some markets for our products.*

But many people have difficulty accepting the success of a few. People's perception oscillates between admiration and jealousy. For example a 40-year-old woman said:

> *People think I am a bitch and are jealous of my success. People always think that a woman who is travelling alone for business is a prostitute. They are used to women who stay at home, cook for their husbands and take care of babies, not women who travel and are successful in business.*

Many see active women as "powerful women" because they have money. Some mentioned that their success prompts others' jealousy. As a 39-year-old Christian woman with four children and one other dependent, working as businesswoman, said:

> *My colleagues and friends thought I was a boastful person. Now, they have started to realise that I am a normal person. They come to seek advice and financial support from me.*
>
> *As you know, we African women have to face a lot a jealousy. If others see you doing well in your activities, instead of asking you how you did it, they start seeing you as boastful because you have money.*
>
> *We have to educate them, because we women have to work hard so as to have our own lives and not depend too much on our husbands.*

Women who experience this type of problem are more isolated and often criticised for their dynamism. Moreover, many people want to profit from these women's efforts. One 52-year-old Muslim woman, who has four children and six other relatives and has opened a grocery store, said:

> *In my business, I have no colleagues but my neighbours don't like me because of the way I treat them. As you know, neighbours like to ask for a loan when they see someone has opened a shop. I always refuse because if you give them a loan, then when it comes to paying it back, there are always quarrels. People do not like to pay back a loan; so they call you bad names. I take care in order to keep my businesses going. In fact, the profit on many items is very small. For example, a Coke crate costs Tanzanian Shillings 4,200, and after sale I get Tanzanian Shillings 700 per crate. So I have to be careful, otherwise I will have to close shop.*

Some informants said they were not preoccupied by others' perceptions. "There are always quarrels, complaints and comments in the workplace." One 23-year-old Muslim woman highlighted the problem of sexual harassment:

> *We, human beings, like to speak behind others' backs. I never asked anything from anybody. I do things on my own with my husband. I don't care about others' perceptions. I will talk to anybody who dares to be with me or talk with me.*
>
> *People see me as I am—an ordinary person; but some perceive me differently. Another problem at my workplace is that everybody wants me. Every man tries his luck. Their approaches are persistent enough to make me unhappy. For example, my managing director does not talk to me because I rejected him when he told me he was in love with me.*
>
> *It has reached the stage that I have started to think how people, especially men, perceived me. Do they think I am a girl to play with, or a prostitute? If I had been an easy-going girl I would have got HIV/AIDS by now, but I have no time for them. I care for my life first.*

Most women want to be left in peace to perform their activities without getting into trouble. Women are in a double-bind situation.

On the one hand they receive the message that they should do things to ensure a better life for all members of the family. On the other, they are poorly perceived because a woman's role is still seen as the traditional one of being at home.

Tanzanian society is built on an ideology of equality. There is therefore a conflict between this and the ideology of individual success. Competition is one of the new rules for survival. One 36-year-old Christian woman said:

> *You have to take care in this city because not all people like you. We are from different places. Personally, I don't even tell them how much I cook for my business. They always ask me how much I cook. You have to think before confiding in people, otherwise you will hear your business details being spread everywhere.*

This creates exclusion. Exclusion originates from specialisation, economic mobility and competition. The city is a place for professionals and specialists. In an urban environment, excluded people are the ones without any professional skills. Inequalities increase. Many of the "winners" see the advantage of individual profit, sometimes at the expense of relationships. Solidarity ties are becoming more flexible. Social distance between family members is increasing, facilitating the emergence of a privileged category that adopts a new mode of life, and favouring the exploitation of clan members who are less privileged.

To an extent one could say that women are now integrating the winners' attitudes and behaviours, even if they do not benefit from many resources or opportunities. Women continue to take care of their family members and relatives. They seem more faithful to their obligations. They are not only in search of profit for themselves, but are fighting for a better life for their children, even in the absence of help and support from others. This is a demonstration of their imagination, strength and flexibility.

Women's perception of life

Women's perception of life depends on their daily experience and on the place they occupy in society.

Of the 68 participants, 37 women felt that "life is hard." They gave the following reasons:

- The increase in responsibilities and the difficulty in satisfying all their family's needs.
- The constant need for cash forces women to work hard or find a job.
- The lack of support for women who are alone; they receive no help from anybody; even the government does not feel responsible for widows.
- Life is not stable because of financial insecurity, added responsibilities and the large number of dependants, which represents a major burden for families and working women.
- Men's oppression and exploitation of their spouses is seen as placing more and more difficulty in a woman's life.
- Life is miserable because divorce is seen as a bad thing for children.

Life was "not good, not bad" for 9 informants. They said:

- They have enough money to be independent.
- It takes effort because a woman alone "has the feeling of not going forward because her responsibilities are constantly growing".
- The extended family is seen as a burden, destroying the resources of a family.
- Employers do not give employees enough work benefits that could profit them and increase their quality of life.
- Life could be better if they did not quarrel with their husbands all the time because of jealousy.
- Being able to afford things brings peace in the house for some.
- Many cohabiting woman said they missed the "respect of marriage", which gave them social recognition and legitimisation.
- Ignorance of the husband's salary.

- The desire of most men to control their wives' wages.

Life was "good" for 7 women for the following reasons:

- A woman and her husband can fulfil all the family's requirements. Family responsibilities are shared.
- It is possible for spouses to make plans for the future.
- Material conditions are good.
- The husband can share responsibilities with a working woman, who is allowed to work or have her own business without experiencing her husband's jealousy.
- Women can afford many things and be independent.
- Enough money brings harmony to the house.
- Women have money and freedom.
- Women who are separated are happy because they feel free.

Life was seen as "better than before" by 15 participants for the following reasons:

- Women feel better since their separation or divorce. They do not face constant battles and are independent. In comparison with the married days of oppression and humiliation, life is good.
- Widows feel free because they have "learnt how to find money."
- Working helps women gain power in the decision-making process.
- Some said it is possible to share responsibilities with a man and live peacefully.
- Freedom to choose and work is wonderful.

Most widows find that life is difficult and that they receive no help from anybody. They have to initiate business, find a job and live on less money than before. They often receive nothing in inheritance. Widows feel that the Government only helps people in high posts.

Married women have more and more responsibilities, and the urban and economic crisis adds to the burden of daily life. Many problems come from the obligation to care for relatives or their husband's family. Women also fear illnesses such as HIV/AIDS due to their husbands' infidelity.

Those who are cohabiting feel that "the respect of marriage" is missing because their liaison is not officially recognised. Marriage is still perceived as the only respectable state for a woman.

Most women who were asked about their perception of their life considered only the material aspects. Few mentioned elements related to psychological, spiritual or emotional wellbeing. Some were concerned about the peace and harmony in the home, and felt that it was a good example for their children.

Are women happy?

Women's evaluation of their quality of life is related to both objective and subjective factors. Objective wellbeing is expressed through material comfort, good health and freedom of expression. Subjective wellbeing is linked to women's perception and representation of their life.

Looking at objective factors, how can material comfort be ensured in the context of an economic crisis? Socio-economic conditions increase the difficulties of everyday life. The constant need for cash enhances the pressure on urbanised women. Struggling to ensure the wellbeing of the family is a daily nightmare. More and more men are "free-riders" as they cannot fulfil their role of breadwinner any more. In Dar es Salaam more and more women bear the full brunt alone, as men flee the burden of family responsibilities.

Health is also a matter of concern. Most informants mentioned severe difficulties linked to accessibility of healthcare, environment and life-style. Women's knowledge about public health issues has increased. Yet, as noticed by Cloutier (1996) and Obrist van Eeuwijk, they lack the means to put this knowledge into practice. In such a situation, public health knowledge becomes a risk because it causes emotional distress. If, on the other hand, a woman has accurate public health knowledge as well as access to adequate financial and social resources, knowledge becomes an enabling factor (2000:254). Women are more directly affected by health issues linked to reproduction. Moreover, most informants said they feared AIDS as they have no control over their sexuality. They cannot ignore their husband's behaviour and do not have the right to discuss it. Many among them feel divided between their social obligations and their apprehension of disease.

Gender and age are among the factors affecting happiness. Women's education and socialisation processes focus more on attention to others. It is seen as a responsibility of women to facilitate satisfaction in human relations. However, as noted by Helgeson (1994), these characteristics can become negative if, for example, attention to others is pushed to an extreme in which a woman's biological and psychological needs are ignored. It is the case of most women of Dar es Salaam who are socialised in that way.

Age has always been seen in Tanzanian society as an essential factor with regard to happiness. Older women gain prestige, authority and social recognition. In the context of the economic crisis, however, it is difficult for older women to be respected and socially recognized. They are considered a burden because they cannot work any more. Some newspapers and magazines such as Femina (1998) have reported cases of old women being immolated in different areas of the country. On the other hand, in the context of AIDS, many older women have to continue to work because they are responsible for their orphan grandchildren.

Among the subjective factors affecting women's happiness, most mentioned the need for harmony and peace in their social relations. In Dar es Salaam, the social relations of women are characterised by obligation and reciprocity. To have good relations with relatives, neighbours and friends makes them happier and more secure. They know they can get help in tough times.

Nevertheless, women still display a reluctance to develop ties with people not seen as members of the extended family. As one female informant said, "Sometimes, women can have a good friend. However, that happens only if we are lucky. We cannot trust others easily because you never know when they will make trouble for you."

More than friendship, attachment to the spouse seems to be the main source of wellbeing. However, few women can claim they are experiencing a good life with their husband. Most women complained of men's behaviour and attitudes. Women who defined themselves as happier were generally those who decided to divorce or to live separately.

Women take refuge in work because it is perceived as having beneficial effects such as the feeling of personal utility, and the creation of new links with others. But it is also viewed as a source of dissatisfaction, due to inadequate working conditions.

Most women confirmed that religion increases their satisfaction in life and provides an efficient psychological support in the face of hardships such as funerals, divorce, unemployment and severe illness, and emotional distress. As believers, they benefit from both practical and psychological support from a faith community.

Conclusion: The burden of tradition

Tanzanian society is based on a dual-sex system in which sex roles are clearly defined and fixed, establishing gender asymmetry and inequality. Judging by the discourses of the informants, both contribute to reinforcing the ideas of masculinity and femininity. Masculinity is supported as hegemonic and as closely connected to the institution of marriage. Femininity is constructed in the context of the overall subordination of women to men through domestic-public dichotomy. Female subordination takes intricate forms grounded in traditional Tanzanian culture and, as observed by Mikell in other African countries (1996:3), in dual-sex patterns transmitted through history. Ties between the social and ideological structures of communities and gender, and familial relations of local areas, are closely woven.

Masculinity and femininity are socially constructed and perpetuate the idea of a social order based on men's authority and hierarchy that is legitimated by the whole social organisation. Men's ideological perception of women frames them as supportive, nurturing, acquiescent, subordinate and familial, not as political persons or authority figures. This ideological framework justifies men's control over them as they view themselves as strong and authoritarian, the decision makers and leaders of the family. Compliance seems to be the only option for women in response to the social discrimination that develops against them. Adapting to men's power, women accept the ideals of nurturance and empathy as womanly virtues. Biology is used to explain and justify this construction. From men's point of view one could say that reciprocity in the couple is a kind of antagonistic complementary nature. Men can do as they wish even if married, while women oscillate from elders' to husband's control. For example, men's authority is derived from dowry payments and the prescription of *"virilocalité"* residence, which procures them *de facto* the legitimate superiority over women.

The institution of marriage is still predominant. It is viewed as the final achievement of prescribed gender relations. There is a consensus on the fact that it brings respect, dignity and community recognition. However, emotional links between spouses are weak and marked by a lack in democracy. Women use marriage as a survival strategy. Men profit from this tradition, and are not willing to challenge a socialisation process that guarantees women all rights and power.

Relations between women and men are marked by a lack of democracy, and a dearth of communication. Women complain about the lack of financial contribution from the husband; as a result of which they have to assume more and more responsibilities. Many women also say they miss affection and tenderness. Indeed, few participants mentioned romantic reciprocity as an important aspect of married life. It seems to be women's obligation "to love their husbands." Many men still believe that they have to show an unwavering firmness towards their wife, as they fear as losing strength. Married life is supposed to be based on a kind of equilibrium that lies on different but complementary prescriptions to be fulfilled by both partners.

The burden of tradition is heavy. Marriage, divorce, separation and remarriage consume a lot of money, and meanwhile children are deprived of resources. Men continue to exploit tradition because they benefit from its advantages provided by customs. Men use tradition to justify their position, for example, describing women's economic activities as flouting tradition.

Women are the losers in the system. They are generally oppressed by men. They play little part in public life, have to obey men without question, rarely own property, and are subject to domestic violence.

Their family of origin usually does not support them in times of trouble. Even if they are involved in double production (i.e., children and goods) for the profit of the husband and his family, they are treated as "strangers." The double work of women profits the husband's family, both financially and in terms of social prestige. One could even say that in some cases it is women's work that enables men to afford another official wife or many concubines, as shown by Dacher and Lallemand in the case of Goin society of Burkina Faso (1992). Indeed, as quoted by Lecarme-Frassy (2000) in the case of Senegal, women are classified under the category of wilderness and seen to be "civilised." Urban Tanzanian women, as women from most African cities, are viewed as uncontrollable and this justifies the desire of many men from Dar es Salaam to be married to rural women, as they are seen as more faithful and respectful of "traditions." The threat of women's insubordination preoccupies men in an obsessive way. It justifies their controlling women's movements, their language, behaviours and sexuality. As most men are used to being in command at the domestic level, they cannot share power. It is the path for violence in gender relations at every level, be it domestic or public.

Not all women accept and reproduce the unequal social order. Gender relations are being differently apprehended. In the urban setting, changes occur as women can no longer tolerate the behaviour of their husbands. They want consideration, respect and control over their lives. Many women refuse to be seen only as childbearers or domestic help. More and more women see that it is possible to get on better without living with a man, and so do not fear to divorce or get a separation. These women seem happier than married women. Women who are young, educated and have financial autonomy are no longer afraid of social marginalisation. In addition, older women who suffered a bad husband for years have also learnt that marriage no longer guarantees security and peace. Even if they live under social marginalisation, other women admire them because they are able to affirm themselves. Younger women may now refuse marriage because their mothers have taught them it no longer ensures their protection. This testifies to the desire to pass from an authoritarian and hierarchical relation to a relation of negotiation and equality. Many women know that this pseudo-legitimacy is socially constructed and imposed on them, and in time they may even be supported by their mothers or other women in the family.

As a result of change, kinship relations have become subject to reinterpretation (Obrist van Eeuwijk, 2000:218). Many women consider that generalised reciprocity is a kinship obligation. No payment or counter gift is expected. Traditionally, many women support a certain number of relatives as a normal commitment. Some informants no longer share this point of view. They consider their contribution as "help," implying the requirement for direct or indirect repayment. Some informants said they preferred to spend money on their children rather than to support relatives from the extended family. They want to dissociate themselves from extended kinship systems, as they no longer have the incentive to invest in the maintenance of kinship ties. Urban life commands new behaviours, which are linked to "modernisation" as exposed by Binsgergen (1999) in the analysis of the life of a young girl in Botswana. New needs emerge such as the necessity of abandoning the "peasant" look by using cosmetics, following a new code of dressing and home decoration, buying more furniture, developing new technical skills, going out more frequently and fostering friendship relations with strangers. What could be called "basic needs" command a constant need for cash, and it becomes more and more difficult for newly-urbanised people to respect their obligations towards kinship.

Women in the city develop new kinds of ties with friends and neighbours, or develop new associations. They are criticised for behaviour that is no longer congruent with tradition. As noted by Gordon (1996:170), the extended family is weakening and individualism is growing in Africa among those exposed to Western culture, urban life, and the benefits of capitalism (e.g., better jobs and pay, science and technology, higher material living standards). Among these strata of society, there is a tendency to reject what Ojwang (1989:5) refers to as the solidarity of kinship that precludes individual distinctions of fortune and status.

Many women seem ambivalent about the new life-style. They know that if they assert themselves they could lose the social insurance that was provided by the extended family. However, most of them—whether separated, divorced, widowed and even married—also recognise that kinship is no longer the best or only source of security and help. That is why more women are developing new associational groups that are not based on kinship relations alone. As migrants, they band together in the city.

Old traditions or habits are in conflict with the new knowledge generated by society, more precisely by the urban context that is increasingly diversified. Circles of socialisation are multiplying, offering new possibilities and choices. Women question their social roles. Nevertheless, the power of social rules and constraints oblige them to act in conformity, even if they would prefer to resist. As noted by Kaufmann (2001:203), a structural dissonance can result from this situation. Indeed, it may divide the logic of identification into two parts: actual marginal life and life in conformity with the norm.

The present dominates the past. But the historical weight of interiorised social memory opposes the domination of the present. Women are still experiencing a double-bind. On the one hand, they are now learning that they can become autonomous. On the other, they still have to respect many social rules. They discover that they must be engaged in contradictory schemes to acquire new habits. Conservative schemes are still present, but in the urban setting failures are also appearing. More and more women are conscious of this fact and are challenging the social construction of femininity and masculinity.

CHAPTER 5

WOMEN'S VOICES: THE PERSONAL EXPERIENCES OF FOUR WOMEN

This chapter presents the life stories of four women, aged from the twenties to the fifties. These women talk freely about their childhood, studies and professional histories. This inter-generational comparison illustrates both the social and the historical construction of gender relations. The women provide a view across different periods: under colonialism, after independence and today. Women's changing reality is compared with Tanzania's national development. Studies in "women and development" show how women's lives have been influenced by different development approaches. Margaret Snyder and Mary Tadesse (1995:8-16) have described the following changes over time:

- The *welfare approach* was popular during colonialism, based on the theory that women are simply passive recipients of development benefits because their major role is in reproduction.

- In the 1970s, a *human resource development approach* was developed that identified women as economic producers and community managers. Its strong development component recognised women's contribution and made women's access to productive resources a development issue associated with increasing self-reliance and autonomy. This strategy reduced the likelihood that member states would be resistant to programmes for women.

- Subsequently, the *equity*[1] *and human rights approach* tried to achieve the goal of equality between the sexes by means of legislation. It focused on inequality between women and

[1] Equality between the sexes was the primary approach of the UN Commission on the Status of Women (CSW) through the 1960s, and it is the strategy of the Convention on the Elimination of Discrimination against Women (CEDAW) today. Equity entered the field when Western women exercised pressure on international development agencies in the 1970s. This occurred after the human resource development approach had gained momentum, so "equity" was the original "women and development approach" (Snyder et Tadesse, 1995: 11).

men and its priorities and strategies confronted sexism and patriarchy by putting in place new legislation that would be more favourable to women. However, there was resistance because this was not perceived as a practical approach; legislation was seen as having limited potential to affect the vast majority of women.

- The *anti-poverty approach* focused on women in attempts to overcome the hunger and malnutrition that accompany poverty. It was a period that focused on income-generating and entrepreneurial programmes.

- The *efficiency* approach was development-oriented and sought to increase productivity in order to enhance quality of life, rather than solely to achieve economic growth. It became market-oriented in the second half of the 1980s, during the global economic crisis and as Structural Adjustment Programmes were introduced. The efficiency approach led to serious setbacks in women's position. Responsibility for health and education shifted to the voluntary sector, and thus mainly to women; women lost family support benefits; and female sexuality became commodified as girls and women tried to support themselves and their children.

- The *empowerment approach* of the mid-1980s recognised that women's experiences vary according to ethnicity, class, history and economic status. It emphasised mobilisation and consciousness rising in women's organisations and grassroots groups, and women's access to productive resources such as land, credit, education and training. The approach was more concerned with personal autonomy to enable women, nations and the poor to make their own choices. Key words were participation and self-reliance.

- Meanwhile, the term *gender* became popular in the late 1980s to replace "women and development." Gender theory is broadly applicable from the household to the international economy.

These approaches have all recognised the need to take into account the contribution of women to development. Nevertheless, there remain many obstacles to women's advancement. Most of these originate in the national and global economy, where few women have a voice. Nor are women present in critical numbers in government, technology or business.

The following presentation of individual life stories shows the influence of national policies on individuals. The patriarchal African State has a powerful influence on people's lives through legislation that directly affects people's choices and lifestyles. To ensure the survival of their households and communities, women are forced to act. How does this affect gender relations and social structure?

The first section introduces a 28-year-old woman who defines herself as a housewife and businesswoman. Despite numerous obstacles, she remains optimistic about her future. The second example is a 35-year-old woman from Musoma who works as a bank clerk. According to her, men still block women's development where they retain power in the decision-making process and continue sexual harassment. The third, a community worker of 43, has tried to offer her children equal opportunities, but she admits it is far from easy. The final informant is 57 years old and retired. She worked as a teacher and later as a school director.

Life stories have been reproduced as told by the informants; the language has only been changed where it was necessary for clarity or to avoid repetition.

ROSE[2]
Age: 28
PART 1: Childhood

I was born in Singida in 1973 and grew up there. We were three children in my family. I have one brother, who is the firstborn, and one sister. I am the third and lastborn. All three of us have different fathers.

---

[2] Fictional name.

Our mother was Christian and she brought us up according to Christian principles. My father and my brother's father were also Christian. Our sister's father was Moslem.

Unfortunately, our mother was not married. She told us that she was engaged to the man by whom she had the first child. He mistreated her, beat her, and did other bad things to her. She left this man and got another one, who was a soldier, and he brought her to Tabora. My mother found that the place was too far from her home and she left him and came back, where she met my father. My father was a student at the University of Dar es Salaam at that time. He met my mother while he was on holiday and he got her pregnant, knowing that he would return to Dar es Salaam. I was born in Singida and my mother and grandmother (my father's mother) took care of me. My father used to visit during holidays, but he never made serious efforts to take care of me because he knew that his parents were doing it. Do you think that a town man, a well-educated man, would come back to live with a woman in the village?

I don't know if my father refused to marry my mother because she was from a rural area, or maybe because he was married to another woman in town, who was better than my mother.

We were living with other relatives. We used to live with my mother's younger sisters. They would come and stay till they got a job. Later, they left us and we lived alone with our mother.

When I was young, I went to school. Our brother used to stay with his father's relatives. To me, it seems that we were treated the same. My brother, when he came to see our mother, sometimes cooked, swept, fetched water and washed his clothes. At our place, in Singida, boys and girls were treated equally.

My father was an engineer, who is now retired. He married another woman with whom he had three children. I am the one supporting him now, as his second wife is dead.

My mother studied up to Standard IV. I think this was due to her circumstances; her parents did not prioritise education. She had more influence on me because I lived with her till I grew up. School was also very important to me because I am now able to read and write.

PART 2: Studies

I started going to school in 1981, when I was seven years old. My mother decided to send me to school. When my mother went to church, I went with her, and I was enrolled in the church's nursery. I studied there until I was old enough for Standard 1. My school was in Singida town. It was not too far from my house, and it was a day school. I was there from Standard 1 to Standard VII.

When I was young I wanted to be a nurse. I remember seeing my aunt, the sister of my mother, putting on a white dress and white cap because she worked as a nurse. I wanted to become a nurse so I could wear dresses like her. I also wanted to go to work because sometimes my aunt gave us cash to buy things. I saw her as someone who was very comfortable in life. She had no problems. I did not complete secondary education because my mother was not able to pay for it, and no relative from my father's side volunteered to pay. As I was completing Standard VII some people came to the district to enrol children as National Service volunteers. I enrolled and went to Tabora.

When I was at school, we were equally treated. I was not aware of anyone being favoured. I saw the teachers treating us equally, and if you made a mistake, the punishment was the same for both girls and boys.

From the way I grew up, I have learned it is very important for girls to get a good education. Nowadays, a woman must be educated to get a good job. And a woman cannot live without a good job. Nowadays, she would end up being nobody. She will not be a woman! She will be harassed even if married. A man sees an uneducated woman as having no importance. She is there only to take care of the children and the household. But if a woman is educated and has a good job, her husband and family will respect her.

PART 3: Professional life

I had to move to Tabora when I was recruited. I lived in the camp with my colleagues. My mother gave me permission to join the army. I liked it because it felt like being back at school. I was in a youth group, called "*chipuzi*" in Kiswahili, and it followed the military lifestyle. When we joined the army for training, we were not paid. We were given a small amount of money, known as our ration, and a small allowance every month. It was for buying soap, lotion, petroleum jelly, etc. The amount of money was very small and it was not enough for someone to buy a dress or cloth.

I am now the one supporting my father and my sisters. I am able to do so because I started a business. So when my brother and sister ask for money to buy an exercise book, it is easy for me to give them that. If they ask a man, he will tell them he has no money. My mother has passed away; that is why I have not mentioned her name. Before she passed away I was helping her, even though I could not do much. I had not started my business at that time and had to beg cash from my husband.

As for the money I get from my business, my husband has no say in it. I always decide what to do with my own money. You know when you are married, you need to live in harmony and advise each other. Sometimes my husband is broke. So we plan together, and he knows if our children will eat today or not, or if I have enough money.

The major problems encountered by a married woman? It depends on how she is and how her family treats her. If a woman decides to do nothing, she will be nothing. If she decides to work hard or make an effort, no one will block her, neither her parents nor her husband.

I don't know what to do to improve my daughter's life, but I know that if a person wants to prosper in life she has to work hard. Sometimes you may try to help people who are not ready for it or who do not understand you. You may give your daughter advice; if she refuses to take it, will you tie a rope to her to make sure that she does what you say? This is why I don't know what can be done for women in general, because if a person does not understand it is useless to try to rescue her. I think we women do not understand what to do. We are not making enough effort to achieve what we need, that is learning how to read and write.

My parents treated boys and girls equally. They sent both girls and boys to school. Nowadays, I ask my son to sweep the floor, fetch water, wash his clothes, make his bed and clean his bedroom. I want to teach him how to cook, but he is still too young to learn.

I will educate my daughter to the level of Form VI and to university or college, and if it is not possible for her to reach this stage, I will let her go for vocational training based on her interests and ability. I will help her develop any activity that will ensure she gets a good job.

Both education and marriage are important for a woman. Marriage gives a woman respect from her parents and the community. She will be regarded as a normal person; the community sees a single person as abnormal. But it is also important for a woman to have a good job. Women who are educated deserve good jobs. Girls should also be allowed to make their own decisions. It is very important to be the one who makes the choices. It makes it easier for you to live comfortably; you can choose your husband freely and then it is easier to live with him. It is really very important to make free choices.

I think that life is now better for women than it was before, for my mother or my grandmother, for example. At that time people followed traditional culture, whereas nowadays people are more likely to live according to mutual respect. Now life is more complicated and people need to help each other. For example, take the dowry issue. People used to pay dowries in cows, according to the value that was put on a woman. Some were married after they had children whereas others married before they had any children. For a woman with no children before marriage, the dowry payment was five cows, while for a woman with children before marriage; the dowry was only one cow or perhaps only goats.

Nowadays, more women know their rights, although village women still haven't caught up, despite media broadcasting. Maybe sending information to women about what they are supposed to do, for example by using ten-cell leaders or through schools, could help. Women should be informed in different ways. This would help those who do not have a radio.

PART 4: Personal life

Marriage is very important for a woman. If you are married and living peacefully with your husband, you can decide to go into business or do something else while your husband is an employee and gets a salary every month. He can help you or advise you on what to do. He will also give you capital without any problem.

I have been married since 1989, for twelve years, and I now have three children. I was married at the age of 17. My husband is Moslem and I was Christian. I changed my religion because he did not like Commissioner's marriage (civil marriage). My Muslim name is Mariam.

I married the man of my choice, although my mother, aunts, grandmother and grandfather on my father's side arranged the marriage itself. I met my husband at the National Service camp. I became pregnant while I was training. I was not allowed to continue and I went back home to Singida. I stayed there for two years. Finally, my husband came to take us up to Tabora, but he was not allowed to take us until he paid the dowry. After that we were transferred to Dar es Salaam.

I met my father after having my first child. I was at home and my aunt came from Dar es Salaam and she asked me to come with her to Dar. My mother met my father and told him that I was in Dar. He came to see me.

I started my business when we came to Tabora. My mother fell ill. I travelled to give her a hand. It was in October 1996 that she passed away. I came back and found my husband had bought a refrigerator. When I saw it, I asked myself what I could do with this fridge. I decided to start selling water and ice cream to secondary school students. I used the money my husband gave me. It took me less than a month to stop selling ice cream and water because secondary school students do not like ice cream. I decided to sell juice. My stock was sold out on the same day, before time. I added one more tray of juice and it sold easily. My husband recognised the value of my business. He is a driver; he bought me five trays of juice. With my earnings I kept on adding more trays of juice and I reached ten trays, each tray containing forty packs. I used to make a profit of Tanzanian Shillings 5,000 per day. Later, my husband went to attend a course and I had to use the money to pay for the family's needs until he came back. I also use my money to help my father and sisters and brother; and I buy things for us, as I like.

I became closer to my father when I had some accommodation problems. I went to stay with him. He was the one who gave us this plot to build a house, after seeing how we were suffering, and because it was our aim to build a house. During that time, I used my money for the family's needs, while my husband's salary was used for construction.

We are both responsible for the children. As I am more at home, I am more responsible for them. For example, if a child falls sick, I will take him or her to the doctor. When my husband comes back, I tell him about it. If there are debts or bills to pay, he gives me the money.

We were both involved in the decision regarding the children's school. I went to register them because their father was at work. He is the one who pays for all their needs, such as fees. We will decide together about the children's future, if God keeps us alive until then.

Our relationship and communication are good. When there is anything to discuss I usually tell him and he thinks about it and makes a decision. He can refuse or agree. If he refuses he will tell me the reasons and give me an alternative. For instance, I told him that selling water and juice was no longer viable when we moved from Mgulani to Charambe. I asked him to open a shop for me. I also asked him to change the set of chairs we have now. He agreed and we got a new set. We have already bought one bed and I told him I want new beds for all the bedrooms. I also told him to buy a farm. We went to see it together and have already made half the payment.

After we have reached a broad agreement, I can decide for myself what I want to do on the basis of what was agreed. If we have agreed, why shouldn't I implement the decision?

I think that I am adequately supported in the decisions I take. But the majority of women are not supported enough. I tell men to take advice from their wives, because sometimes you find a man who has money but does not know what to do with it. He only knows that it is important to buy flour, maize and beans to eat and that is all. If a man listens to his wife, he will prosper. For instance, I told my husband that three children were enough for us. I am not ready to bear another child and he agreed.

Urban and rural women are not equal. Their differences arise from their circumstances and living conditions. Rural women depend on the harvest while urban women can do any type of business and make a daily profit. This is possible throughout the year. In terms of workload, rural women are more burdened. They farm, fetch water, look for firewood and cook food on a daily basis. Urban women, when they are working, have fewer activities and tasks to do at home because they can have a house girl to help them.

When my daughter has finished her studies, I will buy her the tools she needs to start her own business. I will help her find a place to start working.

I don't know why women often think that bearing many children is a solution. I think that the problem is a lack of education. You find women living difficult lives but continuing to bear children, even though they have difficulty feeding and clothing them.

Yes. The choice is there, but it still depends on your being lucky in your choice. You may get someone who beats you or you may get a good man. I have never been beaten all the time I have been married. Most of the time, men want to be listened to but they refuse to listen themselves. Men do not pay attention to what is suggested by their wives. They do not like to be taught by a woman. A man will listen to you, knowing that what you are saying is true, but he will pretend to discourage you to prove that he is a man; he will refuse to be taught by you. However, deep inside he knows that what you are saying is right.

Men feel superior because women stay as housewives while men work. Even some men, who are with a working woman, feel superior, thinking that it is how God made them. But if you look hard, men are no more capable than women. A man is a normal human being like a woman. Yes, if he is your husband, you are supposed to respect him. But he also has to respect you because you are his wife. Respect must be on both sides. If you respect each other, you will live in harmony.

Some people have changed the way they educate men. Our children will be different; my sons are used to cooking, washing, mopping, sweeping and doing any task without thinking that it is only for girls.

Women complain about their relationships with their husbands but they accept the situation because they fear divorce. If a dowry was paid at the time of marriage, and if you had children with a man, the dowry will not be paid back because the woman's family will have spent the money that was given by the husband's family. A woman is also concerned about her children. If she leaves, who will take care of them? Most women decide to stay for the sake of their children.

Sometimes, we see a woman leaving with her children. Each time I ask myself where will she go. It is okay for a woman who can support herself and her children to leave and take her children with her. If you can manage, why continue to suffer in an unhappy marriage?

My advise to other women is that if they stay at home, that they must work hard at anything that could help them develop themselves or to help their family. If a man sees you generating income for the family, he will respect you more. Sometimes, when your husband has no money, he will know that you have enough to buy food for the children. But he can also pretend not to have any money, knowing that you will be able to provide for the family.

CHERYL[3]
Age: 35

PART 1: Childhood

I was born in Musoma in 1968. I grew up partly in Musoma and partly here in Dar es Salaam. I come from a monogamous family. My family was Roman Catholic. We were eight children in the family, four girls and four boys. I am the firstborn. When I was young I lived with my parents. When I reached Standard V, I came to

---

[3] Fictional name.

live with my father's brother in Dar es Salaam. I stayed with my uncle from Standard V till the time I started to work.

I came to stay with my uncle because I was not keeping well, and it was thought best that I stay near a hospital where I could get treatment. That was the main reason. Another reason was that my uncle had just got married. They needed someone who could stay with his wife and keep her company. So my uncle decided to take me. He said I would receive my treatment and his wife would have someone to stay with her.

In my family we were living with many of our relatives. They were all studying. It was as if people came to our house to study.

When I was young, there were a few we had to do like sweeping, washing the dishes, and taking care of the children. Taking care of the children was a task for all of us when our mother wasn't around.

I did all the activities that must be done by girls, such as sweeping, housework, fetching water, cooking, and taking care of children. Most of the time, the boys helped to fetch water. But beyond that they did not help. It was based on the upbringing they had received and very often, it was a problem. You see, my parents were educated and we were living in a town. We were interacting with other people from other places, which was contrary to the custom of our relatives. Our relatives came from the village with a typical village upbringing, where men are not supposed to do these tasks. So it was a problem for my mother to get them to fetch water. Slowly, they came to learn that they each had a duty, such as tending the garden outside our house, or fetching water for the family.

Do girls and boys benefit from equal rights? I can't talk for other people. In my family, our parents, especially my mother, tried hard to educate us equally. She tried to make sure that we all went to school, regardless of whether we were girls or boys. And those of us who were able to study further, did so.

When I refer to my family, I mean my father and mother. My father's brothers and sisters thought he was too religious and did not understand why he was sending girls to school. They felt that girls should be married! In Musoma, girls who get married receive a big dowry. So our relatives told my father that in our tradition girls are not sent to school. They are just sent to primary school and after that, are married. This is done to get dowry to help the family or, if there are sons in the family, to get dowry so that the sons can marry. So you see, girls are valuable for a short time. They are seen as valuable because they bring wealth to the family. At the same time, they are not valuable, especially after they have received the dowry. This is a big problem for a girl child.

A male child will still be valued while growing up. He will be married because the dowry needed will come from his sister's marriage. After marriage, he will continue to live with his father; he will not have to struggle to be independent. Everything owned by his father will automatically be his. It is different for a girl. If she is married to a poor man whose father owns nothing, her life will be a mess.

The highest and lowest price for dowry depends on the clan, family and tribe. For example, at home, if a man marries a woman from our own tribe the dowry will be very high. If the man is from another tribe that does not share our tradition and customs, he will pay less. If the girl is educated or comes from an educated family, the dowry is not a priority with them. The dowry amount has been reducing because of the hardships that people are facing now. Our parents told us that in their time, dowry consisted of 45 or 50 cows, but the day before yesterday my young brother married and he gave 7 cows as dowry. My sister-in-law was married last year with 16 cows as dowry. It depends on the family circumstances. Sometimes they look at the person who is marrying. If he is rich they will ask for a big dowry. *(She refused to divulge the size of her dowry, saying it was her secret).*

My father was an accountant and studied up to Form V. My mother was a clerk, a Standard VII graduate. My parents had a normal life, but it was different when they went back to the village. They were seen as different people, living an unusual life. When my father met his colleagues in the village he was perceived as different because he was able to support his family and lead his own life. At the same time, his wife was also working, which at that time was a stranger thing than it is nowadays. In those days it was very rare to see women doing paid work. That is why so many people came to stay in our house, because they felt they could have a better life with us. For example, when they were sick, they were treated.

Life was difficult for my mother, because the people living at home were from our father's side. So, they had all the rights in the family. Sometimes they wanted to have more rights than the children of the family. Most of the time mother did not like this kind of behaviour and preferred to develop a good understanding with her brothers and sisters-in-law. Our mother tried her best to make sure that the children who were staying with us finished their studies and got employment. Most of them appreciated what she did for them.

Who influenced us? Most of the time, in everyday life, it is the mother who has more influence on her children. She is closer to them and can offer some guidance. Her suggestions are then presented to the father for approval, but most of the time it is the mother who introduces things.

We are grateful to our mother; we thank her a lot. She was the one who taught us so many things. We saw all the efforts she made for the family. She used to tell us that if she had never been to school and gotten a job, she wouldn't have been able to do the things we saw her doing. So we kept on pushing ourselves to study hard so we could get a job and manage our family too. She used to say, "Without a job, I would have failed to do so many things and failed in so many plans." That is because when our father used to reject some of her plans, she used her own salary to implement them. The results were seen as family matters decided by our father, while it was our mother who initiated them with her own money. So the idea of sending children to school came from our mother because education was important to her.

PART 2: Studies

I started my studies in 1978 when I was eight years old. My mother decided to send me to school. I don't know if my parents discussed it first but what I remember is that on the day of registration it was my father who took me to school. It might have been that my mother told my father, so he took me there. My mother had already bought exercise books and pens.

I did primary school at Mwisenge Primary School from Standard I to IV. I was transferred to Dar es Salaam from Standard V to VII. I went to Lugalo Primary School. Mwisenge School was not very far from home. Lugalo School was far from home, so I stayed in Kawe with my uncle and his family. I had to take a bus to school.

I completed my secondary education at Zanaki Secondary School from 1984 to 1987. At home, I was doing household activities like washing dishes, fetching water, cooking and more. At school, I studied; there was also a school farm where we used to farm, play sports and so on.

At my uncle's place, I was treated like a child and house girl. They had no house girl, and there were some young children to take care of. I did most of the chores. When my aunt had a baby, I was the one who did everything for her such as fetching water and cooking. There was a big water problem at Kawe. It was difficult because I was going to school, and each day I had to go fetch water. But I got on well.

I stayed with my aunt until I completed From IV. For Forms V and VI, I was in a boarding school called Rugambwa. I did my National Service and after completing it in 1991 at Ruvu, I came back to stay with my aunt and uncle. I started work and stayed there until 1993, when I moved into a rented room.

My professional objectives changed over time. Usually, youthful aims do change. When I was young, I wanted to become a nurse. But when I was in secondary school, I found I could not do well in subjects that were necessary, like chemistry. Later on, I came to like hotel management, things like cookery and house keeping. I failed at that as well—I was doing fine in nutrition, but when I joined Form V, I did history, geography and literature, and didn't have nutrition as a subject. So when I finished school, I found myself employed as a banker and I did not have time to study hotel management. So it is over with me now. I still would like to be a hotel manager, though.

It is very important for girls to get a good education. Not only for girls but also for mothers. I have seen from my own family, women do most of the things in a family. So, if a mother does not have enough income, she will fail to fulfil some of her plans. It will not be possible for her to get enough income if she has no education. If a mother has money, she can provide excellent things for her family without people knowing that it is the mother who is responsible for the family's prosperity.

Respect for your parents is very important. You have to respect them, whether they give you money or not. It is your responsibility.

Some people do not respect their parents. I think it depends on how they were brought up. Do they value people or things? Although, perhaps, when a parent is doing inhuman things to you or using force, you are not obliged to respect him or her anymore. For example, I respect my mother because she spent time with us. Usually, it is easier to have a closer relationship with your mother than your father. A mother will generally take more time to discuss problems with you. Also, if you have a problem, it is the mother who will notice first. A father can leave in the morning and come back at night when you are asleep; how will he know if there is a problem? And whomever you are close to will influence you more. More than anyone, my mother always advised me to study. She really insisted on education. She always said that education is the door to independence.

My uncle also helped me because he was the one who paid for my education; I stayed for seven years in his house, which is a long time to stay in someone's house. He was not bad to me and did not harass me, and that is why I could study.

My brother helped me to achieve my professional objectives, as he was a banker. He informed me about the vacancies at the bank. This was when I had come back from my National Service. I was still immature and employment was not a priority. But my brother pushed me to apply. At first I did not do it. He called me again to remind me that it was the last day for the application. He really pushed me to make sure my application reached the right person at the right time.

PART 3: Professional life

I started work in September 1991 at the National Bank of Commerce, Masdo branch, as a clerk. The job was advertised in the newspaper but I did not see it. My brother told me about the vacancies for bank clerk and cashier. It was for people who had completed their secondary school education or their national service. I wrote an application and sent it to the bank.

I was called for an interview. Then I was told to make a follow-up visit after one week to check the results. I went and found that I was selected. The ones who had been successful were told to come back the following week to be told our assignments. I went back one week later and I was told to go and collect a letter confirming my place of work.

It is my uncle who gave me his blessing to start work, as my parents were far from Dar es Salaam. I just called them and informed them that I had a job. After one week, I was sent on a two-week instruction course where I was taught what my duties were and what I had to do.

What about my first salary! For me, just out of school, my salary was good. I thought that I had a lot of money because I was used to begging for 200 or 500 shillings. Now I was being paid thousands.

I was still living at my uncle's place and paying him nothing. My salary was just for me to buy my own things. I remember my mother told me that, in order to show people that I was succeeding in life, I needed to work hard and not play. She told me to plan my future, not to spend my money on trivial things but to buy important things like a bed, mattress and utensils. After that, she told me to move into my own place and to live alone to show that I was grown up. She told me to be independent. I followed her instructions and after a short time I was able to live alone.

When I started working, my younger brother (third from me) was in From III. I helped my father pay his school fees; I paid for forms III and IV. After that my father stopped working and our family's income reduced. There were four other children who were still going to school. So I continued to help pay for their school fees and other needs. Later, I brought two of them to stay with me.

This was before my marriage. Now, since I am married, I have bigger responsibilities. My father and mother are retired and some of my siblings are still at school. Before I got married, one of my siblings was living with me; after my marriage, one more was added and he was in secondary school. I was supposed to pay for school fees and other needs. At the same time, my husband has three relatives who needed help. So we continued to help them one at time, in rotation.

I can decide how to use my salary. Since our marriage, we have decided jointly on our aims, so when we receive our salaries, we put the money together, pay our offering to the church, and look at the month's plan. We buy food, pay for electricity and pay bills. You know our salaries are not big! After paying for all these things we have only a small amount of money left and many other expenses. There are emergencies, like I might receive a message that one of my parents is sick. I can send them money straight away and afterwards tell my husband about it. I can decide on things like this; but since we follow a monthly plan for our expenses, emergencies are not good.

I have changed my job because I get a better salary here. My family responsibilities remain the same because the children we are helping are still going to school, and four of them will complete their studies this year. When we are finished with that, we will know if our responsibilities became lighter or not.

At work, women experience many problems. Often women do not succeed in their professional life because women are not like men. Women's hearts are not hard and we live to help. You can define your objective, such as building a house, but if a relative falls sick will you continue to build it? You will feel obliged to help the sick person. But if a man wants to buy a car he will do it, without considering others. A woman's heart is so ready to help!

Women are responsible for the family, for planning, for satisfying the family's needs, unlike men who do not take care of these things. Men will not check if there are enough plates or food in the house when they have visitors. A woman will use her extra cash to buy all these things. Women shoulder major responsibilities for their families before and after marriage. These are the things that stop them from achieving their aims. That's what I think.

As for sexual harassment, I experienced it in my first job. There was a man who decided he would have me. Because he held an important position, he used it to block me. For example, there was a course that I wanted to attend and he stopped me without good reason. He just wrote that there was too much work and that I had to stay because there was no one to fill the gap. This was not true, and the tasks to be achieved were not an obstacle for me. Another course was offered and only men were allowed to go. When you attended this kind of course there were some benefits, like you got a daily allowance for expenses. He wanted people to share their allowance with him when they returned. I think there was no reason for my boss to stop me from attending the course. These things are very common and many women experience them. However, there is no reason to make a big deal of it. In fact, everyone experiences something different.

Improving girls' lives? I think that it is time for parents to recognise that everyone has his or her responsibilities. For example, if you have your own children who need your help, how can you expect to help them if you continue to help your other relatives? It is time to stop helping relatives to a certain extent. Let us try to be like men, who do not go out of their way to help. You put your foot down and say now it is time to shape my children's future. You can achieve your objectives like that.

There are women who really work hard to develop themselves through study and there are others who always think that their husbands will do everything for them. When we were at school we heard girls saying, "Ah! I have someone, a man who is studying hard for me. Somewhere there is somebody cracking his head for me, taking his Master's degree or PhD. Why should I crack my head?" So they didn't study hard for their own future; they thought somebody else would support them. Even as an adult you find the same attitude, you find women who are employed but do not want to buy a plot, because they expect they will be married and their husbands will provide for them. So women's ideas must be changed. They think that if they own property before marriage, it will no longer belong to them after they get married. These ideas are not good, and women fail to perform well or do things that are well within their abilities, just because of this habit of dependency.

What am I doing to improve my daughters' lives? I wish you knew what parents wish for their children. You have good plans and objectives for them, and then you find a daughter who is not serious about herself or has her own priorities. If she likes school, I am ready to pay for it. I remember my mother did not have a big income and she used her salary to pay our school fees. I remember we were sometimes chased from school because we didn't have the uniforms or we hadn't paid our contribution. My father had a big salary but he delayed paying. Our mother would tell us to meet her at her office and she would give us the money we needed to pay the school fees out of advances on her salary. At that time I did not understand the meaning of the word "advance." It is after I started working that I knew its meaning and I discovered what our mother had done for us. At the end of the month, she had no salary left. It hurt me a lot. So if my daughter is able to study, my strategy is to pay for her education, according to my ability.

For a young girl, it is more important to get a job first than to be married. You know marriage is always there, but if you get married without having a job or a salary you cannot be independent. I have seen many friends or relatives who are not respected by their husbands, because they are not contributing to the household. A woman who is not working is just like a child who has never been to school. The husband has all the responsibilities and must work hard. It can reach a point where he sees you only as a burden. So you need to get an education and keep in mind that marriage must come after studies. How is a woman without an education going to run her life?

The way I understand it, "free choice" means something that I have chosen myself. A person can choose without being forced and without fear of what others will think or say. For example, when I chose my fiancé, I was not forced by anyone and had no fear of what my parents would say. I thank them because they respected my freedom of choice. Even in your marriage you might decide to study again. It is you who decide and not somebody else for you.

You know, women's lives are better now. If you talk to your grandmother, you will hear how she got married and lived. It is quite different from now. For instance, my grandmother told me that she had no say in her marriage. She found herself in another house and she was told the man was her husband. She was taken there when she was young, grew up until she became a woman. While she was there, she was used as a tool to take care of her in-laws and the whole clan. Having no power in the decision-making process is contrary to me. Now I work and earn money to satisfy my children's needs and help the people I have decided to help.

A woman can go to school now and compete with men, which is different from the old days when women were not allowed to go to school. In the family you can sit together, plan and decide on family issues, such as about the children, or about building a house. This is so different from the past when women were not even allowed to decide on the number of children they wanted. You were married and it was your duty to bear children.

Nevertheless, there is still a need to educate women to improve their lives. You still find a lot of women who never went to school. There should be seminars or institutions to teach women what they are supposed to know. You know women can sometimes use the excuse that they are not supposed to do certain things. For example, yesterday we were at the bus stop going to a funeral. We could not talk to the conductor and were waiting for a man to come and talk to him. There were over twenty of us, we all had money, but we could not talk to the conductor! You see that there are many habits embedded in our minds.

This is why we need seminars to teach women about their rights, their responsibilities, how they can make decisions to help the family. Many women are not doing things because they are not aware that they can. They do not go to school because they are not aware they are supposed to go.

What is the reason for this? It is related to upbringing, and you find yourself reacting according to it. The ones who escaped from such upbringing, that is from kitchen and household duties are boys. They can work hard and do well at school. Take one woman of my age who has been in the village since she was born. I tell her that I sit with my husband to decide on the family's matters, while she was never told about her rights. She can do a lot of things perfectly but has never seen what other women are doing. So women who have a chance to be successful should go to meet the less fortunate women. They should tell them to work hard to achieve better results.

PART 4: Personal life

I got married in December 1996, when I was 26 years old. I myself took the decision that he was the man I wanted to marry. My father made all the arrangements for my marriage.

Marriage is important for women, but many women think that to be married is the be all and end all of their lives. If a woman is not married, she may think that she can't do anything by herself such as buy a car or build a house. She has no life if she is not married.

There are people who think that if they are married they will have children. Of course, we can have children without being married, but this does not have a nice image in our society. My own parents were married when I was born. So if I say that I want a child, where can I get one? It means that you just go and get a child who will care of you. But God said it is not good for a man to live alone. You may own a car and a house but you will not enjoy life if you are single.

Both of us are responsible for children *(laughs)*. I laugh because the mother's responsibility is greater than the father's. That is not a secret. You may sit down together and plan what to do for the children, such as send them to school, but when the time comes, no money appears from his pocket. If a mother has the money she spends it so they can go to school and have other small things. For instance, if you find your child has no shoes, you will buy a pair of shoes. As I told you, a woman's nature is different from that of a man. The nature of a woman is to be responsible; a man can see a child playing without shoes but he will not react and he won't see that he is responsible for buying those shoes. He must know that it is a bad thing, but if he sees a torn uniform he will not think of buying a new one. Most of the time, it is the mother who takes on the responsibilities.

We sit and plan together for our children's future. We also pray to God to help us. We have two children, and the most fundamental thing for them is education. We sit and plan together then later, during the implementation, one of us may be slower to act. Most of the time, men are slow to act, and finally you may find yourself, as a woman, using the money that you put aside to allow the child to attend school.

We are from the Kurya tribe, and among us it is the father who decides. You may sit and discuss the matter together and agree upon it, but later the family speaker will decide what he wants. Sometimes, a woman is not even allowed to participate in her daughter's marriage arrangements or dowry. She is not allowed to say anything even if she might have seen the groom misbehaving or stealing. The daughter will stick with the man, and the men of the family will not allow the mother to comment on anything that has been agreed by the father and the aunt (sister of the father). Most of the time the father's family has overriding authority in these matters, more than on the mother's side, and in the case of marriage, it is the father's side that has authority. I have heard that there are tribes where the uncles have more say. For us, it is the father and the aunts who have the greatest say.

I thank God because my relationship with my husband is good. Your life depends on how your man was brought up, the family he comes from, or how God made him. Some were brought up in families where the father was always fighting and beating the mother. It will not be easy for such a man to be peaceful with his wife. But for us, our communication is good and I am authorised to decide some things and just give my husband a report. My husband travels a lot, and one day I had a message saying that my mother was very sick. I screwed up all my courage and decided to rescue her. I withdrew cash and sent it to her. When he came back, he had no problem with it, which is different from other people. Although our communication is good, some say that this will change over the years. I can't comment on that.

Women are supposed to have the right to decide for themselves. As I told you, women have more responsibilities in the family than men. So if a woman is not allowed to make decisions, what will happen? If a mother who is responsible for her family has no right to decide what happens, how can the family work? It will be difficult for her. For example, when I was at my parents' place, my mother had a big problem with children from my father's side but she had no authority to tell them off, because they were not from her own family.

Sometimes women themselves spoil their status, like when they overreach their authority. People become fed up with them, and there are some women who harass men. But on the whole women are not supported enough. Most of the time men do not trust women. They are seen as weak and not able to do things. A man often doesn't pay attention to a woman's advice, because men underestimate women. This disease will take years to end. Men have to be taught that there are some women who are as wise as they are. They should learn to respect their decisions. Men should also know that there are men whose decisions are rotten. So if a man's decision is rotten, what should women do?

You can see the difference between rural and urban women by looking at the health of a woman from a rural area. She can be sick and recover without going to hospital or taking any medication. In town, women will take time to rest but rural women do not rest from January to December. Here, women work, and almost all houses in town have a house girl, which is different from the rural situation. When you have a maid to help, you have time to plan your things or to rest, and when you come home from work you will find everything done. In rural areas, when a woman leaves home to go and work in the field she comes back to find nothing done. She still has to cook, fetch water and perform all the other tasks. Here, with educated people, you sometimes find a man helping his wife at home, which is quite unlike rural areas. If you find a man carrying a bundle of clothes to wash, it will be a surprise to most people.

Is there a common vision? I do not think so, because in town we see people or women who went to school and are working. You find yourself learning many things about how to live that were not taught at school. This is different from the countryside, where a person is born, grows up, marries and stays in the same place. You may find a woman who has never been to town, even to her district headquarters. The whole way of looking at things will be different.

My daughter, if God keeps me alive and gives me a good job, will be educated and go to school. If she is educated she will be able to liberate herself and run her own life. If you say, let me build her house or buy a car, she will end up being like a rural woman. She will take things for granted. This is not the right way to liberate a woman. To liberate a woman means letting her run her own life as she wants when her husband is not around or if she is not married. A woman who is not educated will find it difficult to run her own life if she stays single or if her husband passes away. The fundamental thing for me is to give my daughter a good education.

Some women can make their own marriage choices and some cannot. Men will use different tactics to win a woman, for example by using cash, and then you see the woman has no choice. A man can come to your place and study your situation. He starts to give you things you lack and later he will marry you. In town women get married in different circumstances, for example marrying their boss because they are being harassed. In that case, it is not really the woman's choice; she married the man because of the problems she was facing.

Married women still face many problems. A woman can find that she is married to a man who does not allow any discussion and who plans by himself even things that concern her life. For instance, when relatives on your husband's side come to stay with you, they come with all their power and authority, knowing they are coming to live in their own house. Your in-laws come and decide for you. Another problem is financial dependency. Most women do not have their own money. You see that the salary a woman earns is given to the husband. Women then find themselves with a big burden because the money they earn is used for the family needs. For example, my neighbour came to see me because her husband did not provide her with food or clothes. Life was miserable for her. I advised her to look for capital and start a small business. So she went to ask her brother-in-law for money and he gave her Tanzanian Shillings 50,000. She started to sell paraffin, cooking oil, tomatoes and other things in front of her house. The business prospered. When the husband discovered this he stopped supplying things at home. The business then had to feed the family of four people, including his relatives, and she had to find the money for bus fares and so on, till the business died. When the business stopped, the harassment returned as the woman came again to beg money for bread. Moreover, she was now asked what she was spending the money on.

Most women have no freedom to work to generate income. For example, you can find a woman going to Zanzibar on business, buying things there and selling them in Dar es Salaam. Back in her house, no one trusts that she is doing business and not other things. Or if you are working as a banker, for example, sometimes you fail to balance the books and then you have to come back at 8:00 pm, and you find that your husband does not believe you when you say that you were at the office. So there is no freedom to work.

Nor do women have freedom to decide on the number of children they want. You still cannot tell the doctor to give you a tubal ligation, even in a government institution, without the authorisation of your husband. They will tell you to go home and come back with your husband, who, if he is against family planning, will tell you to carry on bearing children until you are finished. If God does not help you to find a man who cares, you will not be able to decide how many children are enough.

A woman cannot even decide to send the child where she wants, because money counts. If a woman wants to put her children in a special school she will not be able to if she has no money, even if her husband is a millionaire. You may be on good terms with your husband, but you still have to do what he wants.

I think it is about time to let our society change. Nowadays most families try to put boys and girls together and treat them equally. In the past, boys sat down beside the father and girls had to stay with the mother. The girls did all the kitchen work and finally had more to do than the boys. But parents who have been to school or gone to town have learnt different things. They've discovered that all children are equal. They are giving them equal tasks to perform and some parents have learnt that they cannot force their children. Perhaps if a boy feels he should continue to help with household chores, he can do it.

A man is not automatically respected because he is the head of the household. Respect has to come from both sides. As for the issue of a man being the head of the family…maybe we can ask God. He is the one who made man first, then woman. We also learnt that when he made the man he said he would make a helper for him. People who read the Bible explain it like that. But men should respect their helpers, because when a man falters, a woman is the one who helps. Her success is your success and vice versa. In community matters and life, I don't know if religion can explain everything.

Some women complain they are badly treated by their husband. Women have nowhere to go to make a complaint, I mean you have to go and tell your story to your husband's uncle, who is also mistreating his wife. Many women are not educated and they do not know that what a man is doing is not right. It is high time to educate both men and women, society at large, that there are things it is not good to do to a person, specifically to a woman by a man.

Women are not willing to leave their husbands because they think that they would have to leave their children behind. As I have told you before, the mother is the one who has all responsibility for the children. You cannot think of leaving your 2 or 3-year-old child behind. You take into consideration that your husband is not a man who feels responsible for his children. He may have the money but he will not take his responsibilities seriously. So you think how much your children will suffer if you leave, and finally, you stay. Other women think that if they leave they will only marry another man who will be the same or worse. They think, "How many men am I going to run from? Maybe be that is how they all are."

You find other women who are afraid of the shame that they will feel in the community. People think the marriage failed because the woman left her husband and came back to live with her parents, as the majority of women cannot afford to live by themselves. So if I cannot support myself, I need to go back home and depend on my parents. It creates embarrassment on both sides.

The dowry is another obstacle, because if you leave your husband's place and come back to your parents, they are supposed to pay back the dowry that was paid for you. When a woman has a problem, she will go back to her parents' place to let them know that she still belongs to them. Sometimes, the dowry was paid a long time ago and has been spent. This is a big obstacle for women.

There are some women who simply cannot stay with their husbands, and leave, despite whatever happens. They are rare and the community perceives them as exceptional women. Whatever they are doing is noted; even if it is a common thing, it will be stated as another reason why she failed to stay with her husband. But maybe it was the man who was to blame.

I would like to tell women that we should have a strategy to become independent in education and economy. It cannot be achieved in one day. Some women have managed it, but in general, the community is not ready to let a woman become independent. The community still underrates a woman, and they are still looked on as strange things. Women with educational and economic independence are there but they are not recognised as men are. They suffered a lot before reaching their present position. So we need institutions to support women who are ready to liberate themselves from the current situation.

Even basic education must be available in rural areas, where women suffer so much. You won't believe that a woman who is in nine months pregnant is still working on the farm. The day she starts her labour pains is the day she comes back from the farm and goes to the hospital. At the same time her husband is sitting in a bar, drinking. This woman is responsible for everyone, and if you ask why she does not rest, she will tell you that nobody will cook for her and that her husband cannot cook because no men cook for women in her society. These women need to be educated so they can liberate themselves. Men also receive a bad education: they are told that women are their enemies within the family and need to be overcome. I don't think that women want to become like men. But they need education, to get a good job so they can support themselves and their families.

MYRIAM[4]
Age: 43

PART 1: Childhood

I was born in Tanga on 7th December 1958, and grew up in the Kilimanjaro region. I come from a monogamous Roman Catholic family. We were eight children; one passed away so then we were seven, six girls and one boy. The one who died was a girl. I am the

[4] Fictional name.

second born in the family, but after the death of my sister, I am now like the first born.

When I was young, we lived with eight relatives. They were my aunt and uncle with their children, from my father's side; and my uncle and his child, from my mother's side. My paternal uncle had two boys, and aunt had one son and one girl. My maternal uncle had only one girl.

When I was a child, I had many duties to perform at home. I swept and washed my clothes and my younger sisters cleaned utensils, cooked, and took care of the other children. I only rarely went to the farm. It was not something for us girls and boys. Most of the time, tasks like washing, sweeping, cooking and dishwashing, in fact cleaning in general, were for us girls. The boys did not do any of these tasks. They played football, or read books or newspapers.

I think that it was like that because of tradition or habits and culture. I don't know why people think these tasks are for girls.

As I see it, girls and boys do not yet benefit from equality. They are not educated in the same way, according to the same principles. You see, most of the time, girls do work for the families while boys do their own things. You can find some families where both girls and boys are equally educated, while you will see that in other families only boys are sent to school. For example, take the area where I am living. I have a neighbour who has four children—two boys and two girls. When the first girl completed Standard VII, they let her be married. The other one is still at home. The family struggles to pay for the boys to go to Airwing secondary school. The person who struggles more for them is the mother, who sells fried fish. I asked her why she was not sending her girls to secondary school and she said, "With the girls you end up wasting your money. Let me educate the boys." So the way the family looks at things also matters.

When I was young we were all sent to school, both boys and girls. We lived with my uncle's son (from my father's side) and he was our father's favourite. You would see our father checking up on him, like if he did a mistake my father asked him, "Why did you make a mistake? Why did you stay at home instead of going to school? You know that all of us depend on you to help your young brothers."

My father never bothered with us, as he never asked anything of the girls. We were just sent to school for the sake of it. There was not a thought in his head about our future. To discuss things he would call upon this boy (our uncle's son) but he never asked for my sister who was older. What can you say? Girls were seen and not seen.

My father had secondary education. He had completed Standard 12 and graduated at that time. He was an employee in the Forestry Department. My mother went up to Standard IV and had to drop out to get married to my father.

My father had more influence on me, perhaps due to financial power. He was the one we were dependent on, and he was the one with income. So you see we had to obey what he said; and what he decided was right.

As for my mother—she was not heard at all. If she talked to my father he only ignored her. He always ignored my mother's view, even if it was good; he would refuse to recognise her opinion. Sometimes, we saw that my mother had changed something by herself, and even if my father had decided it, when he saw what had been done he would become furious and tell us to do things the way he wanted them done. And it was done the way he wanted.

This way of doing created problems, especially when our father passed away, when we had to turn to our paternal uncles for help. They were not ready to help us. They blamed our father for having spoiled us. There was no more support for us.

PART 2: Studies

I started going to school when I was seven years old. I don't remember the year very well; it might have been 1964 or something like that. My father was the one who decided to send me to school. I don't know why my mother did not decide, but I remember that when I was small, my father was the one who sent me to school. He was the one who escorted me there for my first day. I was very young. What I remember is that my father came home and told us that I would go to school tomorrow. I didn't sleep that night because

I was thinking what the school would look like, what would be there. At two o'clock, I went to wake up my father and told him I was ready to go to school *(laughs)*. In the morning, my father took me to school.

I attended nursery school at Lushoto, close to Tanga, where I also did Standard 1, II and III. After that, my family had to move to Morogoro. That is where I completed my primary school, up to Standard VII. I was selected to go to Morogoro Secondary School and I failed to go there because my father was transferred to Kilimanjaro-Moshi. I transferred to Mawenzi and when the school opened I was already there.

I completed my secondary education at Mawenzi Secondary-Moshi, which was from 1972 to 1975. I was supposed to be at school early in the morning. We had duties and when somebody had a cleaning duty we had to come earlier than usual. Before our colleagues entered the classroom, it had to be clean and well arranged, the teacher's chalks and classroom register had to be in place. When the teacher entered, a monitor had to give everything to the teacher. Other responsibilities were related to general cleanliness, in the classroom or somewhere else in the school. We cut grass. I liked art subjects such as cookery, needlework and typing.

School was very important for me because there were sports at school like netball and basketball. It attracted me. Also, I knew that when I was at school, I had time to have friends. I liked sports a lot and that was another reason I did not skip school. Even when there was an emergency at home and I was supposed to remain there, I sneaked off to school.

When I was at home, I helped my mother by doing some small work like cooking. After that, and if I came home early, I used to go to the library. Our house was not far from the library. You could go to the library before going home, or go straight home and later go to the library. During school vacations I used to do some temporary jobs. I was allowed to keep the money I earned. I got used to buying dresses and other small things. I managed to get that job through my friends with whom I was studying.

When I was young, my professional ambitions were quite big. I wanted to be a lawyer. I remember one day, when we had some visitors, there was a man and a woman. I asked my father who they were. He told me that he was our visitor and she was his wife. And that she was a lawyer. I was intrigued by the woman's appearance; she was still young. I asked why she was dressed like she was. My father told me that it was the way lawyers dressed. I said if God wishes I will be a lawyer too. That is what I remember.

But when I went to school, I realised that I couldn't make it. I found myself doing what I do now, that is working as a community development officer. What were the major impediments to my becoming a lawyer? My ability and my intelligence were maybe too limited. I don't know. Perhaps the way I viewed the profession. I mean, perhaps in a family parents are supposed to talk to their children and discover what their interests are, and what they are capable of. But there was nothing like that in our family. This might be the cause for my not having completed my studies in law. I didn't get support, there was no one to push or encourage me. No one was behind me to tell me "do this or that and you will succeed." It is not that I was not capable in those subjects, but information was limited.

.

I studied Kiswahili, History and English at school. My father told me that if I finished school, when I came back home, I would be able to be a teacher at a higher level. He told me that he would help me to complete further studies. This came with warnings that I was not to fare badly in studies or end up pregnant. He was very harsh about that.

My other relatives also studied. My father's favourite went to Tanga and afterwards to America. He never came back from there. Others went to study at the Teaching College. One is at Bukoba. We are dispersed now.

In fact the biggest help I received was from my father. He is the one who did everything for me. After him, perhaps the circumstances of life forced me to reach where I am now. My mother was there, but I don't know how I can explain it to you. For example, when I was at school I was supposed to tell my father what I needed. What could I ask or tell my mother? For me, my father was everything. My mother was just there to cook the food we ate at home. If we were sick, which was very rare, it was my father who sent me to the hospital.

My mother had no economic power and our father treated her as a typical housewife. She had to stay at home; she did not go out to the market or anywhere else. She cooked, ate, cleaned, and went to visit the neighbours if there was a death or any problem.

Why did my father behave like that? One day, I asked him why he treated our mother like that. He told me not to interfere in his business. This caused problems for my mother, especially after my father's death. She had to go out and struggle by herself. The children needed to go to school and my father was no longer there. What could be done? She did not know anything, where to start, what to do. As a result many of our possessions disappeared because people who knew about our properties decided to keep quiet when they knew that our father died. So they took all our properties.

Later, our mother confessed that she didn't like the way our father treated her. She told us not to copy these Swahili customs whereby a woman is supposed to stay indoors, be supplied with everything and just sit there as if someone is doing everything for her. And if a man does not act like that, society will see him as someone who does not take care for his wife. I think my father was brought up that way.

My mom dropped out of school in Standard IV to be married. She did not love the man *(she beat the table to show how her mother was forced to marry)*. They told her, "Whether you like him or not you will marry him. We have done all the preparations." Our father told us that our mother did not love him and that he married her with her parents' permission, because he loved her very much. And that was why he did not want her to have any problems.

PART 3: Professional life

I started working in 1978 as a Community Development Officer at Muheza district in Tanga region. I reported there until January 1979, when I left to attend National Service. I came back in 1980.

Nobody helped me get this job. It was my post after two years at college. I had to move from Moshi, while my parents lived in Tanga. It was the first time I was far away from my parents.

As we had no relatives in the region, the people at the office took us to a guesthouse. They told us they would pay for our rooms for seven days, and after that everyone had to find their own accommodation. Fortunately, my colleague had her sister living there. She went to stay with her. I stayed at the guesthouse and, seven days later, I went to stay with my colleague at her sister's house. Two weeks later, a colleague left and said that her room was vacant. She offered to rent the room to me until she came back from college.

In fact, my first job was not in accordance with my studies. When we were at college, we studied development, which included sewing, handicraft and project writing. We were lost when we started work. For the first time, I had to do cooperative work in farmers' associations, serve associations and audit. I used to go to the association and ask the accountants to give me their record books for auditing. I had to follow someone who knew cooperative work, and so I learnt what we were doing.

My salary was very little. Truly, when I received my salary for the first time, I wept because it was so little. I thought that I needed to pay rent, and I had never stayed alone. I was not used to budgeting for the full month. I had no bed; I had nothing. So I sat down and wept. I told my friend that I was leaving and went back to my parents' place. But my mother told me that this was life, and I should go back and learn. As my father was dead, I had nobody to support me. My mother gave me a bed and some pots, plus the fare back to my duty station.

I could decide what to do with my money and I was not obliged to my family. But I squeezed myself to send my family some money. When I started working, some of my sisters and brothers were still at school and my father was dead. Our eldest sister, whom we were depending on, had also passed away. So our mother was alone and she started to work. The work was for an unskilled person, so she was earning a very small salary. She had money from our tenants because she was renting our house. But it was a very difficult period.

It was before my marriage. When I got married, I told my husband the real situation of my family and asked him if I could send half of my salary to my family to help them. He agreed to that. My salary never changed; only duties and responsibilities changed

Women encounter many problems while trying to achieve their professional goals. We have a dependent character so we mislead ourselves in development matters. We also experience problems with harassment.

Harassment! It is what I have experienced before marriage. For instance, in these offices, when you are a woman, it can be difficult for you. If you are not married, you will receive many proposals from different men. If you don't show interest they may post you to the village. For example, when I reported to Muheza they posted me to Amani, where I have never been before and they told me that the place had a transport problem. I agreed to go. Later on, the boss called me and told me to talk nicely to him, so he could post me to a good place within town. I don't know if I was immature, but I reported the matter to the District Commissioner. After that, a scandal broke out. I told the District Commissioner that I had been told to talk nicely to my boss so that I could be posted within town. The matter was discussed in the Boma and as you know Muheza is a small town. They said, "Look at her she is pretending to be like this and that!" I felt bad and perceived it as harassment.

When I completed From IV, my father sent me to Thika High School in Nairobi, Kenya. I stayed there for almost five or six months. In the sixth month, I went back home to Moshi. I was there till July, when the results were out. I had a letter from the Prime Minister's Office, and when I got this offer I didn't want to go back to the Thika School. This was due to what my father told me before I left for Thika. He said, "Look, you are not going there to waste my money. I am sending you there to study." So when I saw the letter, I saw it as a way to be rescued from this situation of being blamed without reason.

When my father passed away, our relatives created a lot of problems. My mother had to look for a job for the first time in her life, but she was not able to walk a long distance. She found a simple job of carrying files. She left the job when I was working and my sister was also employed. Unfortunately, my sister passed away and my mother was completely frustrated. The same Regional Commissioner who helped my mother find a job organised a plan with people from the coffee board to modify the regulations regarding our house. So tenants could stay there for free for one year in compensation for the money used for modification. They would start paying in the second year. My mom agreed, and this helped her a lot.

I have learnt from my mother's experience not to be dependent on a husband or a child. Things such as death or disease can happen and you will find that life is sour. I have also learnt that if you are dependent on someone, you need to achieve something on your own as well. For instance, if my mother had been able to do something, she would not have suffered the way she suffered.

In my own view, to improve the lives of women, the first thing to do is provide them with a good education. We must educate our daughters because if we educate them they can rescue themselves and become independent. If a woman is educated she will not be married early. The time she is at school will let her mind grow and make her wiser. If she stays at home, after a certain time, she will get a fiancé and be married. By being at school, she will stay busy with school activities, to the extent that she will not think about getting married.

I have two daughters and I am always telling them to be independent. They should not be dependent on someone else. For instance, if there is a house girl in the house, she is there to help. It doesn't mean that my daughters can relax. If they find a dirty plate or unmade bed, they have to wash that plate or make the bed, and later tell the girl that it should not happen again. Or if they go to the farm and find that nothing has been done, they cultivate and then tell the workers that it is not good to let things be. They have to set an example.

My children were born in Dar es Salaam, and this is their hometown. They are Zaramo by tribe. I have a small place like a farm, which they cultivate as a garden. If I had some more money, I would have established a business for them. After finishing school, they could work there. I have also bought a sewing machine on which they are sewing or trying to sew during their vacations. So, they could run this sort of business later. My firstborn has already finished From VI.

I will send her to a computer school for three months, which will cost Tanzanian Shillings 60,000.

I think that it is more important for a girl to get a good job than to be married. To be married is just an outcome not a base. Why not a base? Marriage is there and if you look at the community, they prefer to see you with a partner. But if you become dependent on him, there will come a time where he will harass you. And if you are independent he will respect you. So it is better that you have a good job, and when you find a partner he will respect you.

Women should decide things for themselves. This will make them committed and they will be sure to work hard to make things happen. It is not the same when someone else takes the decision for you. For example, I have decided that I am going to construct a house for my children—a small one, not a big one. If I die at anytime, my children will have a place to live. I sat down and thought, "My salary is not enough even for food every month for all of us to live on." Then I decided to look for other jobs. So these other jobs also helped me. I already had a plot and I managed to make blocks, buy iron sheets, paying the masons, and construct a house.

I think that women's lives today are better than what my grandmother and mother had to go through. Very much! I saw how my mother was oppressed. What made me notice her oppression was the fact that she had no influence in decision-making. She was not allowed to speak and what she said was never considered. It was only our father who could decide and say whether it was bad or good. No one was able to change his orders. He just told her what he did. There wasn't any discussion. He did not beat our mother, but the problem was in the decision-making process. If a child had a problem, my mother was not even allowed to decide or give any advice, because our father decided what to do.

I even told her that I was surprised to see her still normal and not mentally affected. I really felt sorry for her because she could not speak. My father had a bad character. I think our father was treating our mother like a child. I don't know, but I think my father thought that he knew more than my mother.

My mother told us that their marriage was not a voluntary one. Her grandmother selected him for her and forced her to marry him. She did not love him at all, but our father said he loved her so much and she never loved him. He said, “I managed to marry her just because of her parents’ power.” They used to tell us this and we used to laugh.

Life is better today. Women are employed and men are also employed. We see some women who are not married, and they are able to support their children and educate them well. Women have better incomes now.

But women are still dependent. Even their views are still related to dependency. I think it is because of tradition and culture, or the kind of upbringing we get. In reality, we are dependent. The way I see it, the problem is still there.

What could be done to improve women’s lives? First, I think that the lucky women who had access to education should help their fellow women who are not yet educated.

Second, I think parents have to bring up their children differently. Girls should not be educated only for marriage. They should grow up to be independent. If they get married, it should be to someone who is ready to help them. It should be a relationship in which they help each other.

I have two sons and two daughters living with me. Sometimes, you may find my daughters Doreen and Yohara at home. Most of the time, you will find Doreen cooking, sweeping the house or fetching water. If there is nothing to cook, she will prepare some porridge. That’s not like the boys, who go and play football. When they come back from school they know their mother or sisters would have cooked something. One day I asked one of my sons why he was not cooking. He told me that he was playing football. I told him that if he did not cook he would not eat. He thought I was joking. The first day, he went to eat at his aunt’s place. I spanked him for doing that, and informed his aunt that he was refusing to work, so they should not give him food. It was hard for him to wash his own clothes. I am trying hard, but it is difficult; you will always find that a girl does more than a boy.

PART 4: Personal life

I got married on 26th October 1980, when I was 22 years old. I can say that it was my decision. I have been a widow since 1995. I have not remarried.

I think it is better to have a good base in marriage, especially for bringing up children. It is important for the children to experience care from both the parents. The child will learn more by seeing a mother and a father. They will be happy, and there will be love. Also, the child will be spoiled less. Sometimes, you see a grown-up girl who becomes very excited when she sees a man, because she never experienced life with a father. The same applies to a boy who has never been close to his mother. When he is close to a woman he can be confused. He may run away, or have affairs with sugar mommies, just because they are of the opposite sex and he missed that affection during his childhood. For me, marriage is important and necessary for the upbringing of children.

I was separated from my husband for a period of time because we had quarrelled. I caught him with another woman. After that, we quarrelled a lot. I had to leave him and I went to live somewhere else. On his own initiative, he contacted his relatives and he brought them for reconciliation. I agreed and went back. We were separated for six months.

After this incident, we agreed upon some things. I told him that as he was not faithful, he should not expect me to do things for him such as wash his clothes. I also told him that I was withdrawing my money from the joint account we had. We should keep our own money and use it as we want. We had also bought a farm, which he decided to sell. I asked him to pay me back my money, and I used it to buy another farm. He gave me back my money and he changed a bit because things were tough for him. At that time, we had two children. He went to report me to the church, saying that we had quarrelled but were not really reconciled; I was seen as an obstacle. He said that I claimed I had forgiven him. We were summoned to the church and I was asked if I had forgiven him from the bottom of my heart; and if I had, then things should be as they used to be. It was unfortunate for me because the priest was his brother. I saw him oppressing me but I agreed because there were some older people there. We swore. I agreed. They told me to act like a Christian, and as I grew up in a Christian family, I had to forgive my husband and live the way we used to, and have a child because we had reached the point of having no sexual relations. My in-laws insisted on that. They said, "If you have relations, we will know it by seeing you with another child." That is how the quarrel ended.

After this, my husband worked hard even if there were some problems at his workplace. I was pregnant at the time; he never told me about his problems. He just told me that he had to travel to Rwanda, and when he reached there he called me on the phone to tell me that he had problems at his office, and he had to leave. I went to inform his brother who checked up at his office. They told him he was indeed facing some problems. They were looking for him. They traced him to his house, but he was not there. I don't know if those who came to the house were police or not. He called again and spoke to his brother. We owned another farm, and we sold it in order to pay for a lawyer. The case was ended and my husband was dismissed from work. It was difficult for him because he did not get any benefit.

After that he stayed on in Rwanda and Burundi for years. He did not call anymore and I went to ask his brother, who also didn't know where he was. We were living in a parastatal house and were supposed to vacate it. I went to stay with his brother but it was not comfortable to live there. I decided to look for a house, and this is the house we are in now. I also looked for a house girl because I was totally frustrated and I wanted to go back to school. I took my daughters to his sister's place and the boys to my mother's house in Moshi. One girl fell sick and I had to come back from school. Life was very tough.

One day, I came back from school and my husband was at home. When he came back, I was not around. He went straight to his sister's place and asked for me. His sister asked him if he was really serious about asking the question. She told him that his wife was an exceptional person because she did not go back to her parents' house when she was abandoned while pregnant. Now the child is aged five; Yohana was a big boy at that time. His sister told him, "Now you come back in such a condition. Where were you, and what have you done?" He failed to answer.

He was completely changed, and was not the man I used to know. I asked him what happened, and he told me he was sick. I asked him why he had changed so much. Remember, he left while I was expecting. I had a child in 1986 in his absence and he came back five years later, so changed!

I went on telling him that he was not the man I knew. He was in dirty clothes with long nails and hair. You couldn't tell if he were a mad man or normal. Have you ever seen soldiers who stay in the forest for a long time? I told him if someone bewitched you, then they really got you badly. I felt pity for him and I gave him some money to cut his hair. I thought that this was the man I had chosen to be my husband. I gave him new clothes and told him to sit there, and I looked at him to see if he was the one I had chosen. (*She laughed.*) I left for school.

I left him in my house in the absence of the children. I told him to stay there, and I went to withdraw some money. I instructed him to cook and eat because he had *kwashiorkor*[5]. Then I went back to school, and while at I was there my sister-in-law wrote to me saying that my husband was nowhere to be seen. I just said, "He will take care of himself." When I came back I heard that he went to Rufiji and thought that, in his condition, he was going to die. He came back seriously ill and went straight to his sister's place till God took him.

Now I am responsible for my children. Their aunts and uncles are there. But for someone to be responsible, it means they have to take them to the hospital when they fall sick, provide food and so on. Initially I was really frustrated with all these problems. My salary was so little, while the children needed to go to school. All these problems at the same time! So I went to see my brother-in-law who told me that he also had problems because he had no job. I went to see my sister-in-law and she told me that she also had children to take care of. Wherever I went, people told me they had their own problems. I decided to take my children to my mother. When I got there my young sister told my mother, "Why did you take the

---

[5] It is an advanced form of severe malnutrition.

children of my sister while she is in Dar es Salaam? I will have to use my own money to feed them. What are her relatives doing? Tell her to come and collect her children, or you put them on the train yourself." One day, I was at home and I received a phone call from my sister saying that my children were on the train. That is the day I realised I had problems. I did not have a house to stay in, but I came to collect them. My school results were also out, and unfortunately I had to repeat one year. I decided to look for a house girl to stay with my children. I left a note for her to collect my salary and use it for the children. I will never forget that house girl and only God knows where she is. She stayed all the time with my children, while I was in Tengeru until I completed my studies.

You know if you go to ask your relatives for help it does not mean that the help must be monetary. It can be in the form of advice, but you find them telling you that they do not know. Maybe they refuse to be involved in your problems. One day, a sister-in-law helped me by telling me that they were distributing land in Morogoro. I went there and got something, which helped me. The money I had made me strong and it reduced my problems. When we got there they gave us the farm and I received Tanzanian Shillings 300,000, which I never expected. The next time I received Tanzanian Shillings 50,000 and at that time I had some problems, so the money helped me a lot. I was grateful and thanked my sister-in-law for that.

What should one's relations with one's husband be? Before the problems occurred, we were communicating well and our relationship was fine. For example, once, when he was going to buy a farm, he asked me to go with him. I asked him where we were going to buy a farm and he answered that it was in Pugu. When we got there, I told him that I thought the plot was too big. The seller told us that with time the place was going to change and not to worry about it. I also found that the place was far from town in a bush area. I refused completely to buy in that area. We had a joint bank account and he withdrew enough money to buy the plot. I found that I had also participated in buying the land. Sometimes, in buying household utensils, I used to oppose my husband by telling him that we had no house in which to keep them, and I asked him what would happen if he lost his job and we didn't have a house. It was better to use the money to make some blocks. He agreed and we bought iron sheets, and we kept them at Pugu. That was before the problems. After that period, nothing went well.

A woman's decisions are supported when she has economic power. Her decision will be taken more into consideration than a poor woman's decision, even if it is a wise one.

What is the difference between urban and rural women? The first difference is in the work; you will see that a rural woman has more work to do than an urban woman. Some urban women do not have work to do and they stay at home while their husbands buy clothes and food for the family. Their work is to cook and eat and sleep. They are always at home, while those in the village will be looking for firewood, fetching water, cultivating and doing many other tasks. It is a real difference. In town, you find educated women with good jobs. They take care of themselves and they have a good life, compared to women in rural areas.

Urban women know their rights better than rural women because there are so many activities in urban areas. There are many different organisations and people attend workshops or seminars. For example, my neighbours told me that they had been to PRIDE International and Poverty Africa; this is quite different from the situation in rural areas. Women in rural areas do not know any NGOs or organisations. They only know CCM[6].

Improving my daughters' lives? I told you I am not very rich. I have tried to build a small house so that if I die today my children will have a place to stay, even if it is not a very good place. I have also bought a farm plot on which they can plant something to eat. If they starve it will be their fault. I have bought a sewing machine, which they are learning to use during school vacations and if they fail it will be their fault, because you can't do everything for others. If I had enough capital I would have opened a shop for them or I would have bought a minibus and let them count their Tanzanian Shillings 20,000 per day.

---

[6] Chama Cha Mapinduzi (CCM) is the name of the official political party that runs the country since its Independence.

What I have learned from marriage is that married women suffer due to their relatives, especially from the man's side; and it is worse if a man is rich or has economic power. They like to interfere in family matters and it is a problem. For example, you may find a woman married to a man who is financially capable and you will see that his mother, sisters, uncles' children, aunts, they all come to him with their problems. If the man says that he cannot help them, they blame his wife. Sometimes, you will find a woman with problems. If she is working, she will get respect but if she is a housewife, she will have fewer goods and will wait for them to be given by her husband's relatives.

Are woman's own relatives accepted? It depends on the power a woman has. You find some men who do not like their wives' relatives, and you also find women who do not like their husbands' relatives. It is a problem.

Another problem is that women are dependent. You find some who went to school and they still have ideas of dependency. They cannot even decide about a small thing. A woman will worry about how her husband will feel if she does anything, and will wait for someone to tell her what to do.

Other problems are related to health. Women's health is at risk, especially when a man sleeps with other women. And all along, they continue to have a lot of family responsibilities. Most women, who are employed, when they go back home after work, can't decide to stop at a bar for a beer. They will go straight home to see if the children have something to eat or if other things are all right, while a man will go straight to the bar for a bottle of beer with roast meat. When he comes back home he will see that you have done everything. In the morning I am the first person to wake up, though we all go to work. I clean the house and do other things. So you find that women are still burdened.

It is true that men are naturally powerful. It might even be true that men are more intelligent than women. Women who are intelligent are fewer than men. That is my view.

I think that might be because of upbringing. I always think that upbringing results in this. That is how the community moulded us women since time immemorial. We've found ourselves on this track. We have inherited it, and our children will also follow the same system. I think we should have been treated equally as human beings, not as a man or a woman. People are still educated in that manner, even if some are trying to change. People are educating the community, but few among them have changed. Religion, tradition and culture; all these contribute to women's harassment.

Take the example of the Moslem religion. A woman is supposed to wear dresses to cover her whole body and head, leaving only her eyes uncovered. If she is at a meeting and raises an issue, everyone will be on her case, saying that she has a big mouth, wondering how a woman can talk like that in front of men. They will call her bad names like liar, big mouth, prostitute; and if she stands and looks straight at men, that is even worse. They will say how is it possible for a woman to behave like that?

As for the Roman Catholics, you do not see any women as priests, and I don't know why. It is better with the Lutherans because they have women priests nowadays.

What are the traditions and culture at Tanga? For starters, a woman is not supposed to pass or cross near men if they are seated somewhere. If a woman talks to them or sits with them, she will be thought a strange person. In our family, boys used to eat before girls and as sisters, regardless of age, we were supposed to serve our young brothers and remove the plates from the table after they finished eating. The biggest share had to go to the boys. Our mother used to tell us to serve the boys a lot of food and the remainder was to be for us. If they finished eating without being satisfied, we had to go to the kitchen to cook more. After all, we were only girls! In most cases there was nothing left after the men and boys finished, and none of us girls was ready to go back to the kitchen to cook again. Everyone was tired.

Yes, our father and brothers were seated at the table while we were seated with our mother. If visitors came, we used to sit at the table with our brothers. We could use the table only if there was a ceremony at home, like baptism. This was possible because many visitors were there and it was not easy to separate us. But the norm for us was to sit on the mat, serve more food to the boys and if there was any left over, it was possible for us to eat.

Many women complain about their relationship with their husbands because it seems unsatisfactory. Personally, I see that in most cases it is the children who make these women tolerate the situation. Once a woman is married she will not want to move out and leave her children. She does not know where to go if she leaves the house. It is difficult for a woman to bring her children to her parents' house. For example, it is not possible to bring your six children to your parents' house where there are already many other people there, that is your parents, sisters and brothers. So a woman might decide to stay, hoping that maybe the husband will change.

What would happen if a woman tried to behave like a man? For one, the man will try to kill you. For example, if a man catches you red handed with another man, if he is the civilised type, he will just divorce you or tell you to go. If not, he may kill you with a knife. You will have to leave, and the community will look at you as an aberration. And if by chance the man agrees to stay with you, my God! They will say you did something, that is gave him some magic herbs to make him stay with you. But if a man did that, they will tell you to forgive each other.

Women forgive easily because they have a tender heart. Maybe it is because we experience so much pain during labour. Maybe it is our nature.

What can happen if the dowry is not paid? Where we come from, in Tanga, my daughter can be married with three chickens. One chicken can be prepared for our colleagues. Moslems will perform a ceremony, which involves burning incense and rituals. Christians may have some more complicated rituals. So dowry is not an issue, except for those tribes that collect a big dowry. I do not know about them.

AUDREY[7]
Age: 57

PART 1: Childhood

I was born in Ludewa district on 30th December 1944, and grew up in Ludewa-Milo. I come from a polygamous family where my mother was the first wife. We were Christian and members of the Anglican Church.

We were ten children in our family—six girls and four boys. I am the fourth-born in my family. The second wife had four children—two boys and two girls.

When I was young, we did not live with our other relatives. There was only my mother, father and my siblings. The second wife lived with her own children. My aunt and cousins used to visit us. Afterwards, they would go back to their house, because it was not far from where we lived.

I had some tasks assigned to me when I was living with mum. I went to school but I also fetched water, did some cultivation, looked for firewood, cooked and chased birds from the wheat crop. I also chased monkeys away, so they did not spoil the maize. After coming back from school in the evening, we had a rota for chasing away the monkeys. For example, my brothers would be on guard and when they came back they would also fetch the cows from the bush. I used to be on monkey guard after coming back from school. We really shared the tasks among ourselves; so that the person who chased the birds yesterday would chase monkeys today, while the others herded the cows. Our mother used to plan the rota for us. We all knew what our duties were.

In our family tasks were shared equally between boys and girls. Our mother brought us up like that. The boys were quite used to cooking and fetching water. We worked equally.

---

[7] Fictional name.

Nevertheless, girls and boys cannot benefit from equal rights. Girls differ from boys. Girls learn things faster than boys. So, most of the time people depend on girls for doing things, just because they are quicker.

It depends on the way parents raise their children. For example, our mother treated us equally, but this may not work due to the nature of each person. For example, my mother might ask one of my brothers to pick vegetables. However, if she realised that he was too slow, she would stop him and leave me to do it. That is because she would know that I did things faster and in a more efficient way than my brother.

My father was a mason, building brick houses, especially mission houses. My father attended school for a very short time but he could read and write. My mother never went to school and did not know how to write or read. She was a housewife. *(She thought back and modified her statement).* No, my mother used to work for white people. She washed, swept, watered flowers, made beds and sometime fed chickens at the farm. I had forgotten this.

My mother had more influence on me than my father. She is the one who let me and my siblings go to school. My father was around, but was not dynamic. Mum wanted us to do household tasks while we were also going to school. She wanted us to eat well, wear nice clothes and take baths; she really supervised this.

My father attended school for a short while but he did not continue. I told you that men are slow. I think that they are not naturally clever; they are not aggressive or daring like women. Our mother used to do many things. For instance, I remember she built a house. She cleared and levelled the plot, together with a skilled worker who helped her with the construction. Some other people also helped her collect grass for thatching. She also made the local beer. Our father was around, but my observation was that he never seemed to be as involved as my mother.

I didn't know what was important for me, but I think that my mother knew. That is why she sent me to school, taught me how to cook and many other things.

PART 2: Studies

I started school when I was still young. My mother was working, employed by white people, and decided to send me to school because the lady from the mission influenced her. I studied at Milo Primary School. The distance from my house to the school was almost two miles.

I didn't reach secondary school; I just completed Standard VII. In our time, there were very few secondary schools and there was only Tabora secondary school near by. The children who were chosen to attend were those who had first-class scores. I was among them, with good performance, but I was not chosen to attend this school.

I started Standard 1 in 1951 and completed Standard VII in 1959. I attended the Teachers' Training College at Masasi District in the years 1960 and 1961. During my training time and especially during the holidays I used to teach pupils, or sometimes I stayed at home, helping my mother.

What I wanted to do? You know in our time, going to school was very uncommon and the possibilities for what you wanted to do were limited. We were not the ones who decided what we wanted to do, and we were not educated towards being able to choose or to think about our own objectives, because the desire for us to go to school came from the missionaries. They wanted us to study to become nurses or teachers, because a nurse could help to treat patients at their hospitals and a teacher could teach at their schools. So the possibility of thinking about my own future was not in my mind or in the minds of my friends. It was the teachers who decided on our behalf. They even decided which pupil would go to secondary school. If you had your own wishes, you just had to keep them to yourself.

So I achieved the missionaries' goals. This was possible because I was among the best students. I became a teacher; they selected me, I myself never applied to join the college. The white people decided who would go to secondary or another school. Two students were chosen to join the Teacher Training College and I went to Ndwika Mission College. Three were chosen for the nursing school. When my friends came back, they went to work at the mission hospital.

This was the plan made for them by the planners during the colonial times.

Mission people did not think about professions other than nursing or teaching, or about benefit to the African race. As you know, when they came they wanted to educate people to a certain level so that they could serve in their work places. They had schools and hospitals to run, so they educated people to work in these places. They needed a basic education that was not of a particularly high level. They knew that if someone reaches Standard VIII, he or she would have enough knowledge to teach or treat people.

Education for girls is very important because then they can have equal opportunities. Girls are intelligent, with abilities just like men and sometimes more than men. But it is also very important for a girl, or any child, to respect her parents in order to get blessings. It is written in Bible, with the promise of benefits that will follow. For example, the fourth commandment says: *"Respect your father and mother so that you can add more years to live in blessings."* Other commandments are just stated without any promises, for example, you are told to love your neighbour, and not to steal. To be blessed, you must respect your parents. God is God for fathers and mothers, but fathers and mothers are God for their children.

Who had most influence on me when I was young? I had no idea about anything and I just studied without any objective or vision. We were told that only one student could continue to secondary school. It was like winning a fortune to hear that you had been selected and told to go to the mission, collect some money and go to school after receiving a letter. It was something you simply did not expect.

Many people helped me achieve my professional objectives and personal goals, especially becoming a teacher. My brain started to work. I started to think differently because I was able to think by myself and be independent, to choose between things I liked and disliked—to have a choice at all. I was advised to undertake certain studies and one person told me about tutorial college courses. In Kenya there was the Rapid Results College, in the UK there was the British Tutorial College, and there were some colleges in Dar es Salaam. I did some correspondence courses here in Dar es Salaam, and other such courses from Kenya and the UK. At that time, it was very easy to do a correspondence course. You had to send your papers and the results came back very quickly.

PART 3: Professional life

I started work in 1962. I was a primary school teacher at Ibumila, in Njombe district. At that time, when we had completed studies at the mission college, they used to give us posts in their mission schools. So I was posted to one of their schools. I had to move from my parents' place and I went to live in Njombe district. I started by living alone, later with my younger brother, and later on two sisters joined me. I did not have to take permission from anybody. That was not the case. I decided for myself—after all, I was not married at the time.

My first job was in line with my studies; of course these whites knew my educational background and qualifications. I had finished Standard VIII, which allowed me to teach Standards I to IV. I started work at a salary of Tanzanian Shillings 250. I paid a rent of Tanzanian Shillings 36 to a council called the Native Authority, and the remaining money was for my own use. I sent some cash to my parents, paid school fees for my sisters, and I was also able to buy some things. For instance, I bought a sewing machine, a Singer, and I paid for it in instalments while continuing to help my relatives. I also managed to run a shop for my parents. At that time Tanzanian Shillings 200 was a lot of money. Not like nowadays.

I did not change my employer. It was only the tasks and duties that changed. I worked for twelve months as a teacher immediately after completing my college training. I taught Standards 1 to IV for two years. I went for further studies, then came back and was able to teach Standards V to VII in English. Then I left teaching at the primary school level and moved to the college level. I was among the first African women to teach at the college level.

Later on, in 1969, I did school inspector training. I worked as an inspector for a short time and continued to teach at different colleges, for example at Tosamaganga in Iringa, at Mpwapwa in Dodoma and Chang'ombe in Dar es Salaam. I was also a Tanga Municipal Adult Education officer. Later, I became a school inspector until I retired.

I used to decide on how I was going to use my money, even after marriage. I managed to pay for the education of my sisters and my brother until they became independent. They all became employed. I got married after this, when I could use my money for my family, to educate my children, for household needs, to build a house and for family development.

What are the barriers to women achieving their professional objectives? I have already said that we women are faster and more dynamic than men. Women are intelligent, wise and knowledgeable. I would like to say more now about the knowledge that women have. Their knowledge is wisdom and ideas. This helps them in taking care of their children, household matters and all household development. A husband might be there, but he will not know that a child is sick, or needs a school uniform. A woman will deal with these problems while a man cannot. A woman is capable; it is written in the Bible. She is the one who goes to bed late and is the first to start work early in the morning. She is the one who makes sure that everything at home is in good order, by supervising the children and casual workers, and building a house. For men, the Bible says they have to respect their wives, but it is not stipulated how they should operate in the house. So the Bible gave men just this one duty, and gave all the other duties to women, who are more capable. Look at what women can do! Women do everything in rural or urban areas, whether they are intellectual or illiterate women. Everything is left to women, and in fact that is too much.

It is also written in the Bible that a man is the head of the household. This just has to be. Because of this, a woman has no freedom to say, let me go and look for a plot. She might have some money to build a house. Many people in town provide security for themselves by building a house, and they are able to do so because they have money. They are educated, unlike rural women.

What could be done to improve girls' lives? You know, when I was young, there were some people from Community Development who used to go from one village to another to teach women how to cook, how to dress, how to take care of or serve a man, how to make beds. In the villages someone might come from the farm with mud all over their body and go to sleep without washing. The people from

Community Development taught them that this is not good, and that they need to take a bath. They were reaching very isolated villages. This helped those who never went to school; at that time school was for only a few people, not like now. It gave them the chance to open up their minds to knowledge, and also taught them to be hard workers. You know, we need to teach people to work hard because this gives them a certain vision. When you visit people who are not developed, you can move them some steps forward by providing education and encouragement to do more. Nowadays, community workers are found in urban areas. I am not sure if they are at the district level or the regional level or at the headquarters. These people are educated to know the procedure for doing things. Many women are still not aware of what they can do. They just know that a man is supposed to cultivate, bring in money, send the children to school and take them to hospital if they fall sick, and build a house for the woman, while the wife must stay at home waiting for her husband to bring her everything. There are still women of this type and this is due to their lack of education.

Tradition and culture have become muddled because of a lack of education; if people had been educated they would not be so confused. It is like this because most people are used to seeing women and children in the kitchen. This is men's rules and procedures, tradition and culture. And maybe those who stay in the kitchen, women and children, are not aware that staying there does not give them any dignity. It is a male idea that women should stay in the kitchen, and most women and children find it okay. But men should be told that they could work in the kitchen just as well as women.

I really worked hard to improve my daughters' lives and make sure that they were getting a good education. They are educated because I am educated. In our family, we are all educated and I contributed a lot to my brothers' and sisters' education. God blessed me because I sent my daughters to school, and they are all doing well and help me now. I thank God because his promise to me has been kept. He said, I will bless you and all your children, and he has. I am living in a comfortable house, wearing clothes and eating food my children have bought for me, using the perfume they got me. They give me everything I need. They have even given me a car.

I succeeded in improving my daughters' lives by using my money in businesses like poultry farming or charcoal selling. I have done so many different kinds of business, almost all the businesses found in the world! It was not big business but things like selling vegetables, cultivating enough vegetables to sell, selling beans and chicken; it all came out of my salary and I did it by myself, with my children. They are now more educated than I am. I worked hard to be sure that they would go to school. I really worked hard for that.

It is not bad if you remain single because you can produce for yourself and live a nice and comfortable life. But it is written that you should marry. You will do the same tasks whether you are married or single. You know marriage and education are good, but it depends on what you plan and work for. All is well if you marry the man who was planned for you by God. But you may pick someone who will not be good for you. With a good man, you can plan together and live comfortably. Both will want the same things—to buy a house and have children. They plan together for the family and listen to each other. They become one group made up of father, mother and children. But families like that are very rare.

You may pick someone you met in the train while travelling to Kigoma and decide to get married a few months later. You don't know where he comes from, and you will have misunderstandings because you do not speak the same language. You will find that he does not help you, he doesn't notice when you are sick, that you are going to the antenatal clinic or that you have delivered. He does not know that his children need to go to school, or that there is no more sugar at home, or that there is a need to buy a plot and build a house, to or visit a parent. He does not know that plans should be made together.

If you marry a man like that, you will be in trouble all the time. You will use your own money for regular family needs, and he will count on you for everything. This kind of man will not be thinking of you. So, this is not the one meant for you. If a man is meant for you, you will always love each other.

What does it means to decide by yourself? God gave both men and women brains and intelligence. It is inherited. The wisdom of men and women is equal. God never differentiated, that women should have less intelligence and men should have more. God distributed these attributes equally to men and women. It may happen that there is a very stupid man and a woman who is very intelligent, or the other way round. This is God's wish and it is not to do with human ability. So, as I have said, being a woman means having the ability to decide on your own and to make the right choice. If we say that a man has to decide for a woman, does it means that he is more gifted than the woman? From my own experience in marriage, I see that women can be very clever, sometimes even more than men are. I do not talk about only intelligence, but about knowledge and wisdom. Women think well and they have the capacity to develop their home in a dynamic way. The husband should respect his wife's suggestions, for example she may tell him to build a house and he should agree, and make sure that they can achieve this goal. A woman is the key advisor. If you see any home that is progressing well, you know that it is due to the woman.

Life is better now compared to the days of my mother or grandmother. At that time, women's oppression was greater. Nowadays, men know that women can do things, and that they are not just like a cow or a tool they have bought. Men do not beat their wives as they used to. At that time, beating wives was normal and a man's right. Now things have changed.

Change starts at the household level and spreads to the village, ward, division, district and national level; it disrupts the community. Change mean development, but it does not always mean that it is positive. It is sometimes negative. For instance, the television is a product of development and progress, but it is also destructive. It destroys home life because we can see advertisements that are not good. TV influences people's life through advertising. You can see children in the streets repeating what they have seen on TV. It is different from the past. We need to be careful when changes occur, because there is no way to escape development.

Because of development, women have had the opportunity to go to school. They are aware of their rights and the fact that they have even more ability than men. Even women from the village understand that they can participate fully in development. One woman can initiate a project such as a poultry farm, gardening or cultivation. Many are aware of sources of loans to start a business, or know how to start their own groups in order to get more money. I have not seen men doing this. Some women start flower businesses, run exhibitions or salons, open boutiques or run catering services. You see them in the marketplace. It is the same if you go to the village. Women sell the vegetables they have produced, and finally they are able to establish themselves alone or make a joint venture with other women, or to start an NGO. They can start anything and run it, and other people for their own development and that of their families will bless them.

Women are aware of their own development and understand what they need to do. But I think that women still need help in the villages because services are missing. Community workers should travel and visit people, to help improve women's lives in rural areas.

PART 4: Personal life

I am married and I live here by myself. My husband lives somewhere else, where we used to work. He comes to stay here for a short time and then goes back. He is around.

I have been married since 1973. That makes it 28 years. I was born in 1943. That means I was 30 years old when I got married. Women are supposed to get married younger than I did. My marriage was my parents' decision and I don't know if dowry was paid. In part, the decision was not mine. The dowry was paid without my knowledge, because I remember writing a letter to my parents advising them not to take the dowry, as what they had received was enough. They did this in my absence.

At that time I was teaching at Mpwapwa College. You know my parents and my husband are from the same tribe, and we lived not far from each other. His and my parents lived in the same village and they managed to organise our marriage once they learned we were talking to each other. They said that we were old to be married. They did it in a hurry. You must know that in the village they like their daughters to be married. I was late, I delayed it because of my studies and also because I wanted my sisters and brothers to finish their studies. I was relaxed about it, but the decision was mostly my parents'; I was only partly involved.

If you say that people have freedom to decide for themselves, they will know if getting married is important or not. I don't know if marriage is in fashion or not. God said that Adam needed someone as a wife, so it is biblical. It is not essential to get married. Someone can decide to stay single and have a comfortable life and make her own products, study, build her own house, communicate with other people, have friendships with other, without needing a husband. Sometimes, single people have better lives than married ones, but that should be their decision. Most people think that marriage is important because it is something biblical, and the community insists on the importance of it. People also like weddings because there is food to eat, dancing and celebration, because people who are just married do not know about the long-term consequences of marriage. The woman just thinks about the nice dress she gets to wear.

If I were single in today's day and age, I would never bother to look for a man to get married. I would concentrate on God.

Who is responsible for children? Both of us were responsible for our children. But, usually, the woman is the one who plays a bigger role. For example, right now my husband is not around while the children are here; automatically I will take care of them. I was the one who was responsible for them and made decisions for them, although they also made their own decisions. It depends on how the children see the household; whether they think that it could be too much for their mother. My children were used to deciding for themselves, but I also helped and advised them in some cases, for instance on school or job matters. Sometimes, when their father was there, we used to sit and take decisions together.

For a large part of my life, I have lived alone with my children, especially when the children were young. I took care of them and gave them all they needed. I think that if you are a mother, you know what your children need. You have to be strict with children to make sure they go to school and complete school courses. You need to be strong, especially single mothers. I advised my children to look for a good job where they could get a good salary and live comfortably. They all went to school. I advise them to look for more money, and to work harder in order to make more money. I tell them look for opportunities. We all work hard; they help me and I also help them.

Yes, it is possible, if you recall what I said about a good husband being one who respects his wife. It is in the Bible in Proverbs. So a woman can make decisions. Otherwise the household will be a shambles. You will see grass growing up to the doorstep, or you will see a household without animals or crops. Can you buy poultry if you cannot make a decision? Have you never seen women going to buy chicken feed, cement for building, or carrying crates of drink to sell? Sometimes a woman will decide while her husband is there. Others build houses without telling their husbands, for example my husband did not know about this house and he first saw it when it was finished. I decided everything myself.

When you have children, boys and girls, you will see that the girls are more dynamic than the boys. That is why Adam was deceived by Eve in the garden. That is how they are. God asked Adam what he was doing and he answered that he was hiding himself because he had eaten the fruit, which was given to him by a woman. That is why women are clever, and why they can overthrow empires.

There is a difference between urban and rural women. Rural women are not exposed to sophisticated life, the way urban women are. For instance, urban women have access to loans, groups, they can work with computers, they can surf the Internet, they watch TV, and so on. Urban women are exposed to more development than rural women. Rural women fail to keep up because of poor communications. They do not own a telephone or TV, cannot read newspapers, and there is no Internet; even regular mail is not available. Their development depends on political decisions.

Many problems arise because men are cowards. They have been told that they are the head of the household, and when they realise that women can do things like buying a plot or cultivating land, they think that women do not respect them. You will see a woman buying a uniform for her child; it is obvious that a woman always assesses the situation and then takes action. A man might think that this woman does everything by herself and she does not respect him anymore. The issue is not lack of respect, but you can be sure that conflict will start because of this.

Some women wash their husband's clothes and iron them, and then the man thinks she is hinting that he is a dirty man. He will go out to look for a woman on the street, and he will look for an uneducated one because he knows he has more chance to oppress her. Most men prefer to get married to an uneducated woman. They are afraid of educated women because they think they will be overtaken. This is due to cowardice; the man is the one who creates conflict and misunderstanding in the house, not the woman. When a woman gets married, she knows that it is full stop for her, which is not true for men. When a woman does anything, the man gets scared and associates everything to a lack of respect. You see a man having an affair with the house girl, knowing that she will always be in his power.

In my case, my aim was not to be married. I wanted to choose a handsome man to have three children with him, and after that I wanted to take care of them. I had no idea about marriage and I had many fiancés. I decided that I wanted children without being married. In the end my family arranged my marriage, but I decided to accept it. People say, "The one who chooses a coconut will end up picking a rotten and unripe coconut." It is a choice I wanted to have, but I never made it. Choice for women is very important.

No, men are not more intelligent than women. They are the same. I remember when I was at the Adult Education Institute for my diploma. We were taught about inheritance, psychology, philosophy and intelligence. Just as a man can be intelligent, so can a woman. This is God's will, and what decides the intelligence of a child is not human ability but God's wish. It is inheritance through reproduction. I cannot agree with the statement that men are more intelligent than women.

We need to respect each other. I told you that it is written in the Bible that a good man is one who respects his wife. He respects her for what she does, and not just because she is his wife. It is a must for a man to respect and take care of his wife, even if the woman is a millionaire. A man is the head of the household, and even if he has a small salary, he is supposed to keep it for his wife. It is good to respect each other. A man is supposed to be responsible for the children, to buy clothes for them and send them to the hospital, to buy clothes for his wife and pay for food. He is also supposed to take care of the house, see if it needs painting, if there are beds in the house. That is the meaning of "head of the household." Respect is a two-way affair.

Married women accept difficulties with their husband for the sake of their children. These children come from her womb and may be the only ones she has, whereas a man can have these and others here and there. So she might stay with no food, no electricity, no sugar and no salt. A woman stays for the sake of her children. Some women also contribute to their marriage problems; they go looking for a man. For example, I had one fiancé at Mpwapwa who was a doctor, and he was very handsome. I saw him with open eyes, and he ran from women who were after him. He was clean and, with the title of doctor, nurses flocked to him, TTC students flocked to him, and I saw him struggle to hide himself. They were all after him; some even went to see him for treatment when they were not sick. And sometimes, he failed to escape. It is the same with married women; they use different tactics to get somebody else's husband.

I read the story of a white woman whose husband left her with a child. The new woman living with this man knew that he was married to a white woman, left behind at a hotel. If she had been good, she would have said, "No, let me look for my own husband." Why can't she look for her own husband and love him, instead of taking someone else's? I don't understand, because there are many men around.

That is human psychology, which I really don't understand. These are human beings' weaknesses and the work of Satan; if you know God, it will not happen.

Conclusion

In these sections there have been no comments on the women's discourse. The women have been allowed to express themselves as they wish.

The next chapter will present an analysis of women's voices on the four topics presented here. It outlines different moments in the country's history and the various political, economic and social changes that have had an impact on women's lives, either facilitating or impeding their development. Individuals can also make choices and develop different strategies under specific circumstances. They are marked by diverse events, living in a complex society in which structural changes put pressure on people's behaviour.

CHAPTER 6

WOMEN AS NEW INDIVIDUALS AND SOCIAL ACTORS

The following chapter introduces an analysis of the similarities and differences occurring in the four life stories. It also describes some changes in the areas associated with the sexual division of labour, power relations, and the daily life experiences of men and women.

An analysis of the similarities and differences in women's life stories shows the importance of the environment and of historical processes in building up the "plurality" of individuals. It is not easy for men and women to distance themselves from socially constructed gender categories. Individuals are confined in a system that confirms and reinforces the structure of the personality and reproduces the system through ideological and justice institutions. Inequalities are present and interrelated in representations, in the work place, in the constructions of femininity and masculinity, in *habitus* and habits.

Nevertheless, contradictions emerge as individuals living in the city are more frequently confronted with new information or situations. The system becomes more open as individuals adapt themselves in a continuous reformulation. Thus, the interaction between men and women is a good example of both continuity and changes.

The second part of this chapter reports some students' comments on four different topics related to gender relations: marriage, respect, humiliation, and women earning more money than their husbands. The conservative views of younger individuals demonstrate the persistence of social memory.

Finally, the chapter ends with a discussion of the changes and challenges in gender relations in the city of Dar es Salaam.

Across different historical periods

Four life stories. Four different contexts. Four generations of women. How varied are the lives of women in Dar es Salaam? How have they changed since 1944, when the oldest woman interviewed was born?

To what extent is the situation of women connected to changes in Tanzanian society?

Of the four women who gave in-depth interviews:

- The oldest was born in 1944; she was 57 years old at the time of the interview.
- The second was born in 1958; she was 44.
- The third was born in 1968; she was 34.
- The fourth was born in 1973; and she was 28.

Thus, two women were born during the period of the British Protectorate. The oldest participant completed her studies and started working during colonial rule, while the second began primary school after Independence. The third started her studies after the Arusha Declaration, and the fourth went to school in the early 1980s; this period was characterised by a national economic crisis, followed by the implementation of a Structural Adjustment Programme. These four life histories are therefore closely linked to four significant periods in the country's history.

The colonial regime in most African countries, as shown by Mikell (1996:17), introduced capitalist economics and the ethics of Western Christendom. Four factors were significant in establishing a new form of gender bias: 1) *Christianity*, with its notions of monogamy and female subordination; 2) *westernised education*, which gave preference to men; 3) *differential marriage systems*, with Western marriage guaranteeing women access to property rights that women married under traditional law could not claim; and 4) *alternative legal systems* that supposedly acknowledged African women's rights (although in practice colonial magistrates often treated women as minors in need of male guardians).

The colonial regime distorted the gender hierarchy already present in African culture. The linked processes of colonial domination and capitalist penetration interacted with traditional culture, increasing the workload for women relative to men, and also created a dynamic of individualism, which resulted in gender inequalities for ordinary women (idem). The colonial regime envisaged men, rather than women, playing the major economic and political roles. The colonial state's interest in controlling and extracting from African women was narrowly focused on their sexuality and their role in social and biological reproduction (Geiger, 1997:22).

At Independence on 9th December 1961, Tanganyika declared war on three problems it had inherited from the British administration: poverty, ignorance and disease. The philosophy of "social equity" was adopted via a massive state commitment to social services. The institution of universal primary school, which began in 1974, was ordered to offset gender, class and urban-rural differences. Ship (1988:157-160) noted that the 1968 government statistics for primary school enrolment indicated a ratio of 1.77 boys to 1 girl in rural areas. The urban ration was 1.22 boys to 1 girl. The 1978 statistics revealed that the gap was decreasing between both urban and rural areas, and between boys and girls at the level of primary school. However, dropout rates were higher for girls in both urban and rural areas. In 1960, female students represented 15 percent of the total number of students as, in 1975, they represented 31.9 percent of 12,261 students enrolled in vocational schools. Of the 38 vocational schools, 17 admitted only males, 16 admitted both males and females, and 5 admitted only females. No females were enrolled in agriculture, masonry, carpentry, auto mechanics or air conditioning. Sexist attitudes about appropriate gender roles were reflected in the content of programmes.

For example, the number of women who were educated increased; a quota system or separate selection process for secondary school girls[1] was instituted after Independence to encourage girls' access to school. However, women were not integrated into decision-making or planning at every level of the government. Male biases resulted in few women being chosen for political activity or posts that could influence the decision-making process at national and local level.

After the Arusha Declaration in 1967, major changes in the Government policy occurred. Socialism and self-reliance became the

---

[1] "Following the same principles as the quota system for region and district, girls' results in the Standard VII examination are separated from boys; a certain percentage of girls are selected for Form 1, according to the scores. In Dar es Salaam day schools and those of other towns, 30% has been the common quota. As a result, many Form 1 girls have performed much more poorly than boys; just as many boys and girls from disadvantaged districts have performed less well than those from educationally developed districts. If there were no district or gender quota system, there might be no girls at all in secondary school in some areas, and some districts (and ethnic groups) would find themselves without any secondary school enrolment" (TGNP, 1993:83).

guiding principles; the Government introduced centralised planning, nationalised the major means of economic production, and regulated free market practices. Social services such as education and health were free. "All these steps—economic diversification, and the expansion of social services—cost large sums of money, which neither the Tanzanian government nor its population could afford" (TGNP, 1993:45). Consequently, the country became dependent on external input of capital, primarily from official donor agencies.

The number of women educated continued to increase, but they were still excluded from the political game. A campaign for adult literacy was launched and universal primary education was instituted. More women now migrated to the city; colonialists had blocked urban migration of indigenous Africans, especially women. From 1968 to 1978 the gross domestic product (GDP) increased, but declined from 1979 (UNICEF, 1990:6). The deteriorating quality of education and health services forced families to reconsider their economic strategies. The country was firmly enmeshed in the global economic crisis as a result of debt, donor dependence and continued export orientation.

In 1986, the Structural Adjustment Programme's conditions were accepted by the Government, which thereby acquired access to renewed financial support from the IMF and other donors. The introduction of the Structural Adjustment Programme affected women directly, as they had to support families as the quality of education available at all levels declined. In these circumstances, many children were withdrawn from school on a temporary or permanent basis, as their financial contribution was seen as necessary for household survival. Thus, girls' possibilities for continuing further studies were affected: post-primary and secondary training and education had lower female enrolment and a steady decline in female students, reflecting the disinvestments in postgraduate education. Government priorities shifted from human to more economic preoccupations.

> *Corruption and nepotism have radically increased with liberalisation and structural adjustment, rather than the reverse. Poverty and rising costs of living have bred growing meanness of spirit at all levels of the society. The gap between rich and poor has contributed to sharpened conflict along*

class, ethnic, gender, religious, and national lines (TGNP, 1993: 46).

The economic crisis increased hostilities between men and women, and between people and the state, as subsidies for housing, medical care and education were cut. Women noted that they bore the brunt of economic reforms. Many became aware that women's conditions were deteriorating, reflected in rising infant and maternal death, and the feminisation of poverty. Women saw the need to address their subordinate position in the public arena. They already perceived, as pointed out by Omari and Mbilinyi that "they were born to be less equal" (2000:292-314).

According to TGNP's report of 1993, female enrolment at primary level increased from 42% in 1974, to 46% in 1979, to 49% from 1984 to 1991 as a result of the policy of Universal Primary Education (UPE) and the practical support and cost-sharing of parents and communities. Dropout rates for girls tended to be lower than those for boys, contrary to expectations. However, during the last years of primary level, Standard VI and VII, girls are frequently withdrawn from schools by parents to undertake puberty rites or because of pregnancy[2]. Although official education policy is to reduce gender inequalities, many inequities remain.

> *The lack of women in higher levels of employment and education can explain the perpetuation of institutionalised sexism in all spheres of society. Grassroots women lack enough educated women with a gender perspective, with whom they could network and develop broad alliances for political section. Skilled human resources are necessary components in the struggle for gender transformation of the society, and are more powerful when they belong to Tanzanian communities (TGNP, 1993:88).*

Disillusionment with political parties, as they perpetuated the historic exclusion of women from decision-making, has forced Tanzanian

[2] "In 1991, 45,487 children dropped out of the primary school system, 48% of whom were girls; 2946 dropped out because of pregnancy, 2917 died, 2653 for other causes, but 36,941 dropped out because of 'training.' The meaning of the concept, training, appears to be *unyago* and *jando* or puberty rites. In the past children missed two or three weeks of schooling, but now puberty rites have become a rationale for withdrawing children from school completely." (TGNP, 1993:82).

women to create many organisations that focus on concrete organisation building. "Dealing with the challenge of everyday survival, women have created associations that contain the beginnings of the kind of society they desire: more inclusive and participatory at all levels and that is organised along lines that are meaningful to the people themselves at the grass roots" (Tripp, 1996: 305).

Women's personal life and social contradictions

Women become "resilient" if they have the capacity to overcome society's obstacles. Resilience is produced through various determinants; among them the weaving of self from social discourse and images. Thus, each person gives a private meaning to events because things and events are perceived in various ways. A multitude of responses are possible to the same situation.

The four women who present their own stories come from four different areas of Tanzania—none were born in Dar es Salaam, but all migrated to the city for different reasons—and are linked to four different historical moments.

These women work in different economic sectors according to their educational level. The two older women have been involved in the public sector as teacher and community worker. One younger woman in her 30s has been incorporated in the private sector as a banker while the younger one, in the informal sector, identifies herself as a businesswoman. The two younger women had less education than the older ones. This reflects the decreasing educational provision due to the economic crisis in Tanzania.

Childhood and socialisation

The four life stories show the strength of paternal authority; the mother's confinement to domestic tasks and lack of power in decisions over family matters; the use of physical, mental or psychological force or violence against women; and the division of labour between girls and boys, and men and women. They show the continuity of the patriarchal ideology, which states that unpaid work to benefit others is women's work, while men control the decision-making process.

From childhood girls learn they cannot participate in the decision-making process even for questions that directly concern them. They are excluded from family and political life because of their sex. Their role is confined to domestic duties and the care of others, whereas boys benefit from recognised and legitimised power and respect, because they are viewed as the "head of the family." While still very young, all four women perceived the negative attitude and low status that was accorded them.

Three of the informants feel sorry for their mothers' situation. Except in the case of Audrey's mother, the others were unable to participate in the decision-making process and were excluded from socio-economic life. They had no influence or economic power. The father had all the rights and no obligation to inform his wife of his decisions. All informants saw the effect of this kind of situation on the mental health of women.

Unequal treatment of boys and girls is apparent in these four life stories. As is normal, the four women underwent their apprenticeship in social roles throughout their childhood, in which boys were more favoured than girls. Boys were not obliged to participate in domestic tasks while girls were assigned specific jobs that they had to perform on an everyday basis. Because of prevailing gender stereotypes in society, the gender division of labour starts and is maintained at the family and household level. In most families, girls are expected to help with domestic chores and are assigned specific tasks such as cooking, fetching water, cleaning, sweeping and taking care of younger children. By contrast, boys get time for leisure and can concentrate on their studies. Unlike girls, they will be encouraged to pursue further studies. Under the ideology of biological determinism, girls are seen as naturally devoted to others because of their strong maternal instinct, while boys are seen as natural leaders.

Thus socialisation processes, which start at the family level, perpetuate women's inferiority. Social roles are learned, as patterns of masculinity and femininity are maintained in daily life. In the four situations, the father had the ability to impose the orientation of the situation and to set the terms in which events were understood and issues discussed. The four life histories also evidence the social distance between a girl and her father. Very often, the father is called her "guardian." Usually, except for the case of Miriam, the father is not present in daily life, and inspires authority, respect and "evasion of attachment." The reproduction of the system is reinforced by the attitude of the father, and the exclusion of women from decision-making. It is also perpetuated linguistically through the use of proverbs and rituals that reinforce men's prestige and authority. All these things influence young boys and girls, who very early internalise the sexual inequality in the mental structures that are built up by such practices.

Access to study and personal objectives

In three families (except Miriam's family), the father did not value secondary education for girls. In general, as one informant said, the value of a girl is of short duration. However, all four were encouraged by their mothers to continue their studies, and some even paid for it! The three fathers did not seem to be concerned about their daughters' future. It has great consequences on women's future as "the low participation of women in education means low participation in formal employment and in executive posts which include decision-making bodies. This eventually determines their social status in society as well" (Omari and Mbilinyi, 2000: 301).

None of the four participants achieved their personal aspirations. Reasons for this that were cited included the lack of parental attention to their children's aptitudes, parents' arrangements for their children's future life and/or marriage, the respect of customs and tradition in such things as puberty rites or initiation periods, and the social obligation for children to respect their parents. Lack of money and of access to school, and early pregnancies also counted among the major impediments. The lack of information on career opportunities and poor school performance also acted as powerful deterrents to young girls choosing their future careers. The possibility of making real choices is greater for girls nowadays because they receive more information than previously, and more families let young girls choose their future occupation. Post-primary education for young girls was dominated by domestic sciences and training for gender stereotypical jobs. Women were assigned jobs in education, nursing and community services—all occupations in which others' development and well being is the main issue.

In addition to family factors, the general social and historical situation of the country determined the choices each girl made about the completion of her studies. For example, in the case of the 57-year-old woman, the Mission authorities took the decision.

In summary, it is clear that power relations impose limits on the choice of future life. Authority oscillates between the State and the father, the mission and other institutions. The father formulates ideals and morality, and asserts his hegemony over each member of the family. Nevertheless, for the four women, their lives became more social and less dominated by the family. School, teachers, exams, quarrels and so on organise the milieu that influenced the private life of each. They were exposed to new ideas in the learning process. This helped them to fight tradition and to distance themselves from the old social schemes.

Professional life

Professional integration marked the moment when all became autonomous and learnt how to cope and manage by themselves. The four women all estimated that their salary was "too little" for their expenses, especially because they had to support their families financially. This again shows how the sexual division of labour is achieved: women occupy secondary posts that are viewed as gender-specific because they are more oriented to others' welfare. The two older ones, who became a teacher and a community worker, did not choose their careers by themselves, but were assigned to a specific job by the authorities[3].

[3] As quoted by Omari and Mbilinyi (2000:301), "the increase of girls in education schools may be an indication of a change of attitudes among parents towards education for girls. But it could also be a result of the existing educational structure in the country whereby there are more secondary schools for boys than for girls or for the two together. As a result many qualified primary education girls are left out in the selection process for the secondary schools. So when private secondary schools are available, 'enlightened' parents send their daughters to these institutions for further education. In areas like Kilimanjaro, Kagera, Mbeya and Iringa, where the level of education among women is high, this possibility is particularly strong."

- Woman in her 50s: A teacher and later a school inspector. The mission authorities gave her job to her.
- Woman in her 40s: A community worker. Her assignment was made by Government authorities
- Woman in her 30s: A banker. Her brother helped her find the job.
- Woman in her 20s: A businesswoman (informal sector).

The oldest woman's career reflects the Tanzanian context of the 1950s in which education was accessible to women through the mission establishments. Women became professionals in teaching or nursing. This period prioritised welfare-type approaches to women's problems, emphasising the importance of the family and the need to defend it from the ravages of capitalism by strengthening women's capacity to do domestic labour and child-rearing within the home, while the male breadwinner worked for wages to support his dependants. The education system imported European values about motherhood, marriage and the family. Elite women were more affected by this.

The second informant was born in 1958, which means that she started school after independence. She became a community worker. The strong political mobilisation, favouring social equity, had accelerated the implementation of universal primary education and adult literacy programmes. Nevertheless, women's access to work was restricted by the authoritarian tendencies of political leaders in sustaining the bureaucracy, placing artificial restrictions on salaries and prices in the market, limiting women's involvement in decision making, and attempting to silence them in the civil service.

The situation of the two younger women is different. One was born in 1968 and the other in 1973. Their access to education was limited by the economic crisis that affected the country. The rising cost of living and the obligatory contribution of families to school fees forced some parents to limit their daughters' access to school. Many estimated that they did not have enough money to pay for school requirements. In the 1980s and after, the familial and domestic crisis was visible in the high number of children abandoned and begging in the city streets, and in the level of domestic violence and child labour.

The implementation of the Structural Adjustment Programme (SAP) affected the feminist struggle for social justice, equality and human rights. The SAP focuses mainly on efficiency. It undermined the minimum liberal achievements of the 1970s and early 1980s. The double burden on women is still apparent: women are involved in various productive activities that are not paid adequately, and they also have to perform unpaid work as they are responsible for children, the sick and elderly.

During their professional life, all four women were confronted with the problem of sexual or other harassment at work and in other public spaces. They all talked about their inability to be heard by the authorities, who do not take sexual harassment seriously. Among the most common types of harassment mentioned by the informants were sexual proposals by bosses, the use of "bad" language, the obligation to provide bribes on a regular basis to a boss in order to stay in a specific post, denial of access to training and thus to promotion, and general blackmail over new posts and higher wages. A study conducted by Joyce Shaidi (1991) proved that 95% of female respondents had experienced some kind of harassment that was manifested through unequal access to on-the-job training, unsystematic procedures for hiring job applicants and monitoring job performance, greater workload at home and in the community, and lack of support in childcare.

In spite of all the problems the four informants encountered, they recognised the importance of access to work for women's independence and ability to make choices. They mentioned the need to work hard, to get access to better posts, and develop knowledge and a different vision of life. Urban women today know more about their rights than before. Many women now know where they can get credit or loans to initiate income-generating activities, or start new associations and groups. A major difference between the women of today and yore is the awareness they pay to their own development. However, efforts must continue to be made to inform them and transform old customs and traditions that block women's development. The notion of dependency should be taken out of young girls' heads by teaching them to fight against cultural constraints that prevent them from acting.

The informants mentioned many other changes. They said that even if life is difficult, women involved in work activities outside the home provide new models for others. Many young women and girls now perceive the importance of having a professional life; among the suggestions made by participants, education for girls appears as a priority. It is seen as fostering the capacity to make choices, through financial independence and greater access to information.

Nevertheless, it is clear that women still have little influence in the workplace, where they are confined to the informal and tertiary sectors and the bottom of the occupational ladder, with low wages and few opportunities for on-the-job training and advancement. The attitude of men acts as an impediment to job opportunities. Men develop solidarity to protect their behaviour and use sexual harassment as a way of excluding women.

Personal relations and daily life

Femininity and masculinity are socially constructed through apprenticeship in specific social roles, based on the opposition of masculine and feminine in a dual-sex model. Sexual practices are organised in couples and heterosexual relations. In Dar es Salaam, ties between spouses are usually weak and flexible. Principles of reciprocity are more to do with families than with spouses themselves.

The four informants related significant common traits and characteristics of emotional relations. Marriage is still seen as conferring prestige, ensuring social recognition and respect. A shared life is viewed as essential for having and bringing up children, ensuring the psychological well-being of the offspring. Divorce is seen as dishonour and divorced people fear losing the respect of the community. Women's greatest fears are related to divorce; they worry about losing their children and are afraid of "the eyes of other people in the community."

According to the women's statements, the parents in all four cases made marriage arrangements. Families and relatives have a tendency to intervene in marital problems, forcing spouses to reconcile without taking into consideration the level of problems they encountered.

Parents and direct relatives still put severe pressure on the couple to have many children.

Their family of origin does not support married women. Once they are married they have to manage by themselves. In the case of problems with their husband, they are told to accept the situation because "it is the life of marriage." In reality, no one is interested in reimbursing the dowry.

The husband's relatives represent a huge burden for married women. In the case of inter-tribal marriage, children are identified with the father's tribe and village. Marriage can impose a change of religion on women, and might also be followed by problems of identity.

Child education is one of the major responsibilities of the mother, even if she does not herself have the necessary resources to offer her children a better life. The four mothers all want their children to succeed and have a better life than they did. Education is seen as the main means to achieve it. All four informants believe that both the partners, that is the father and the mother, must ensure a child's upbringing and education.

Older women do not recognise marriage as providing financial and emotional security. Most of them have been disappointed by marriage and are bitter. They discourage their daughters from getting married or tolerating selfish behaviour in a partner. From their point of view, marriage is a necessary evil. They still believe that the presence of a father is necessary for ensuring the emotive equilibrium of children.

Among the positive changes, younger women informants seem to communicate more easily with their partners than was possible for the two older women. The participant aged 34 said she did the budget with her husband in order to share family responsibilities. The younger woman aged 24 said she was able to influence her husband's decision making. It seems that younger women are sometimes able to influence their husbands, even if officially the men still have the last say. Nowadays, more women are conscious of the importance of educating their daughters, and of the need to develop professional skills and become financially independent. They provide more support to their daughters than before.

Similarities and differences between four generations of women

Women continue to experience gender-based violence causing physical, sexual, and psychological harm or suffering. All these acts occur in both private and public life.

Legal codes and customary practices still treat women as second-class citizens, denying them the right to own property, to travel, or to gain access to economic and productive resources. As a consequence they lack the power to make informed choices about their general life.

Women are afraid to confront their husbands or any kind of authority, reflecting their dependence on goodwill, and the lack of an autonomous base and practice. The opinions of young women show that girls still believe in marriage and most of them want to get married; most young women or girls are not educated to challenge men's authority; and girls are not educated to think of developing their own future for themselves and by themselves. Most of them still think that they must live under the authority of a husband who can do everything for them.

Differences appear between different generations of women. Today, women tend to say that their lives are better than those of their grandmothers or mothers. Girls have greater access to education, even if job opportunities are still weak. Younger women are more likely to say they can make personal choices about their future. That is different from older women, who said mission organisations or others told them where to go for further studies. The lack of information and personal objectives was a fact of life for some of the first women to be educated in Tanzania.

Nowadays, young women try to make their own choices and are more ambitious. Nevertheless, they still experience many impediments despite official government encouragement.

Many accept that marriage is no longer mandatory. Older women perceive that marriage is no longer the first priority for young girls. They prefer to see their daughters developing their own skills instead of being dependent. It is common to hear older women complaining about the behaviour of the young. They think that young girls want to live an easy life, and do not make enough effort to become independent. They are not seen as profiting enough from all the opportunities offered by urban life.

Students' vision of gender relations

The tensions and contradictions of urban life necessarily shape the kind of accommodation that individuals make. However, such accommodations do not result in uniform changes, as they are not experienced in a uniform manner. The population is socially and culturally diverse (Campbell, 2000:38).

With the aim of evaluating younger people's perception of change, young women and men at Form IV level in a public school of Dar es Salaam wrote some dissertations during November and December 2000. This work was done in the framework of Community and Civic Studies. Four different issues were proposed to female and male students. A total of 68 texts were collected. The findings are presented here.

Students talk about marriage

Students were asked: Is marriage important for you? Explain the reasons for your choice. What do you expect from your wife/husband?

Eight students (three males and five females) answered this question.

The women

The women who answered this question said marriage was important because:

- It is a human right to be married and to choose a partner.
- Marriage provides respect, prestige and social recognition.
- It allows us to love and be loved by somebody.
- It allows us to have children who will be educated by both parents, and to perpetuate generations.
- It is God's will.

- It helps us obey cultural and social factors, and develop relationships between different families.
- It helps us share responsibilities, life and experiences with somebody.
- It prevents venereal diseases and prostitution.

Most women aged around 20 identified a man's role as controlling everything and everyone in the family, because "women are weak in decision making when you compare them to men."

What women expect from their husbands
• To share common values and ideas
• To be more educated than them
• To share everything
• To be a "generous" person who fears God and behaves well
• To be a happy and courageous person
• To give advice, respect, and to listen to, support and love his wife
• To develop harmony between the spouses, without superiority

<u>The men</u>

Marriage is also seen as important because:

- It is a way of being socially respected and recognised as a mature person.
- A woman can provide assistance.
- It provides a sexual life without the risk of venereal diseases.
- It gives children and a family.
- It "increases his personality, i.e. a man will have somebody to brush his shoes, wash his clothes, and do other things to make him look smart."

One student, aged 20, made a study of marriage issues. The findings of his survey proved that 50% of people who are married enjoy life more than those who are single.

Only one participant, aged 24, said that marriage was not important to him because it is a complicated and frustrating affair in which people seem to be more tied down, not free and happy. His personal reasons for disliking marriage are related to his need to be free and able to do what he wants, when he wants, without any restrictions.

Second, he dislikes risky things and he refuses to be tied to any person because he feels that it is impossible to know what another's behaviour will be like. Third, he refuses to increase poverty by raising more mouths to feed, as he cannot afford to take care of himself decently. Finally, he does not want to trust anybody other than himself in terms of sexually transmitted diseases. He does not want to risk his life through marriage.

What young men expect from their wives
• To be a friend and companion and give full support, be it financial or otherwise
• To love her husband
• To give advice or information
• To be a good mother and have a stable family
• To be a happy, gentle, trustworthy and honest person

Politically speaking, men are the head of the family and leaders of clans. They represent the family's authority and are leaders of society. Young men expect to be the head of the family in all areas including the economic, social and political. Most young men (and women as well) consider that women have to respect all men in general. From an economic point of view, men are seen as "the head of the family" and usually, they fight for the family's basic needs. From a social point of view, women have to respect men. This originates in religion, tradition and customs, and education. In religious activities, men come first and it is God's will for women to respect all men as "he created Adam before Eve." From an Islamic point of view, as written by a 19-year-old woman who quoted many *sura* of the Koran, "Women believe that men differ from them because they are more powerful than women. In Islamic law, women are told by God to respect men." Most traditions teach girls and women to respect men because "they will be married. In marriage, women have the obligation to control and keep men's wealth."

What is new in terms of respect?

The question asked was: Do women have to respect men in general? Does this answer come from a specific tradition or belief? Can you explain this tradition or belief? Where did you learn it? Nine students (five males and four females) answered.

Most young men and women agreed with the tradition of respect. Two girls said that both persons in a relationship should be respected by society, as both should respect each other. One 20-year-old woman added that respect should be based on the age and position of the person, not just on sex.

Female and male answers were almost the same. Women must respect men in all economic, social and political activities for the following reasons:

- *Economically:* Men have the obligation to satisfy all family needs, just as women have responsibility to control and manage the wealth of men. Women must respect men in all daily activities and follow their advice and decisions.

- *Socially:* Women are taught respect for men through religion, education and marriage. In religious activities men come first. It is God's will because he created Adam before Eve. Islam also teaches that women must respect men because they are inferior to men and incapable of making the right choices. In education, women must follow regulations such as how to dress, talk and behave. In traditions such as the Haya, Kerewe and Hita, men are used to being respected by all women because they will be married.

- *Politically:* Women must respect men because men are the head of the family and leaders of the clan.

Women's underdevelopment and humiliation

The question was: Many women say that men are the cause of their underdevelopment and that men oppress women. Do you think this is true?

30 students (17 male and 13 female) responded.

Most believed that men are the cause of women's underdevelopment and those women are humiliated by them. The reasons they gave were as follows:

<u>The women</u>

All female participants agreed with this statement. For them, men are the cause of women's underdevelopment in the social, economic and political fields. The situation starts in the family and spreads to society in general.

In the social sector: Sex segregation starts at birth, a girl being less appreciated than a boy. Girls are perceived as weak, stupid and lazy. The practices of dowry and early marriage are detrimental for girls because they cannot develop skills or study. Girls do not have control over their own bodies, as they cannot even decide the number of children to have. The division of labour is unequal and most girls and women are obliged to perform household duties. Women are deprived influence in the decision-making process. If their husband dies, their son will be the "head of the family." Traditional beliefs and cultural practices are detrimental, as women's development is not supported if old customs such as early marriage, polygamy, division of labour, sex segregation, are perpetuated. One 19-year-old young woman wrote:

> *Women are seen as "tools for men." They are viewed as a tool of pleasure through prostitution and marriage; as a tool for giving birth, because most of the time women do not have the right to determine the number of children they are going to have. Usually, men decide it. This fact affects women's health.*

In the political field: Women are not allowed to speak in public, so they cannot participate in community and public life. They do not have the right to intervene in family matters. There is unequal access to leadership so that women cannot affect policies. They are still consistently deprived of fundamental rights.

In the economic sector: Women are denied access to many posts and professions because of male institutionalised domination. Very often, they suffer from sexual harassment. Moreover, their husband deprives many women of the right to have a job outside the home. They are very often not paid for their work. Women become dependent on men who often spend their money outside the family "for luxuries while the family does not have the basics."

Some mentioned that women contribute to their underdevelopment by a lack of solidarity that exacerbates feelings of jealousy and distrust. Biological events such as maternity are also viewed as impediments to the social elevation of women.

The men

The men who agreed with the statement gave the following answers:

Cultural beliefs, tradition and division of labour assign gender roles in which women are confined to household activities. They are not authorised to develop skills or productive activities. They do not have control of their own body, and in many cases, are denied access to family planning. They are more subject to physical chastisement and rape. Sometimes they do not have equal access to food. In education, priority is given to boys who are seen as true workers. There is also the problem of sexual harassment from teachers at secondary school. Sexual harassment is also endemic at work.

Women are socially perceived as weak and needing to live under the authority of men. Early marriages oppress women, while in polygamy, women are used as a workforce and the husband benefits from their work. Inheritance customs, including levirate, give priority to men. Women are not allowed to possess land or any means of production. In politics, men lead and women are ignored, seen only as bearers of children and implementers of men's decisions. They have no freedom of speech in public. Consequently, they cannot have any influence in the decision-making process to effect change. Religion also favours men over women, as God created men first and made women secondary.

Some of the young men who agreed with the statement made suggestions for change. Some said there was a need to educate people and insert new ideas that favour social, political and economic development. The Government should pass new laws and help women better their condition.

Other male students disagreed with the statement. They pointed to other elements of the same determinants as causing the underdevelopment of women, because they influence women's life differentially. For example, they said that the level of women's education is not adequate to meet all technological and scientific needs. They make little effort in studies and other activities. They do not prepare for their future because they think "it is men's affair." Some argued that many women encourage the gender division of labour because they are lazy and allow men to manage their lives because it is easier, while they are more interested in marriage. These young men agreed that religious beliefs encourage women to stay at home, and do not allow them to develop skills or study.

Some added that women "are naturally more limited than men" and have an inferiority complex about their inability to compete against men. Some participants believe that women contribute to their underdevelopment because they are more committed to family matters, and lack solidarity. Nowadays, women can benefit from more opportunities than ever before. They have to realise the role they could play in development.

One 21-year-old man wrote, "If women are involved in development it is only because of the men who helped them. If they exist it is because of men, and without men no women would exist. It is called the 'struggle for existence' and only the fittest of the fittest shall survive."

Women earning more money than their husbands

The question was: What do you think of a woman who is earning more money that her husband?

23 students (12 females and 11 males) answered this question.

The women

Young women recognised that a woman earning more money that her husband could bring both benefits and conflict to the family. Nevertheless, most said that a woman "always thinks about her family and makes sure that family life is up to standard." One 19-year-old woman wrote:

> *Mostly, when a husband earns more money he forgets everything about his family; he disappears for a while and when the money is finished he comes back home. But a woman will always have a merciful spirit; she will use her money to improve the family's lifestyle.*
>
> *The house where a woman earns more money than a husband will always keep the peace and everything will stay as it should.*

Women could help family welfare and development by contributing to normal daily requirements and education, the bank account, or investment in different businesses. Women in that situation should feel proud of what they are doing, as they contribute significantly to reducing the "dependency rate of the country." All family members, including their husbands, should respect them and allow them to participate in the decision-making process at home.

Nevertheless, all female respondents thought that a woman in such a situation should continue to "respect her husband." One 19-year-old woman wrote, "It would be better for the woman's earnings to be included with the husband's, and for them to plan together according to family requirements."

Young women are proud that nowadays women are more educated and have access to business. They are "good examples for those who think that women are inferior people." But few of them consider that women deserve respect as men do, as was also shown by Coquery-Vidrovitch (1994: 318) among young girls in Guinea. They all seemed to accept the assigned social role they had integrated since childhood.

The men

The male respondent's opinions differ from the women's, and resemble their older male relatives. Some felt this situation could lead to conflict, including divorce through problems over possessions. Many women might spend money on trivial things, neglecting the family's needs. African tradition could be abandoned because the wife could replace the husband as head of the household. As a 21-year-old male student said:

> *A wife could exploit the whole family by bringing her relatives to live in her husband's house, leading to bad feelings, quarrels and family disintegration. A woman can become the decision-maker in the family and pay more attention to her investment than to the family itself. Money should be used for family needs, and to buy productive assets. In a normal family the man has to be the decision-maker; both parents are equal no matter who is earning more money, but the father must be the head of the family.*

According to the men, a woman in this situation:

- Will not respect her husband because having more wealth than her husband would make her feel superior.
- Will spend a lot of money on trivial things, contrary to God's law.
- Will not take care of her family.
- Will do "evil things" such as looking for another man with whom to commit adultery; this could lead to the moral deterioration of the family.
- Will want to take part in the decision-making process.

The real problem is related to the decision-making process. For these young men, a woman in this situation could want to have more influence in family affairs. She could try to control her husband. Eventually, the husband's orders would not be respected. "It will lead to conflicts because each one will want to be respected. Money could be spent on her relatives while her husband goes without money."

They all said this situation would lead to breakdown and misunderstanding in the family. One 21-year-old man wrote, "African families require a man to have the final say and to have power in family affairs. No woman should intervene when a man takes a decision." He added that such a woman could be careless about her husband although "a woman is supposed to take care of her husband. That means she should provide food obediently, dress appropriately and taking care of any matter related to her husband. A woman has to satisfy her husband."

Only two students (one aged 20 and the other 21) said that this situation could have a positive impact. They thought it could contribute to national and family development. The woman's role would be recognised, as woman would acquire more influence in the decision-making process and more independence though their participation in economic development. It could also help to reduce prostitution and facilitate women's development of skills.

However, there was a consensus on how the money earned by women should be used. All eleven participants wrote that the money should be used for the family's daily needs, education, building a house, clothes or investments. Young men use a socially accepted ideological framework to justify their argument.

For instance, one student mentioned that a well-educated woman who knows her rights and duties would help her husband and contribute to family development, whereas other women would tend to misbehave.

In summary, young men and women's perceptions of gender relations are related to an extremely conservative social ideology of natural complementarity between the sexes. Social pressure that obliges a young woman or girl to look for a husband is still strong. A man is viewed as a protector for his wife and children. Girls and young women integrated and internalised the idea of male domination. This must be related to education and socialisation processes, and to the mode of social reproduction.

Undeniably, these young women are participating in an internal social contradiction. Urban life and confrontation lead to new ways of thinking and living and to new models for women, and potential conflict between two action schemes—one that is incorporated, and the other that is learnt. The first one sees women perceived as the guardians of tradition, while the emerging model places them in a trajectory of autonomy, as shown by women succeeding in different fields of activity. There is a confrontation between two differently structured knowledges. The social context brings a new reflectivity. It is through reflection and experiences that young women could develop new attitudes and changes. However, the stated opinions of young women show that these new schemes have not been integrated into their logic of action. Although girls recognised the importance of marriage, they all admitted that men were the cause of their underdevelopment. There is a paradox emerging from these answers.

Social construction of gender relations

Changes in gender relations reflect the enhanced educational level and professional activity of women, increases in consumption, and the transformation of work and of organisations. What are the consequences of this? Does it produce more democracy at every level of the social structure? How do actors define the norms of their actions in the new context?

Long social memory

Mechanisms of the domination, subordination and impoverishment of women are linked to Tanzanian socio-historical conditions—the social construction of femininity and masculinity and the way that the dual-sex system is socially managed. The economic logic and mechanisms of the world of work, which express the sexual division of labour, cannot entirely explain women's dependency and subordination.

The social structure is the final determinant in gender relations. Social structures are applied through discursive and non-discursive practices such as language, institutions (family and kinship at the micro-level; media, workplace and markets at the intermediary level; and the State at the macro-level), organisation of space, rules and laws, religious and scientific statements, philosophical justifications, religion and morality—the total of what Foucault (1976) calls "dispositif," Bourdieu "habitus" and Kaufmann "habit." An analysis of discursive and non-discursive strategies indicates how the structure reproduces sexual inequality and supports stereotypes. Hierarchy, subordination and complicity are bound to internal relations of the gender order, and this is doubtless both a product and producer of history.

The differentiation of tasks, roles and space between the sexes establishes a hierarchical organisation of society, governed by men at the top. Authority is in the hands of men who benefit from the knowledge, legitimacy, recognition and submission that comes with authority. Power is exercised over other individuals in such a way that their behaviours, actions, and even thoughts, are directed.

However, many men in Tanzania abuse their power and authority in their search for prestige and domination. They seek to maintain a relation of order, control and reciprocal obedience and submission. Interpersonal relations, seduction, confidences, guilt, blackmail, authority, and information management are among the tools used to influence others.

A structure of inequality prevails and involves a massive dispossession of social resources. Most African men, as Njoki Ndungu (1999:7-10) said, sustain their dominance through constant demonstrations of violence. In Tanzania, rates of violence against women are staggeringly high and the situation is reinforced by legal and culturally recognised and regulated practices:

- Within the home such as wife battering, sexual abuse of female children, marital rape, emotional and mental abuse, female genital mutilation and other traditional practices harmful to women, non-spousal violence, and violence in relation to exploitation;

- Within the community in incidents of violence such as rape, sexual abuse, sexual harassment and intimidation at work, in educational institutions and elsewhere; in trafficking in women and forced prostitution;

- Within the country through physical, psychological and sexual violence perpetrated or condoned by the state;

murder, systematic rape, sexual slavery and forced pregnancy are common.

Men who abuse women are unlikely to perceive themselves as deviant. On the contrary, they usually feel they are entirely justified, that they are exercising their right. They are authorised by an ideology of supremacy (Connell, 1987:83).

The strategies and mechanisms, which allow the reproduction of gender injustice, are related to:

- *Symbolic order:* The subjugation of women is performed through language, traditions, rituals, myths and body mutilations. This has a profound impact because it is related to the unconscious domain and taken as naturally given. Social order and body "habitus" are mechanically reproduced.

- *Ideological order:* The dominant culture is transported by different social institutions that serve men's sexual and material privileges. These include educational institutions, family, and legal institutions that play an important role in the perpetuation of sexual inequalities by imposing the *status quo* of a sexist superstructure.

Alya Baffoun (1992) has described how feminine and masculine natures are unconsciously implanted in early childhood, including the child's characteristics that are usually seen as innate. The educational process ensures that girls develop their maternal instinct, as they receive dolls to play with and other gifts that teach them how to perform domestic tasks. In Tanzania, as shown by Omari and Mbilinyi (2000: 293-294), songs and sayings embody traditional attitudes and help shape a girl's attitudes and perceptions. The socialisation process creates inequalities between the members of the society that are based on biological sexual differences. Most people see these inequalities as "natural."

Generally, as Baffoun presented, women internalise this unequal social order; rejecting it can bring them close to madness or depression. Men can develop a double attitude—one related to authoritarianism and indulgence. They may use their privileged status to exert power abuses on women, or they may feel guilty and unsatisfied. Most of the time they justify these privileges by the biological order. Most women are conscious of being dominated but they cannot act against all its mechanisms. Nevertheless, although its acquisition may be imperceptible, what is acquired is always transformable.

Reproduction of domination

Male domination has been maintained through time by many institutions.

- *Ideological institutions:* Tanzanian social structures depend on the female-male division. People take their "place" and relations are anchored in objective, social and cultural reality. These relations result from social, interactive and subjective determinants. As Omari and Mbilinyi (2000:296) said, "By the time the girl reaches school age, she has already been conditioned and socialised to think and believe that her place in the society has already been determined by others. She has no alternative but to follow the prevailing norms, customs and value system."

Male-female relations are inscribed in the culture. In Tanzania as a whole, and within the family, gender relations are hierarchical. This originates from a subjective feeling of superiority or inferiority that has developed over time, through differential social construction of personality for men and women.

The male power structures use schools to reproduce the culture and values, which force women to take up "subordinate positions" in the labour force. Culture has been seen as a justification for the unequal distribution of knowledge between female and male students in African schools. Children are socialised at an early age into the sexual roles they will perform in their adult lives. School reinforces these assigned roles by producing trained men and women to be engaged in their divided roles from one generation to another (Shifferaw, 1992:89).

In Tanzania, as outlined by Omari and Mbilinyi (2000:301), the school enrolment of girls consistently decreases as they ascend the education ladder. The completion rate is also lower as girls are withdrawn from school for early marriage, pregnancy or initiation rites. Shifferaw, writing of Zambia, showed that "the democratic question of women's access to equal education in all areas and subjects has been considered nihilistic and not appropriate for Africa at the present time."

- *Law and justice institutions:* These institutions are not favourable to women. The legal code has been used for legitimating the patriarchal control of women and still coexists with common law based on European precedents. Traditional laws still remain in use, although they vary from place to place. They cover gender division of labour, bride wealth and male control of household and family income, especially big income (TGNP, 1993:71). Thus, men and elders use traditional law to promote their own interests and block economic and social change.

Nevertheless, the new legal code provides some means for women to escape patriarchal authority. For instance, sexual offences, child marriage or the killing of widows can be defended in court. Although the decision-making process is still dominated by men, women can benefit from legal clinics even if their participation in decision-making bodies is low. The case of Aloya, a young Maasai woman reported by Hodgson (2000:200-219), illustrates that men can sometimes support women's rights. This young woman took her father to court rather than marry according to his will. A "disobedient daughter," she directly challenged her father's authority and the authority of local elders, lineages and clans. She also challenged the definitions of father and daughter. The case is complex but the important point is that she won. The magistrate, who was a man, supported Aloya in her confrontation with her father. Hodgson noted that this illuminates how certain gendered relations of power in one patriarchal society are maintained and might be changed. Aloya's father and elders used many strategies to defend their "legitimate" authority over her. They oscillated between threats, appeals to tradition, customs and culture, father's rights, and the natural and immutable deference of daughters. Her father in the courtroom cursed Aloya, as he physically and morally marginalized her by obliging her to live outside of Maasai society. Nevertheless, the

Maasai elders have had to reshape their patriarchal structures of authority to accommodate changes in the state legal system and case law; they installed one of their own as a "Chairman of tradition/customs" and this has been accepted by the state.

This case illustrates the complex collaborations involved in maintaining or transforming any gendered configuration of power. In order to maintain their hegemony, patriarchies must accommodate the shifting structures of power within and through which they operate.

Social norms are printed in the body and instilled through socialisation and ideological processes termed "symbolic violence" by Bourdieu. For example a woman must be reserved, stand correctly and keep her gaze downcast, and may not express herself in public. In comparison, a man must be active, move fast and may talk freely. The socialisation process establishes a fundamental hierarchy between sexes. This distinction is expressed through social behaviours in keeping with masculine and feminine roles. It confirms the domination as it is fixed in psyches and bodies. Everyone acquiesces with the social game, which is governed by the logic of difference and domination.

Symbolic violence means training thinking processes by making dominant representations appear natural. This is developed through institutions and authority. The series of pressures that are engaged in gender relations and their internalisation-reproduction are a cultural "habitus" for the group, and are part of the dominant culture.

Women themselves contribute to the reproduction of this unequal sexual order.

- Many women are conservative; they prefer to maintain the *status quo* related to their social position. They perceive their subordination to men as normal or desirable—even educated women support these assumptions. They develop and encourage an attitude of non-confrontation as a result of their political and economic vulnerability, and reluctance to incite male anger and retaliation (Gordon, 1996:84).

- Once they become mothers-in-law, older women do not defend women's rights. On the contrary, they will privilege their son's point of view against their daughters-in-law and have an intensive interventionist attitude. This is what women call "harmony" and obedience.

- Higher-class women are likely to use their social class privileges to overcome some of the difficulties they face because of their sex in acquiring certain knowledge or obtaining better jobs. Rich females may obtain jobs in the male-dominated sector since they have the education necessary to compete with their male counterparts. They do not represent the majority of African woman, who are at a lower economic level.

- Poor females struggle to gain access to any form of education and to survive in all areas of the labour force. Their work is not recognised and they are unable to get the necessary education or training with which they might improve their living conditions.

- Women avoid confrontation, refusing to assert themselves or establish their own rules, to earn money, to have their success recognised or to have their own space and time.

For their part, sons recycle their fathers' schema and reproduce sexual inequality.

- Men treat their wives badly, while at the same time idealising their relationship with their mother and recognising that their father did not treat her with justice, tenderness or recognition.

- Men use tradition as a refuge. These tradition and beliefs are not questioned. They were developed without the knowledge we have today about the basic needs of human beings. The low status of women is based on the cultural foundation that ownership and prosperity are male domains. As was shown by Obbo (1980), there is an agreement between ordinary men and the male elites on controlling the African women's morality. Indeed, "women should be kept pure for the sake of African authenticity." Maigenet Shifferaw (1992), in the case of Zambia, demonstrated that women are still perceived as bearers and carriers of culture, whenever this culture is not antagonistic to the male-dominated social order. Socialisation processes coach females to fit into the accepted values and norms of the dominant culture. Women are pushed into "the culture of silence." If they demand their democratic rights they are accused of disturbing the social order and of being a threat to African tradition in which:

> *Women, as bearers of African culture, should be protected, with or without their consent from the corrupting influences of Western culture such as cosmetics, wigs or short dresses. Women should be kept pure for the sake of African authenticity. In many ways it is an attempt to reconcile the dilemmas posed by conflicting ideas of individual advancement based on self-interest and choice on the one hand, and the community at large, on the other (Shifferaw, 1992: 88).*

Changes and challenges

Generally, the male informants have little incentive to support women's struggles for equality, as gains by women can only threaten their class interests. Nevertheless, men are not a homogenous group; they do not all share the same ideology. For instance, many women said they had received money from a man, whether the father, husband, friend or relative, for initiating income-generating activities, or to enable them to complete their studies.

As people accommodate to economic crisis in an urban setting, conflict can result. As noted by Gordon, "underdeveloped capitalism is in crisis, however; and capitalist expansion is blocked in part by African patriarchy. This hurts men as well as women, and could provide some basis for changing gender relations" (1996:102).

In the case of Dar es Salaam, what has changed in the sexual division of labour? Is there a difference in the sexual power structure? Are femininity and masculinity constructions being challenged?

Changes in the sexual division of labour

The sexual division of labour is related to the organisation of housework and childcare, the division between paid and unpaid work, the segregation of labour markets and the creation of men's and women's jobs through discrimination in training and promotion. The research demonstrates that unequal wages and uneven exchange are still the norm in Dar es Salaam.

Women constitute most of the informal labour force and occupy the lowest posts in the formal sector. In Dar es Salaam, women from all ages still perform most domestic work. They are involved in all reproductive activities but they do not benefit from similar rights of access to resources such as land, credit or decision-making. Women on the city streets sell food, garments and a variety of crafts. They work in typical feminine jobs and are marginalised in the management of their societies because of occupational gender typing. As shown by Meena (1992), states in the East African region are pursuing development strategies while ignoring gender differences in planning, implementation and evaluation.

Men of all ages generally refuse to perform domestic tasks because they consider it a woman's duty. Women have to perform all these activities on a daily basis with little help in the way of technology. Nevertheless, a few men are willing to "help" their wives as they can see the benefits.

The following changes have been described:

- *The organisation of housework and childcare*: Work is generally redistributed among women rather than from women to men. Women in urban areas contribute more to the cash requirements of the household. Sometimes, they exercise more control over the use of their contribution. As already noted, a few men encourage their wives to work; and in households where women exercise control over increased incomes, the children's situation is improving as they go to school, eat better and receive medical treatment when sick. Children benefit more from income under the control of their mothers than income controlled by fathers (UNICEF, 1990:108). Men tend to spend more income for their own personal consumption such as alcohol, mistresses, food or entertainment. It is clear that members of the household vary in their contributions.

Women express greater willingness to live alone, which is more acceptable in an urban area. Alone, they cope with new difficulties in daily life and are the main providers for their families. However, women frequently do not control the essential resources that are needed for effective action. These resources include time, which is constrained by the demands on a woman's time for production and domestic chores.

- *The division between unpaid and paid work:* This remains mostly the same. However, some women recognise that men, for example their sons, should be involved in and share domestic tasks. When men perform household chores, the gender relations become more egalitarian.

- *The segregation of labour markets, and creation of separate men's jobs and women's jobs:* The sexual division of labour demonstrates that men are mostly involved in activities requiring professional and technical skills, whereas women dominate in areas of self-employment or non-skilled labour.

- *Discrimination in training and promotion:* As men occupy most management posts, other men are favoured for training to acquire skills and knowledge. Most women do not have access to such training. Consequently, the pay of women and men remains unequal. Women are denied access to training as men block the acquisition of skills and knowledge.

Sexual discrimination differs between higher and low-class children. Higher-class females are enrolled in educational streams that lead to good job opportunities, while poor women struggle to gain access to any form of education. Women from higher classes have the capacity to choose the subjects to study. They have the education necessary to compete with their male counterparts and consequently have a better chance of obtaining jobs in male-dominated sectors.

- *Choice of vocation and competition with men:* Through increased access to information, women now know more about new opportunities for study and occupations. Some women have the opportunity to choose their future job. As more women have access to studies and job opportunities, competition with men increases.

Modifications in sexual power relations

The second aspect of gender relations is related to the sexual power structure. It refers to the components of authority, control and coercion that are exercised through the hierarchies of the State and business, institutional and interpersonal violence, sexual regulation and surveillance, and domestic authority and its contestation.

Discrimination based on sex still exists, exemplified by the poor implementation of laws, difficult access to education for girls, and the continuity of traditional puberty rites. Many informants claimed that it was the father's attitudes that denied them further education. Although they were allowed to work, and to relocate to find a job, all families keep an eye on women and young girls as they make decisions about their future. The needs of the group still dominate over the individual's goals and objectives. In the family the power structure is reproduced not only because of the capacity of the father to decide for all its members, but also through force or domestic violence. Bateson (19730 and Laing (1976) demonstrated that strong emotional pressures are placed on family members without any open display of power.

Changes include the following:

- *Hierarchies of the State and business:* Women and young people, traditionally subordinated to old men, challenge patriarchal power. They ask for more democracy in resource sharing. Women seem to be gaining more influence in the decision-making process. They are also fighting for more democracy at the political level. Tanzanian leaders at the State level have been forced by international agencies or donors to modify legislation, including positive discrimination for women. Tanzanian State leaders have signed an international convention against women's discrimination. Legislative reforms such as the Sexual Offences Special Provision Act of 1998 amended some articles of the Law of Marriage Act of 1971 to increase protection of children and women. Association such as TAMWA (Tanzania Media Women Association) and TAWLA (Tanzania Women Legal Association) that are concerned about women's rights have arisen. Many organisations are involved in legal education for women. They organise workshops on human rights and encourage collective action. Increased access to political life, including getting more women endorsed as candidates, facilitated the opening of women's units in the bureaucracy and special welfare programmes. Some Tanzanian women participated in an international conference organised by the United Nations. However, attempts to introduce equal opportunity policies have challenged the sexual division of labour and provoked resistance.

- *Institutional and interpersonal violence:* Increasingly, women refuse to live under violence and challenge it by separating or getting divorced. Women know they can refer to numerous associations to have their rights protected. More and more disputes between men and women are resolved in court. The use of force between family members has become a public issue, with campaigns against domestic violence, child abuse and incest. The greater presence of feminism, or at least of women's organisations, favoured the adoption of new regulations guaranteeing respect for women's rights.

- *Sexual regulation and surveillance:* The marital sexual relationship can itself embody power. Generally, the husband takes the initiative in defining sexual practice. An increasing number of women, fearing STDs, use contraception, and many women use family planning services without their husband's permission. More and more women want to restrict the size of their family, whereas men put pressure on them to have more children.

- *Domestic authority and its contestation:* The interplay between structures within the family is evident. Wages and careers affect domestic power; in turn, domestic power affects the definition of labour. Women succeeding at work develop a different image of femininity and gender relations. Men fear the professional involvement of women, as it affects gender relations, while women can use this strength in power struggles with men. The stake is in the familial sphere and is related to power relations, and relations of dominance between men and women.

There is a paradox in that men are not much involved in the day-to-day activities that most immediately affect the situation, and in general are not the targets of information about how to improve the well-being of the household. Nevertheless, they control most of the resources. Women have little control over basic resources but they receive information from many programmes. To change this paradox requires men to be given more information about the well-being of women and children, and the consequences of actions taken to improve their situation.

Changes in constructions of femininity and masculinity

The third aspect is linked to the social construction of femininity and masculinity. This deals with day-to-day gender relations, including feelings of trust, jealousy and solidarity in marriages and other emotional relationships.

Changes include the following:

- Women receive new messages about gender relations. They know they can perpetuate the tradition but now they are also confronted with a new model, more oriented towards autonomy. Many realise that a degree of reflection is needed to ensure either change or perpetuation of the so-called tradition.

- Tanzanian women analyse the rules, and reflect on the reasons for the constraints imposed on them. Some simply refuse to conform while others adapt more docilely. Women are no longer bound to pre-designed social gender roles.

- Women know they have to look for support in partners who share common goals and interests. Some look for new ways to empower women in society. Changes take time, as the evolution of social structures and women's role redefinition must be conducted at different levels. However, the gap between higher and lower class women is widening. As a result, poorer women perceive upper class women more as speculators who benefit from their class position.

- Many women's associations are creatively pursuing their objectives despite multiple constraints. Women's associations recognise that emancipation requires a revolution in habits and custom. This means that women develop goals that distance them from the subordinating social milieu. This capacity should be developed, as Amougou suggested (1998), in a qualitative and quantitative way—qualitative in its capacity for analysis and critique, quantitative in its capacity to mobilise more women.

- Distrust and jealousy characterise most marriages and gender relations. Today men are less responsible for their family than before, and women accuse them of being more selfish. Men themselves use the language of solicitude such as "I am only doing this or that for your welfare." For example, many Muslim men said that women are like flowers and therefore have to stay at home as they are too weak to do other jobs. This is a dangerous trap; the protective behaviour hides men's vested interests.

- Changes in the family as an institution reflect migration and the arrival of capitalist market relations. The pressure is not all in the same direction. As they develop new models in urban life, women learn of new possibilities. However, they still attach great importance to kinship obligations. Creighton (2000: 125) noted that, "It is maybe plausible to say that kinship remains central to the moral economy of Tanzanian society." The question is how the moral economy will be altered in future under the influence of economic liberalisation and legal changes.

- In rearing children, women invest more, and are entrapped because they know they will have to abandon the children to the father in the case of separation or divorce. Some women still show a great degree of psychological independence, because they manage, in tough situations, to ensure a better future for their children. However, more and more women now leave *with* their children, because they know they can support them. They refuse to see their children become the captives of a future stepmother.

- In many families, daughters are *more* positively perceived than boys. They are seen as more responsible and serious. An increasing number of mothers, and even fathers, put pressure to ensure they are educated or help them to acquire better skills, which are needed for good jobs.

There are clearly problems in the double language and double thought of women in Dar es Salaam. Most accept ancient customs such as initiation practices, arranged marriage, and genital mutilation. Their justification is that these are a part of tradition and customs—obeying them is essential to their identity. This rationalisation allows women to accept their social definition as persons who are naturally fitted only for domestic work. It is also a way of defending their African identity against western values and attitudes.

CONCLUSION: Resiliency and marginalisation

The four life stories, other informants' points of view and the students' comments, all delineate the strength of patriarchal society, its characteristics, mechanisms and "habitus." In Tanzania, patriarchy is not yet a memory; it will be here for some time to come.

In a paper of 1995, "The decline of patriarchy," Ehrenreich demonstrated that the decline of patriarchy has been particularly pronounced in American culture. As indicators of this situation, she identified the following:

- The rapid rise in the number of families "headed" by women and an equally rapid drop in the number of "traditional families" composed of a male breadwinner plus a woman who is a full-time homemaker. The rise in female-headed households represents choices exercised by women, but also changing male attitudes.

- A declining interest on the part of men to support women as wives and full-time homemakers.

- Also on the part of men, a declining interest in children. Men are less insistent than before in claiming that these children are genetically theirs, to "claim their seed" and so on. Men are increasingly unwilling to take responsibility for their offspring.

- The diminishing sense in the American culture that women need "protection."

- The embracing of American consumer culture by males, so that men no longer need a woman to express their social status.

Enrenreich also claimed that the most decisive factor indicating the end of patriarchy is the decline in male wages. "Males have seen their wages declining by 20 percent from 1971 to 1991." This is followed by the end of the idea of protectiveness on the part of men, and the disintegration of the patriarchal family as known.

The end of patriarchy could be used to forge new associations between the sexes "together against our common sources of oppression—perhaps especially the market forces, which, more directly than ever, impinge on the lives of men and women throughout the world, and which have done so much to destroy the so-called traditional family and patriarchy itself" (ibid: 290). However, in spite of the rise of new ways of living for men and women in America, it seems that "as men continue to turn away from being protectors of women and become increasingly *predators* of women, women will continue to make themselves more masculine, if only for purposes of self-defence" (ibid). Gender struggle still exists. The end of patriarchy does not automatically mean women's liberation; it could also indicate new forms of exploitation and degradation. Women now face male domination, which takes different forms.

What about gender relations in Dar es Salaam? If we look now at the indicators identified by Ehrenreich in a context of American gender relations:

- There are more women acting as head of households for diverse reasons: individual choice, rise in "polyandrous maternity," an increase in male free riders, increasing poverty, or as a result of divorce or separation. Koda found that in 1995, women headed 18.6 percent of households.

- The decline in men's interest in supporting women as full-time housewives, as men themselves do not find it easy to make a living in the city. Many withhold the cash support they used to give to their women.

- The declining interest in children is not as marked in Tanzania. Reproduction is at the core of sexuality. Abortion is still illegal in Tanzania, and a woman needs her husband's written consent and authorisation to get contraception; often, men will not authorise their wives to go to the dispensary when the children are sick, because they fear they will make use of the family planning services. This situation also prevails in many other African countries, for example Kenya, as shown by Mwenesi (1995). Men still claim children as being genetically "theirs" and try to protect their "seed." For instance, many refuse to use condoms for protection against venereal diseases or HIV/AIDS. They perpetuate the situation with many different concubines, by having children outside marriage that they refuse to officially recognise. In the event of the death of the husband, his relatives are less interested in being responsible for these children, and more interested in inheriting material goods. It is now common to see a widow living alone and responsible for her children, without receiving any help from her husband's family. More and more men default on their child support; they refuse to take responsibility for their offspring. There is a paradox in this situation—men put pressure on women to have children but refuse to take care of them.

- Men still perceive themselves as women's protectors, and view women as unable to manage life by themselves. According to most male informants, women need to be protected from other men and society in general. Usually, they invoke biological or religious principles to justify this. This view of the situation is related to the construction of femininity and masculinity that clearly delineates who does what and what options are open to each sex. These ideological considerations may suit women who are financially and emotionally dependent on men, while others see it as infantilism.

- The consumer culture is a novel factor for people living in the city. They become attracted to new consumer goods. Few men can afford such luxuries, but they usually give their own pleasures priority over their children's needs. Thus many women prefer life without a husband because they perceive them as "eaters of resources." Men still need women to express their status and they are often dependent on women for their daily needs; laundry, food preparation, child care and domestic duties take up a large amount of time, but it is not conceivable for men to perform such domestic labour.

As with America, the most important factor influencing changes in gender relations in Dar es Salaam is the decline in male wages and the difficulty that most men have to make a living in the city. The introduction of the Structural Adjustment Programme has created more and more problems for men, who cannot adequately supply their family's needs. Increasingly, they depend on women for their physical survival. According to the research findings, it is clear that men are dependent on women for ensuring their day-to-day physical survival and for having children. Most men seem less interested in supporting a woman as a full-time housewife. However, they continue to profit from the social rules that place them as head of the household and decision-maker, and which allow them to exploit their wives.

Nevertheless, certain women assert themselves individually against "habitus." Women today want to have a say in the decision-making process, to be able to implement their choices and to live without violence against them. They want respect for their rights and to be perceived as a whole person. They today want to create new emotional ties with men, and reject the absence of communication that prevails in male-female relationships. These women become resilient and show that they have learnt that something else is possible. They are often separated or divorced, refusing to tolerate the bad behaviour of their husband. They want a better future for their children, without having to support an irresponsible husband or aggressive in-laws. Many young women are even encouraged by their mothers not to get married. Older women have become disillusioned with married life and prefer that their daughters become financially independent or study for a longer period, rather than enter married life.

The price paid, as mentioned by many informants, is living alone without a partner. Women who could be seen as "resilient" are usually socially isolated.

In these circumstances, can we say that women from Dar es Salaam are living out the patriarchal system? Patriarchy implies mutual obligations—protection from men and subordination for women. There are some indications of change, but not always in positive ways that could benefit both sexes. Women are still seen as minors by men and the State authorities, living under the rule of the father, the husband, male elders, the State and religious leaders. However, the obligation of protection has not been honoured. Women of many countries are struggling for their survival in the face of male domination and violence. Women live in dangerous environments in many wards of Dar es Salaam; they feel insecure and fear being raped, injured or killed[4]. The ideology of complementarily thus hides relations of exploitation and discrimination. Women labour without benefiting from social acceptance and recognition, and they accomplish everything under the threat of violence.

The study illustrates the need for women to resist the subordinate position that has been constructed for them in the society. It shows the potential that women have to resist, by providing alternative models through their greater insertion in production and in social critique. A culture of oppression can be converted into one of liberation only when the oppressed take some action to create an alternative for themselves (Meena, 1992:12). Women from Dar es Salaam are changing images and deconstructing gender-stereotyped roles. However, the social system and structure must also be challenged. The dual-sex system is based on a masculine form of domination in which women cannot be involved in decision-making

---

[4] See the study done by CARE in 1996, in which women clearly expressed a growing feeling of insecurity in the city of Dar es Salaam. Many gave it as the first priority for justifying the authorities' intervention.

in communities or families. Emancipation requires the critique of socialisation processes, differential education and values linked to citizenship.

Women are ready to challenge patriarchal gender relations. However, it is evident that men are opposed to this challenge. They refuse to see their current advantages replaced by obligations.

Joan Mapunda says her business is good. Indeed, she has been able to initiate other activities and has had to find new employees to work with her. She says her life is now stabilised.

She has discovered many women's associations. She was a member of PRIDE, but not for long, as she did not have enough time to attend their seminars. Anyway, she said there was nothing to gain from that association, as they are too money-oriented. Moreover, it only provides small loans, which members are supposed to reimburse each week. It is sometimes difficult to reimburse.

She also joined a group funded by Poverty Africa, which functions more like an *upatu*. She obtained a loan that she wants to reimburse quickly, because the faster you return it, the lower is the interest rate. Poverty Africa also provides courses on business management. She adds, "As we meet many other people, it is possible to share more ideas, advice and even find new markets. For example, if you talk with a woman who owns a hotel, she may be in need of chickens or goats. In fact, it is a place where we can learn what others did to succeed." However, Joan says that many credit associations do not reach targeted people. "Leaders should be committed and have humanity, that is the heart to help people."

Joan says she has been receiving help from her husband for a while now. He supports her in her new activities, as he sees all the advantages that come from them. For example, he went to the Sabasaba International Trade Fair and saw women working in different fields. So he asked her to go and see her fellow women, and find out how they operate their business. Then she went to the fair and got a lot of new ideas.

Seeing the benefits from her activities, she decided to help her neighbour who had a very difficult life. She advised her to start a Mama Ntilie business. "In fact, we have formed a partnership. She prepares the food that I try to sell it. Each night, I give her back the money, even if the food is not sold. I just buy it and give her the money to encourage her to continue her business instead of staying at home, waiting for her husband who is doing nothing for her."

Joan's husband gave her a plot at Kibamba. She plans to build a nursery school, as there is no school in the area. For now, she is looking for sponsorship to start the school and find teachers.

"In our compound," she says, "there are many activities done by women. The media should cover that so that we are better known. People will discover what we do. It could be a good way for getting markets for the products we make. There are so many things that could be done but we need training and new skills."

On the subject of enhancing women's lives, Joan says, "We women have to love each other. You meet women who help men but let their fellow women down. For example, women themselves complain that if you have a woman-boss, it is better to quit the job, as she will not help you. It is true that we are not used to being leaders, and that could be why we feel so proud in front of other women.

"Most women in the city forget their fellow women in the hinterlands. They are not ready to help those women in the rural areas, as they do not consider them as civilised as they are. We should develop community participation to enable women to participate in matters related to their wellbeing and to make them aware of their rights. Most women from rural and urban areas do not know what is going on in the world!

"Nowadays, my children are happy because they do not miss anything. They go to school, eat good food and receive more attention from their father. In the beginning, he did not take care of them. Now he sees the importance of his children. Nowadays, the world has changed, as girls are the ones who help their parents. Compared to boys, who do not take care of their parents and wives' relatives, girls worry about them with all their heart. So the belief of our parents, to educate a boy because he will remain in the house and take care of them, has failed. Now parents realise that it is better to educate both girls and boys, because they don't know who will come to help them.

"The family is important. Some families still believe in oppressing a woman. Very often, women have no say in front of their husbands. If they say 'bring me your salary', they have to agree because they fear divorce. But me, I do not have these problems any more with my husband. Whatever I decide is all right with him.

"It took me a long time to come to that point, I have been beaten, discouraged in my production activities, and threatened with divorce; but that time is over. My husband is more helpful than before. Since we have been able to establish better communication, it seems that our life is quieter and we have more egalitarian relations. There are still many other things to improve, but I see that my children are learning something from us. I wish I really help them to prepare for a good future."

The study examined gender relations in the urban context of Dar es Salaam by the year 2001. It assessed the impact of changes on gender relations, on men and women's behaviours, on dual-sex system and ideology, and on the subjective meaning of the gender system for women and men who are confronted with new contradictions. Women's involvement in economic and productive activities that are earning them more than their husbands has been used as the indicator for analysing the complex interaction between the three most important structures of gender relations, i.e. the sexual division of labour, the sexual power relations and emotional relationships.

Thus, women's perception of life has been compared to men's representation of women's roles and of gender relations. Traditional patterns in gender relations have been opposed to changing ones, and the relationship between the daily life of women and their broader social concerns has been clarified. Constraints that women have to face and the new opportunities offered to them might affect the gender ideology that is still prevailing nowadays. Women's involvement in productive activities affects gender relations. Indeed, what are men and women doing while confronted with changes?

From a theoretical perspective, the concepts of social action, agency, *habitus* and habit, plural actor and resiliency occupy a very important place. They illustrate the construction of gender relations. The Tanzanian patriarchal social organisation determines a type of gender relations organised under the ideology of complementary nature and protection based on a dual-sex system. It starts with biological differences for building up a social system that leaves profound traces in all representations, institutions, *habitus* and habits. It shows to what extent the social organisation and the system of relations and interrelations is not favourable to women.

The first chapter concentrated on an overview of the urban environment of Dar es Salaam by the year 2000. The city is under the influence of a national economic crisis. Life conditions of the populations are exacerbated and close to the limit of survival—in such a context creating competition, exclusion and concurrence. The contextualisation exhibits the capacity of resistance of the population to structural, conjectural and punctual crisis. People display a great capacity of creativity and adaptation, while living in extreme conditions of poverty. The informal sector is expanding and recruits the majority of new migrants to the city, and as Rutashoybya (1995:271) mentioned, "It has affected virtually every member of the society, including women, the elderly, children and workers, both high and low income. Even wage workers in Tanzania depend primarily on the informal sector." Therewith, in spite of poor life conditions, people are active and they develop survival strategies. Life in different wards is the pale reflect of the lack of a serious policy of adapted development. These life conditions mark the growing research for security and the utmost of chances for ensuring survival.

The theoretical concepts of structure, agency and habits were useful to capture the anthropological subject. The agency capacity allows people to see themselves in the present (experience, daily life), in the past experience, and to make projections in the future. It refers to the capacity of individuals to embark on processes of autonomous self-realisation. The action which is taken determines the meaning or sense that is given by the plural actor, which is confronted to a "dialectic relationship with 'social structures' and 'embedded in social relations' (Lister, 1997:37) in a multiplicity of contexts that are not homogeneous and help developing new habits and resiliency."

The second chapter focused on the first structure of the gender relations associated to the sexual division of labour. It shows the persistent inequalities in the division of labour. Most women have to combine reproductive and remunerative activities because the traditional role in the family is maintained and is combined with responsibilities for providing cash income. Women are involved in specific fields of the informal sector that are related to skills developed in the household, compatible with their reproductive activities, and which require little capital investment and knowledge. Indeed, most of them are founded in service-oriented activities such as food, handicraft, small retail businesses, hair saloons, poultry and animal husbandry. Very few among them can perform larger-scale activities such as import-export or trade with foreign countries.

Many problems hinder women's performance in production activities, such as a lack of education, capital and managerial skills; a dearth of relevant and adapted technology, markets and time. The complex bureaucratic procedures and constant sexual harassment impede them for securing their activities. The root of the situation is related to the social construction of femininity, which favours the extension of stereotypes, attitudes and prejudices placing women in a subordinate group, as they are perceived as weak, dependent on men and housekeepers. Indeed, as mentioned by Connell (1987:106), the sexual division of labour is a constraint on practice that becomes a social rule by allocating specific people to specific work, and in the design of the work. The creation of mechanisms such as special training and skills development expresses the powerful system of social constraint that is exercised against women. As women do not occupy leadership and management posts, men are favoured to them for having access to training and better job opportunities. Without doubt, the sexual division of labour has to be seen as a larger pattern, a gendered-structured system of production, consumption and distribution. Indeed, the hegemonic pattern of masculinity in organising the solidarity of men becomes an economic as well as a cultural force. Consequently, women lack confidence as the socialisation process places them in a specific and deep-seated situation that disadvantages them from birth.

Women's involvement in production activities is seen has having a different impact. Women informants confirmed what Koda (1995:152-153) identified as the positive impact of the economic crisis on women of Dar es Salaam. Indeed, despite increased responsibilities and conflict, it gives women greater power financially, socially and politically. It also altered power structures within the household. For instance, women are increasingly being accepted as equal partners in development and, at the household level, they participate in the decision making, challenging by that way the old system of socialisation. Some even confirmed their determination by preferring social marginalisation—by being divorced rather than accepting poor life conditions with an irresponsible husband.

However, many women suffer from the situation. On the contrary, Campbell (1995) noted persisting gender inequality, as expressed in the earning power of respective partners at the household level, increasing the burden of work and responsibility for women and challenging their financial autonomy. It reinforces female dependence, exacerbates marital relationships and develops more inequitable gender relations.

In Ghana, according to findings of the study of Ohenaba-Sakyi's (1999:185), women and men alike had independent sources of income, exhibited some control over how the money they earned should be disposed of, and contributed to various household expenditures based on reflections of their "gendered" roles, responsibilities and obligations. Attitudes about occupational, administrative, and political leadership preferences in Ghana for the most part are "traditional." There is still the stereotyping of jobs into feminine and masculine, as defined by customary practices, in spite of the high educational aspirations that most parents have for their daughters and sons.

The result of an international meeting that was held in Paris in 1994 (Bisillat, 1996) demonstrated that some punctual qualitative studies on women head of households[1] have been done. However, few were supported by comparative and synthetic data. The researches had little impact on policies. Concepts and statistics practices still give an

---

[1] In 1978, the International Centre for Research on Women (Washington, D.C.) focused on the unknown situation of women as head of households in spite of their important role in the process of development. In 1988, the Population Council initiated a research programme on family structure, families with a woman as head of the household and poverty. In 1990, the United Nations tried to support, in vain, what had been initiated.

inexact measure of the phenomenon. The results of research are not used, as the political recommendations are not applied, whereas political engagement of governments of the Southern hemisphere is quasi non-existent. Research processes on the issue show the difficulty in defining the term "head of household." The actual definition does not allow the identification of women as headship, as the term head of household is profoundly connected to its patriarchal origin in which only men are viewed as playing this role. A re-definition of the term challenges the social order that is based on women's submission, control of their labour force, their sexuality and offspring. Most women in this situation must remain in a *de facto*, and not a *de jure* situation, with the consequence that they are not politically recognised. Indeed, many stakes of power and resource sharing are behind these quarrels of definition and terminology. Being a woman and female headship bring new discriminations, as women are affected in their access to resources (land, housing, credit) because they are not recognised in this role. They are socially marginalised in societies that do not allow women to be emancipated out of classical family structures. They benefit less from allocations, or public resources and social networks.

A study that was conducted by Lachaud (1997) in five West African countries (Burkina Faso, Cameroon, Côte d'Ivoire, Guinea, and Mali) on women's participation in the urban labour market demonstrated that inequalities related to gender are still existent in countries that are profoundly touched by economic and social crises. The process of social exclusion exposes strong inequalities between men and women according to the access to goods and services, social rights and the labour market. Women are mostly involved in the informal sector of the economy and earn less money than their male counterparts, and even if they are doing similar jobs women's profits are less than those of men.

In these five countries women's status (mostly married) is fragile as they lack control over the resources of the household and opportunities for profits. Lachaud identified three main factors blocking the promotion of women: a) the economic crises that exacerbated tensions and competition between individuals, b) the traditional society and, c) the lack of political willingness to reduce gender inequalities. Strategies developed by politicians still refer to traditional values, politicians being more preoccupied by the survival of the party. Among recommendations, the author suggests that the strategies of international development agencies such as UNDP should be supported for enhancing women's promotion[2]. Other recommendations are related to the promotion of education, development of professional training, and facilitating access to capital and credit for women to avoid their social exclusion.

Findings of a research that was conducted in 23 different countries and compiled in the book *Voices of the Poor* (Narayan et al, 2000:131), demonstrate that "traditional gender roles of men as providers and women as homemakers are highly uneven, with their roles uncertain, men and women express confusion and experience difficulty in establishing new interdependent partnerships." The pressure on women to secure a livelihood is far stronger today and reports from nearly all communities narrate the trend of an increasing number of women entering into temporary wage employment and informal commerce. Poor people mentioned male unemployment as the principal factor driving women to work; but other important factors include improvements in women's education status, greater awareness about rights, and increased access to information (media), credit, and NGOs supported activities. This was reported for Egypt, Ghana, Malawi, Nigeria and even Somalia. Women's discussion groups estimate that women are breadwinners in almost 70 percent of the households.

This situation increases the work burden of women, as men do not participate or help out more with housework and childcare. Casual work by women does not merit additional help with household chores from husbands. In certain cases, a positive link is found between women's earning capacity and their role in household decisions. But in some others, domestic abuse and violence increase as men suffer from unemployment and loss of economic power, and women's economic power is perceived as a serious violation of the accepted gender norms (Narayan et al, 2000:115).

Debates on economic reforms that have developed over two decades of adjustment in Africa reveal their negative impact on women, gender equality, and society in various countries and sectors. Gaps

---

[2] The 1995 UNDP strategy proposed the elimination of juridical discriminations, the modification of social and institutional norms, the fixation of 30 percent for women's participation and the promotion of key programmes for offering new opportunities.

still exist in the knowledge of economic reforms and their impact on the feminisation of poverty, gender mainstreaming, and the reliance of micro-credit.

The Gender and Economic Reform in Africa (GERA), an action research program focusing on gender-sensitive economic policies[3], has made important contributions to the creation of gender-aware economic policies in Africa. Among them, Joanna Kerr (2000:268-277) mentioned the making of economic policy a gender issue, forging an explicit research and advocacy link, facilitating strategic alliance, and the creation of African ownership by the direct implication of researchers in the definition of critical problems met by women. As a unique initiative in its focus, governance and methodology, GERA has sought to give African women a voice to demand policies that lead the lives and livelihoods of dignity for themselves and their communities. However, Kerr (2000:277) noted that in spite of all successes attributed to the commitment of women, the action-research projects have not radically transformed macroeconomic policies as the politics of economic reform, and the powerful institutions that define and implement these policies are not easily influenced. Despite their significance, and although their entrepreneurial activities are essential to the functioning of their societies during the creation and implementation of public and private sector development strategies, women rarely receive formal recognition or assistance in these largely unheralded roles. In fact, women's enterprises are often prescribed by municipal regulations, and they may be subjected to harassment by local authorities. Globalisation and is consequences oblige poor people to cope with illegal activities. However, traditional laws and social stigma oblige women to turn themselves on activities that are not officially recognised but that profit the official economy.

---

[3] The programme Gender and Economic Reforms in Africa (GERA) was initiated in October 1996 in Accra, Ghana. It is an initiative of the North-South Institute (NSI) and a group of African gender researchers and advocates from across 12 sub-Saharan Africa countries (Burkina Faso, Cameroon, Chad, Ethiopia, Ghana, Kenya, Mali, Nigeria, Tanzania, Togo, Uganda and Zimbabwe). The ultimate goal is to develop alternative approaches that ensure gender equity and economic justice. The programme also aims to provide critical analysis, through research and advocacy, of economic reform processes in Africa from a gender perspective. Even if research on gender and economic policies exist, the links between this and analysis and policy changes are extremely weak. Financial and technical support has been provided for 16 GERA action-oriented research projects that have been conducted in African countries.

The third chapter illustrated the second structure of gender relations through power relations from the State to the family level. The family is not seen as homogeneous but as a milieu of interweaved relationships extended in time, extensive in contact, dense in their interweaving of economics, emotion, power and resistance (Connell, 1987:121). In Dar es Salaam there is a clear sexual division of labour inside the family (Obrist van Eeuwijk, 2000; Campbell, 1995). Furthermore, the power-relations structure shows that women do not participate in the decision-making process and are constant subjects to physical and mental violence. Many women fear their husbands and that explains why they do not confront them. In many circumstances, marital relationships embody power, for example the husband defines sexual practice, decides on family planning acceptance, or decides for his daughter's future. What about the idea of women's protection? The emotional relations are not clear as far as fear, distrust and violence are at the core of the situation.

The State is engaged in ideological activity on the issues of sex and gender. For example, it regulates workplaces and families; provides schools; builds houses; and attempts to control sexuality by providing access to contraception, trying to control venereal diseases and Aids, and by legislating, for instance, the age of consent for marriage. It manages institutions such as marriage and motherhood, and by that plays a major part in the constitution of the social categories of the gender order. The State owns an important role in sexual politics. In fact, the Tanzanian State is historically constructed as patriarchal in a political process that institutionalises hegemonic masculinity and expends great energy in controlling it. The condition of women does not receive enough attention at the national level as women are only seen as consumers of state services. Indeed, women's organisations have little impact. The growth of the State's interest in regulating sexuality made legislative and public policy domains particularly attractive fields for political and intellectual struggles around sexuality. Religious backlash against women is done by using the notion of protection.

The nature of the Tanzanian state system is patriarchal, which has resulted in the hierarchical structure of the states' apparatus. This is not just the case in Tanzania, as it has been proven by the findings of the analysis of women's situation in many other West African countries. In the case of Nigeria, James and Etim in "Feminization of development processes in Africa" (1999) conclude that leading economic and political institutions are hierarchically structured and gendered. This interchange, which is based on the instant gratification of one gender group, has resulted in one's gender's manipulating and controlling the other. The consequence of the politics of gender has resulted in the leaving behind of women as a vital segment of Africa's human resources and created a significant vacuum, in combination with other variables, for the developmental process of African states. The State needs to start from a standpoint of mutual support and respect for achieving the long-awaited sustainable development, which means to reject patriarchal values by establishing another set of social, political and economic traditions.

Most of the interviewed women were not able to achieve their personal objectives and goals because they could not decide by and for themselves, as they lived under the authority of male elders of the family. They also referred to religious control, which is still exercised over women, specifically in Islam. Nevertheless, in spite of all these impediments, some women have been able to find a way to develop new trends.

The fourth chapter summarised the type of emotional relations that prevail between women and men. It refers to the social construction of femininity and masculinity and the social roles attached to it, and gender arrangements in a context based on the dual-sex system. This is in marked contrast with social roles, as far as gender is identified as a social construct.

Sexuality and gender are seen as two separate systems, which are interwoven at many points that vary historically and cross-culturally (Vance, 1995:39). The solidarity of a heterosexual couple is formed on the basis of some kind of reciprocity, rather than on the basis of a common experience or situation, as is the case in the structures of labour and power (Connell, 1987:113). It is the fact of many couples living in Dar es Salaam. Indeed, it seems that a couple's daily life is more often than not composed of social obligations linked to the social roles of men and women.

Therefore, multiple inequalities are revealed in the Tanzanian couple, which are marked by an unequal exchange and greater power for men, who are permitted promiscuous sexuality, while it is forbidden to women. It seems that women are "trafficked" and sexualised as objects of heterosexual desires. In marriage and relations to men, some women look more for security than sexuality. The balance of power in conjugal relations, in some cases, appears not to have been changed. Married women lack control over their sexuality and management of fertility, and still face high pressure from the social environment to give birth regularly and to have large families.

Brand, in her study done in Mali, found that the urban economic system affects the sexual order. She observed through her fieldwork that:

> *The gerontocratic control decreases through the loss of economic power over young males. Patriarchs can no longer afford to pay for their son's marriage, as a result of which arranged marriage is giving to a more or less free choice of partner. Prolonged schooling, unemployment and low salaries, in combination with the new economic responsibilities to be shouldered by young men, contribute to the rising age at first marriage. For men, it is not the wedding, but the cost of putting up and maintaining a new household that looms as threshold against early marriage (2001:303).*

In Mali and in Tanzania, postponement of marriage has created a new stage in life—the phase of adolescence that contributes to the creation of a separate youth culture. It creates and feeds a conflict of generation, as the experience of young people today differs in many ways from that of past generations. Rules of avoidance and shame have been loosened a great deal over the past generation. In Tanzania, the world is rapidly urbanising, with many more young people living in unstructured and impoverished conditions. The explosion of telecommunication across cultural boundaries and the increase in travel, tourism and migration also appear to be influencing the sexual behaviour of young people by providing models, pressures and opportunities for sexual encounters (Fuglesang, 1997:1246). Women tend to remain single for a longer period as fathers exert less authority over their daughters' choice of partners, and their sexual and fertility behaviour. In certain cases, friends and neighbours become more important that relatives.

The sphere of gender relations is also affected, as women tend to take over economic responsibilities from their husbands. The foundations of formal power appear to be eroded, even if women continue to pay respect to the husband as representing the authority in the home. Some couples have to communicate more directly and more intensively with each other. This is also confirmed by a study done in Senegal by Lecarme-Frassy (1993, 2000). The division of families follows the influence of economic exchange, urban migration, and urbanisation into smaller units, weakening traditional prescriptions that manage social relations according to a specific hierarchy. Spouses' relations evolve through a setting up of contract-based links and negotiations. Gender stereotypes and the systems that they generate, and which generate them, are not immutable. But they are confronted with fierce resistance to change (2000:239). Indeed, men do not ignore the fact that they do not respect the terms of the contract any more, which includes care of the spouse and children, respect and lack of violence. The concept of human rights penetrates into the social body, and an increasing number of women refuse the exacerbated forms of male domination as the law ensures them with personal rights (1993:685).

It was also confirmed by the study of Oheneba-Sakyi (1999) in Ghana.

> *Joint decision making in children's educational matters, purchase of household items, the family size and contraception was higher for women who possessed some autonomy by way of higher education, urban living, and freedom in their choice of marriage partner. Thus, the observed patterns in family communication and decision making reflect a changing society where the influence of education "emancipates" women (and to some extent, men) from the traditional practices that recognize the man's authority in certain familial domains (1999:185).*

The fifth chapter introduced the life histories of four women, whose ages ranged from the 20s to the 50s. It facilitated an inter-generational comparison for identifying common traits or differences in women living in the same country but at diverse periods of time. Of course, women do not represent a homogenous social group, and are differentiated by factors such as age, wealth, religion and status. However, they are living under the influence of the State's political decisions. Life stories showed the importance and impact of political decisions on women's lives, and their influence by offering or retrenching new opportunities to women. In this section, women's voices and words are transcribed as they express themselves without any revision from the author.

The following chapter offered an analysis of these four life stories. It outlined the influence of successive decades as it illustrated all progress in the 1970s and early 1980s. However, the economic crisis and implementation of Structural Adjustment Programmes imposed significant socio-economic and political challenges to both men and women. Indeed, women had to develop new survival strategies in a context where their conditions were deteriorating.

The students' point of view is characterised by a very conservative spirit towards gender relations and women and men's roles. At first glance, it seems that nothing changed in Dar es Salaam. Most male students present a more conventional view of gender relations. They present a stereotypical notion of men and women's spheres, of the family being headed by a man, and of typical social roles of men and women. It seems they all wish the same situation to be reproduced. Indeed the male students' view illustrates the lively influence of African patriarchy, and of underdeveloped capitalism. They all favour the reproduction of male privilege.

Therewith, female students also tend to reproduce the same official discourse and act in conformity with the social structure of gender relations. Nevertheless, some contradictions emerge as they identify the social relationships and discriminatory barriers erected by the patriarchal system. They know that it is more difficult for them to gain economic and political resources necessary to improve their lives. However, even if they recognise the necessity of distancing themselves from old beliefs and tradition, they do not incorporate new habits. Reflection is not yet completed. Thus, the problem lies in the incapacity of the system to offer more opportunities to many youth, as development is not yet a reality.

The patriarchal state continues to be supported on local and personal levels through men's authority. Male control tends to become higher when they loose the material and financial assizes of their authority (Labrecque, 2001:110). They put more pressure on women to have a greater number of children as a demonstration of their masculinity or virility. The root cause of women's integration and change for a better life lies in the traditional prejudices and stereotypes found in society, held by both sexes, and the construction of femininity. Women are seen as inferior, existing only as appendages of men (Rutashobya, 1995:276). Societal gender prejudices and stereotypes have undoubtedly had an adverse impact on women's ability to do more meaningful work. These prejudices have created a gender gap in almost every walk of life, i.e. education, employment, politics, technology, legal rights, resource ownership and the like (idem: 276).

Contradictions and paradoxes are numerous. Changes also appear.

Women's perception of their life is clearly more positive. Urban women evaluate that they have greater opportunities than their rural counterparts. Access to more information on their rights provides women with a higher esteem of themselves. They look for more equitable gender relations. Indeed, single women or those who got separated or divorced show that women can express themselves out of a marriage relation. But even if they increase their quality of life financially, most mention that they are socially marginalized.

It's clear that the patriarchal situation prevails, and women have to struggle to get new rights and be empowered. They have to be on the move, which means they have to develop qualitative and quantitative approaches for getting their rights. They must develop new measures, which will make gender and feminism acceptable in the region, and sensitise the whole society to fight gender prejudices. Women's condition should not be mixed up with development issues, as the main impediment lies in the social system itself.

Indeed, patriarchy occurs in capitalist and socialist systems (Caldwell, 1982; Croll, 1986; and Mies, 1986) and was present in the precapitalist familial mode of production. The tendency is to keep women under male control within the extended kinship system by keeping them economically dependent on men and family. The prevailing view is that gender inequality and the sexual division of labour are natural, rather than socially constructed. Generally, men struggle to preserve Tanzanian patriarchal relations and other customary practices which represent alternatives modes of survival that do not entail total subordination to capital. Indeed, this is based on the patriarchal idea that the production of goods is separate from the production of people, and that women's primary role is the latter while men's role is the former. It creates a fundamental relational asymmetry between women and men. Women bear the burden of reproduction and the maintenance of human resources with little help from men. Such expectations prevent women from competing with men on equal terms.

Capitalist and African patriarchy benefited from and cooperated in controlling women and creating a sexual division of labour that subsidised men and the capital economy. However, capitalism also modified gradually and unevenly, gender relations as it promotes capitalist economic interests or Western patriarchal conceptions. It also generates social changes that can provide new opportunities and rights for women.

For example, the opportunity for women in Dar es Salaam to earn money is an important first step in loosening the bonds of patriarchy, rooted in a precapitalist and underdeveloped capitalist society. Blumberg (1995:1-3) asserted that "women's control of income is the most important predicator of gender equality and women's empowerment." It provides financial independence from men as it promotes self-esteem, gives women more power in the decision-making process at the household level, and prepares the way for "class-consciousness" and collective organising among women.

Blumberg's observations are confirmed by the case study of Santhiaba, a ward located in the town of Pikine, Senegal (Abdoul, 2001:169-201; 2002). In the framework of local development, women initiated income-generating activities, developed initiatives and collective mobilisation, and created new structures and diverse networks that acted on the community's life. It provided them with a relative feeling of security. Gender relations in the urban environment of Santhiaba, even if they are still marked by socio-cultural values of the patriarchal system, are changing through the recognition of women's participation in the decision-making process in initiatives and community affairs. Their new economic empowerment provides them with an increasing social recognition; they have more power in the decision-making process at the household level as they have developed a relative autonomy in the management of their budget. In the management of local development, they are increasingly perceived as essential protagonists. Residents recognise their dynamism and good manners in economic groups. However, men continue to refer to discourses in which they use tradition or religion, and many women are still receptive to it. But these reference frameworks are not immutable. Urban life and deep changes create a new vision of the world, and women affirm themselves in these changes. Their successes in economic groups allow them to act through various activities related to community interest. It is a proof that habits can evolve. Representations on gender roles and the respective social status of men and women are out of step with concrete reality (2002:95-96).

The same evolution is also observed in the case of the women of Burkina Faso, who are involved in the management of environment in an association called Lagem Yam (Tall, 2001:135-167). Their involvement contributed to a change in gender relations and policies related to it. Obviously, women got more work, but they developed a job and gained autonomy acquired by their earnings. Their action resulted in social recognition and value of their work.

However, the capitalist mode of production is nascent in Tanzania rather than dominant. Although there is a growing bourgeoisie, the bourgeoisie's strength is largely dependent on the State rather than having an independent base in the economy. The Tanzanian bourgeoisie has been a largely comprador class; modern sector manufacturing and other productive enterprise are dominated by foreigners and parastatals. This bourgeoisie remains weak because it is unable to command the forces of production through extensive private ownership of manufacturing enterprise or land (Gordon, 1996:38-39). The current liberal capitalist reform mainly offers opportunities.

As mentioned in the introduction, through the globalisation process, women can be both empowered and disempowered. Through the interviews we can affirm that women's existence is transformed through their introduction in the labour market, be it in the formal or informal sector of the economy. As mentioned by Kabeer (2002:111), from the structural perspective, there is a transformation seen through the labour market, management of domestic activities, marriage practices and migration. Women's work has introduced a greater diversity in the social picture. From an individual point of view, changes occur as some women are now able to affirm themselves in the existing gender-relations system, some enhance the lives of their children, others succeed in the realisation of their dreams or in renegotiating unsatisfactory relations, and others escape patriarchal relations. If women are able to implement their personal or collective objectives in households, one could say that the earnings of women favour their autonomy. In fact, women are empowered in spite of all the difficulties they encounter.

In this context, are men and women ready to challenge their gender relations and social structure, and propose a new type of society?

What will be the long-term effect of feminine resiliency? How will it be possible to challenge the changes that slowly appear?

How could men and women work together to overcome patriarchal oppression? Gender equality could benefit men and thus gain men's support, as has been achieved in most developed countries. Social changes can erode patriarchal gender attitudes and more egalitarian attitudes can be developed. Nowadays, some men encourage their wives in their activities, and daughters are seen as more important than boys. They put in place some grounds for greater gender equality. Others recognise that old customs and traditions affect women's lives and are influenced by ideals of gender egalitarian relations.

The current liberal capitalist reform offers opportunities for those who have become rich through corruption, speculation, government positions and favours, and exploitation of workers. Only a radical change in governance and state policies, and organised popular movements for equitable development can ensure that capitalism benefits more than just a few—be they women or men. After all, gender equality is not about an equal sharing of poverty and powerlessness, but about empowering all people and improving their lives (Gordon, 1996:75).

REFERENCES

ABBOTT, Elizabeth, *Histoire universelle de la chasteté et du célibat*, Montréal : FIDES, 2001.

ABDOUL, Mohamadou,« Organisation de nouvelles activités économiques des femmes et accès aux décisions : une étude à Santhiaba au Sénégal », in VERSCHUUR, Christine et Fenneke REYSOO (dirigé par), *Genre, mondialisation et pauvreté*, Cahiers genre et développement, no. 3, iuéd-efi, Genève, l'Harmattan, 2002 : 93-99.

ABDOUL, Mohamadou, "Les rapports sociaux hommes-femmes à travers les activités économiques féminines et la gestion du cadre de vie », in François HAINARD and Christine VERSCHUUR (eds), *Femmes dans les crises urbaines*. Relation de genre et environnements précaires, Paris : Karthala, 2001.

AFSHAR, Hale and Stephanie BARRIETOS, « Introduction: Women, Globalization and Fragmentation", in Haleh AFSHAR and Stephanie BARRIETOS (ed), *Women, Globalization and Fragmentation in Developing World*, Londres: Macmillan Press, 1999.

ALLOO, Fatma, "Using information technology as mobilizing force" in MITTER, Swasti and Sheila ROWBOTHAM (eds), *Women Encounter Technology*. Changing Patterns of Employment in the Third World, London and New York: the United Nations University INTEC Institute for New Technologies, published in association with the UNU Press, 1995: 303-313.

AMER, Sherif and H. THROBORG, *Health Coverage in Urban Dar es Salaam*, International Institute for Aerospace Survey and Earth Sciences (ITC), 1996.

AMOUGOU, Emmmanuel, *Afro-métropolitaines. Émancipation ou domination masculine?*, Paris : l'Harmattan, Études africaines, 1998.

ADULT MORBIDITY AND MORTALITY PROJECT, *Policy Implications of Adult Morbidity and Mortality*, Dar es Salaam, 1993

BAFFOUN, Alya, "Les stratégies de reproduction de l'ordre sexuel inégalitaire- Analyse de la dyade Mère-Enfant", in *Association of African Women for Research and Development/Association des Femmes Africaines pour la recherche et le développement (AFARD-AAWORD)*, Occasional Paper Series No 5, Dakar, 1992: 41-79.

BATESON, G., *Steps to Ecology of Mind*, Paladin: St-Albans, 1973.

BAYLIES, Carolyn and Janet BUJRA with the Gender and AIDS Group, *AIDS, Sexuality and Gender in Africa,* Collective strategies and struggles in Tanzania and Zambia, London and New York: Routledge, 2000.

BERGER, Maurice, Brian WALLIS and Simon WATSON (eds), Picture Essay by Carrie MAE WEEMS, *Constructing Masculinity*, New York and London: Routledge, 1995.

BINSBERGEN, Win van, "La chambre de Mary, ou comment devenir consommatrice à Francistown, Botswana », in DE LAME, Danielle et Chantal ZABUS (sous la direction de), *Changements au féminin en Afrique noire*. Anthropologie et littérature, Volume 1 : Anthropologie, Paris : l'Harmattan, Montréal : l'Harmattan Inc., 1999 : 37-87.

BISILLAT, Jeannine et Christine VERSCHUUR (dirigé par), *Le Genre : un outil nécessaire. Introduction à une problématique,* Cahiers genre et développement, no.1, Paris : L'Harmattan, Montréal : l'Harmattan Inc., 2000.

BISILLAT, Jeannine (sous la direction de), *Face aux changements les femmes du sud*, Paris : l'Harmattan, Montréal : l'Harmattan Inc., 1997.

BISILLAT, Jeannine (sous la direction de), *Femmes du sud, chefs de famille*, Paris : l'Harmattan, 1996.

BLUMBERG, Rae Lesser et al. (ed), *Engendering Wealth and Well-Being: Empowerment for Global Change,* Boulder: Westview, 1995.

BLUMBERG, Rae Lesser, "Introduction: Engendering Wealth and Well-Being in an Era of Economic Transformation », in Rae Lesser BLUMBERG et al. (ed), *Engendering Wealth and Well-Being : Empowerment for Global Change,* Boulder: Westview, 1995.

BOURDIEU, Pierre, *Le sens pratique,* Paris : Éditions de Minuit avec le concours de la maison des Sciences de l'Homme, 1980.

BOURDIEU, Pierre, *Raisons pratiques*. Sur la théorie de l'action, Paris : Éditions du Seuil, 1994.

BRAND, Saskia, *Mediating Means and Fate*. A Socio-Political Analysis of Fertility and Demographic Change in Bamako, Mali, Leiden, Boston, Köln: Brill, 2001.

BROWNMILLER, Susan, *Against Our Will: Men, Women and Rape,* Harmondsworth: Penguin, 1976.

BRYCESON, Deborah F., "Gender relations in rural Tanzania: power politics or cultural consensus", in CREIGHTON, Colin and C.K. OMARI (edited by), *Gender, Family and Household in Tanzania*, Aldershot, Brookfield USA, Hong Kong, Singapore, Sidney: Avebury, 1995: 37-70.

BRYCESON, Deborah F., "The Proletarianization of Women in Tanzania", in *Review of African Political Economy*, no. 17, 1980: 4-27.

CALDWELL, John, *Theory of Fertility Decline*, New York: Academic Press, 1982.

CALHOUN, Craig Edward LIPUMA and Moishe POSTONE (eds), *Bourdieu: Critical Perspectives*, Chicago: The University of Chicago Press, 1993.

CAMPBELL, John, Race, class and community in colonial Dar es Salaam: tentative steps towards an understanding of urban society" in C. Creighton and C.K. Omari (eds), *Gender, Family and Work in Tanzania*, Ashgate: Aldershot, 2000: 17-44.

CAMPBELL, John, "Conceptualizing gender relations and the household in urban Tanzania", in CREIGHTON, Colin and C.K. OMARI (edited by), *Gender, Family and Household in Tanzania*, Aldershot, Brookfield USA, Hong Kong, Singapore, Sidney: Avebury, 1995: 178-203.

CAMPBELL, John, Joachim MWAMI and Mary NTUKULA, "Urban social organization: an exploration of kinship, social networks, gender relations and household and community in Dar es Salaam", in CREIGHTON, Colin and C.K. OMARI (edited by), *Gender, Family and Household in Tanzania*, Aldershot, Brookfield USA, Hong Kong, Singapore, Sidney: Avebury, 1995: 221-253.

CAPLAN, Pat, "Monogamy, polygyny, or the single state? Changes in marriage patterns in a Tanzanian coastal village, 1965-94", in CREIGHTON, Colin and C.K. OMARI (edited by), *Gender, Family and Household in Tanzania*, Aldershot, Brookfield USA, Hong Kong, Singapore, Sidney: Avebury, 2000: 44-67.

CARE TANZANIA, *Dar es Salaam Urban livelihood Security Assessment*, Tome 1: Design, Background, Strategy, Data Collection and Analysis Methodology, prepared by Rose Rutahakana, CARE Tanzania and Dan

Maxwell, IFPRI/NMIMR Ghana, Dar es Salaam, Tanzania; Tome 2: *Data Document*, Collected by Rose Rutahakana, CARE Tanzania, Household Livelihood Security Coordinator, and Michael D. DeVries, Assistant Country Director, Dar es Salaam, Tanzania, 1997.

CHABAUD-Rychter, Danielle, FOUGEYROLLAS-SCHWEBEL, Dominique, SONTHONAS, Françoise, *Espace et temps de travail domestique*, Paris ; Librairie des Méridiens-Klincksieck « Réponses sociologiques », 1985.

CHAMBERS, Robert, "Editorial Introduction: Vulnerability, Coping and Policy", in *IDS Bulletin*, Vol. 20, no. 2, 1989: 1-7.

CHAZAN, N., "Gender perspectives on African States", in PARPART, Jane L. and Kathleen A. STAUDT (eds), *Women and the State in Africa,* Boulder: Lynne Rienner,1989.

CLOUTIER, Luce in collaboration with Miriam Bisanda, *Quality of health care in Dar es Salaam*, Dar es Salaam Urban Health Project (DUHP), Dar es Salaam, Tanzania, 1998.

CLOUTIER, Luce, *Perception of health and illness among various groups in Dar es Salaam,* Dar es Salaam Urban Health Project (DUHP), Dar es Salaam, Tanzania, 1996.

CONNELL, R.W., *Masculinities*, Berkeley, Los Angeles: University of California Press, 1995

CONNELL, R.W., *Gender & Power. Society, the Person and Sexual Politics,* Stanford, California: Stanford University Press, 1987.

COQUERY-VIDROVITCH, Catherine, *Les Africaines.* Histoire des femmes d'Afrique noire du X1Xe siècle au XXe siècle, Editions Desjonquères, Paris, 1994.

CORCUFF, Philippe, « Justification, stratégie et compassion. Apport de la sociologie des régimes d'action », in *Correspondances*, no. 51.

CREIGHTON, Colin, "Kinship in the urban setting in Tanzania" in CREIGHTON, Colin and C.K. OMARI (edited by), *Gender, Family and Work in Tanzania*, Aldershot, Brookfield USA, Hong Kong, Singapore, Sidney: Avebury, 2000: 67-138.

CROLL, Elisabeth, « Rural Production and Reproduction : Socialist development Experiences », in *Women's Work,* Leanor Leacock, Helen I. Safa, et al (eds), South Hadley, MA :Bergin & Garvey, 1986.

CORDONNIER, Rita, *Femmes africaines et commerce. Les revendeuses de tissu de la ville de Lomé,* Paris : l'Harmattan, 1991.

CREIGHTON, C., "Kinship in the urban setting in Tanzania", in C. Creighton and C.K. Omari (eds), *Gender, Family and Work in Tanzania,* Ashgate: Aldershot, 2000: 67-137

CREIGHTON, Colin and C.K. OMARI (edited by), *Gender, Family and Work in Tanzania*, Aldershot, Brookfield USA, Hong Kong, Singapore, Sidney: Avebury, 2000.

CREIGHTON, Colin and C.K. OMARI (edited by), *Gender, Family and Household in Tanzania*, Aldershot, Brookfield USA, Hong Kong, Singapore, Sidney: Avebury, 1995.

CYRULNIK, Boris, *Un merveilleux malheur,* Editions Odile Jacob, Paris, 1999.

DACHER, Michèle en collaboration avec Suzanne LALLEMAND, *Prix des épouses, valeurs des sœurs : deux études sur la société Goin (Burkina Faso*), Paris : L'Harmattan, Collection Connaissance des Hommes, 1992.

DE LAME, Danielle et Chantal ZABUS (sous la direction de), *Changements au féminin en Afrique noire.* Anthropologie et littérature, Volume 1 : Anthropologie, Paris : l'Harmattan, Montréal : l'Harmattan Inc., 1999.

DE ROSNAY, Joël, *Le macroscope. Vers une vision globale,* Paris : éditions du Seuil, 1975.

DELPHY, Christine, *L'ennemi principal. 1. Économie politique du patriarcat*, Nouvelles questions féministes, Paris : Syllepse, 1998.

EGBO, Benedicta, *Gender, Literacy and Life-Chances in Sub-Saharan Africa,* The language and Educational Library 16, Series Editor: Professor David J. Corson, The Ontario Institute of Studies in Education, Clevedon, Buffalo, Toronto, Sydney: Multilingual Matters Ltd, 2000.

EHRENREICH, Barbara, "The Decline of Patriarchy", in BERGER, Maurice, Brian WALLIS, and Simon WATSON (eds), *Constructing*

Masculinity, Picture Essay by Carrie MAE WEEMS, New York, London: Routledge, 1995: 284-291.

FAPOHUNDA, O.J. and FAPOHUNDA, E.R., *The working mothers of Lagos*, Report of a study submitted to the Interdisciplinary Communications Committee of the Smithsonian Institution, Washington, DC.: "Female and male work profiles" in Oppong, C. (ed): *Female and male in West Africa,* London, George Allen and Unwin, 1983.

FIRESTONE, Shulamith, *The Dialectic of Sex,* New York: Morrow, 1974.

FOBLETS, M.C., « Les enjeux des femmes sud-africaines et des traditions locales, entre la nouvelle constitution et les exigences du droit international », in DE LAME, Danielle et Chantal ZABUS (sous la direction de), *Changements au féminin en Afrique noire.* Anthropologie et littérature, Volume 1 : Anthropologie, Paris : l'Harmattan, Montréal : l'Harmattan Inc., 1999 : 235-259.

FORSTER, Peter G., Anthropological studies of kinship in Tanzania », in CREIGHTON, Colin and C.K. OMARI (edited by), *Gender, Family and Household in Tanzania*, Aldershot, Brookfield USA, Hong Kong, Singapore, Sidney: Avebury, 1995: 70-118.

FOUCAULT, Michel, *Histoire de la sexualité. La volonté de savoir,* Tome 1, Paris: Gallimard.

FOUGEYROLLAS-SCHWEBEL, Dominique, « Travail domestique », in HIRATA, Helena, Françoise LABORIE, Hélène LE DOARÉ, Danièle SENOTIER (sous la coordination de), *Dictionnaire critique du féminisme*, Paris : Presses Universitaires de France, 2000.

FUGLESANG, Minou, "Lessons for Life-Past and Present Modes of Sexuality Education in Tanzanian Society", in *Social Sciences & Medicine*, Vol. 44, No. 8, 1997:1245-1254.

GAIDZANWA, Rudo, "Bourgeois Theories of Gender and Feminism and their Shortcomings with Reference to Southern African Countries", in *Gender in Southern Africa. Conceptual and Theoretical issues,* Ruth Meena (ed), Harare: Sapes Books, 1992:192-125.

GEIGER, Susan, *Tanu Women. Gender and Culture in the Making of Tanganyikan Nationalism 1955-1965,* Portsmouth: Heinemann, Oxford: James Currey, Nairobi: E.A.E.P., Dar es Salaam: Mikuki na Nyota, 1997.

GEISLER, Gisela, "Women are women or how to please your husband: initiation ceremonies and the politics of 'tradition' in Southern Africa", in GODDARD, Victoria Ann (edited by), *Gender, Agency and Change. Anthropological Perspectives*, London and New York: Routledge, 2000: 56-86.

GIBBON, Peter and Phil RAIKES, *Structural Adjustment in Tanzania, 1986-1994.* CDR.

GIDDENS, A., *La constitution de la société. Éléments de la théorie de la structuration*, Paris : Presses Universitaires de France, 1994.

GODDARD, Victoria Ann (edited by), *Gender, Agency and Change. Anthropological Perspectives*, London and New York: Routledge, 2000.

GORDON, April A., *Transforming Capitalism and Patriarchy. Gender and Development in Africa,* Boulder, London: Lynne Rienner Publishers, 1996

GOVERNMENT OF TANZANIA, Tanganyika, African Population of Tanganyika, East African Statistical Department, Geographical and Tribal Studies, 1948, Government printer, Dar es Salaam, 1953.

GUYER, J.I., "Linear Identities and Lateral Networks: the logic of polyandrous motherhood", in C. Bledsoe & G. Pison (ed), *Nuptiality in Sub-Sahara Africa*, 1994, vol.10, p. 231-232.

HAICAULT, Monique, "La gestion ordinaire de la vie en deux", in *Sociologie du travail*, No. 3, 1984 :268-277.

HAINARD, François et Christine VERSCHUUR (éds), *Femmes dans les crises urbaines*. Relations de genre et environnement précaires, Paris : Karthala, 2001.

HARTMAN, Heidi, « Capitalism, Patriarchy and Job Segregation by Sex », in. EISENSTEIN, Z. (ed), *Capitalist Patriarchy*, New York: Monthly Review Press, 1979.

HAULE, Tabu, *Impact of Divorce on Children. A Case Study: Mwenge Ward*, A dissertation submitted in partial fulfilment of the requirements of the Degree of Bachelor of Arts (Sociology), University of Dar es Salaam, Faculty of Arts and Social Sciences, Department of Sociology, March 2000.

HELGESON, Vicki S., "Relation of agency and communion to well-being: evidence and potential explanations", *Psychological bulletin*, November 1994, Vol. 116, no 3.

HIRATA, Helena, Françoise LABORIE, Hélène LE DOARÉ, Danièle SENOTIER (coordonné par), *Dictionnaire critique du féminisme*, Paris : Presses Universitaires de France, 2000.

HODGSON, Dorothy L., « My daughter… belongs to the government now: Marriage, Maasai and the Tanzanian State", in CREIGHTON, Colin and C.K. OMARI (edited by), *Gender, Family and Household in Tanzania*, Aldershot, Brookfield USA, Hong Kong, Singapore, Sidney: Avebury, 2000: 200-220.

INTERNATIONAL WOMEN'S TRIBUNE CENTRE, *The Tribune. A Women and Development Quarterly.* Women Moving Human Rights Centre Stage, International Women's Tribune Centre, Newsletter 58, New York, May 1999.

JAMES, Valentine Udoh and ETIM, James S. (eds), *The feminization of Development Processes in Africa.* Current and Future perspectives, Westport, Connecticut, London: Praeger, 1999.

KABEER, NAILA, "Nécessaire, suffisant ou insignifiant? Femmes, salariat et rapports de pouvoir au sein du ménage », in VERSCHUUR, Christine et Fenneke REYSOO (dirigé par), *Genre, mondialisation et pauvreté*, Cahiers genre et développement, no. 3, iuéd-efi, Genève, l'Harmattan, 2002 : 107-113.

KAUFMANN, Jean-Claude, *Ego. Pour une sociologie de l'individu*, Paris : éditions Nathan, 2001.

KENNEDY, Paul, *African Capitalism: the Struggle for Ascendancy*, Cambridge: Cambridge University Press, 1988.

KERR, Joanna, "The GERA Program: From Learning to New Visions", in TSIKATA, Dzodzi and Joanna KERR with Catht BLACKLOCK and Jocelyne LAFORCE (eds), *Demanding Dignity: Women Confronting Economic Reforms in Africa,* The North-South Institute and Thirld World Network-Africa, Ottawa: Renouf Publishing Co. Ltd.; Accra: Third World Network-Africa, 2000: 267-277.

KILONZO, Shabani, "UPATU- A social security system for the poor", in *The Express*, 1994: 14.

KODA, Betha, “Democratisation of social relations at the household level: The participation of children and youth in Tanzania”, in CREIGHTON, Colin and C.K. OMARI (edited by), *Gender, Family and Household in Tanzania*, Aldershot, Brookfield USA, Hong Kong, Singapore, Sidney: Avebury, 2000: 237-266.

KODA, Betha, “The economic organization of the household in contemporary Tanzania”, in in CREIGHTON, Colin and C.K. OMARI (edited by), *Gender, Family and Household in Tanzania*, Aldershot, Brookfield USA, Hong Kong, Singapore, Sidney: Avebury, 1995: 139-156.

KRIEGER, Judith, “Entrepreneurs and Family Well-Being: Agricultural and Trading Households in Cameroon”, in SPRING, Anita and Barbara E. MC DADE (eds), *African Entrepreneurship.* Theory and Reality, Gainesville, Tallahassee, Tampa, Boca Raton, Pensacole, Orlando, Miami, Jacksonville: University Press of Florida, 1998:147-169.

LABRECQUE, Marie France, « Présentation. Perspectives anthropologiques et féministes de l’économie politique », in Anthropologie et sociétés, Université Laval, Québec, Canada, vol. 25, no 1, 2001 : 5-22.

LACHAUD, Jean-Pierre, *Les femmes et le marché du travail urbain en Afrique subsaharienne,* Paris : l’Harmattan, Montréal : l’Harmattan Inc.., 1997.

LAHIRE, Bernard, *L’Homme pluriel. Les ressorts de l’action*, Paris : éditions Nathan, Collection Essais & Recherches, 1998.

LAING, R. D., *The Politics of the Family, Penguin: Harmondsworth, 1976.*

LAMPHERE, L., H. RAGONE and P. ZAVELLA, “Introduction”, in LAMPHERE, L., H. RAGONE and P. ZAVELLA (dir.), *Situated Lives. Gender and Culture in Everyday Life*, New York, Routledge, 1997: 1-17.

LEACOCK, Leanor, Helen I. SAFA, et al (eds), *Women’s Work,* South Hadley, MA :Bergin & Garvey, 1986.

LECARME-FRASSY, Mireille, *Marchandes dakaroises entre maison et marché.* Approche anthropologique, Paris : l’Harmattan ; Montréal : l’Harmattan Inc. ; Budapest : l’Harmattan Hongrie ; Torino : l’Harmattan Italie, 2000.

LECARME-FRASSY, Mireille, *Marchandes à Dakar. Négoce, négociation sociale et rapports sociaux de sexe en milieu urbain précaire,* Thèse pour le doctorat de l'École des Hautes Études en Sciences Sociales (E.H.E.S.S.), Paris, 1993.

LE COUR GRANDMAISON, Colette, "Contrats économiques entre époux dans l'Ouest africain", in *L'Homme,* X1X (3-4), Paris, juillet-décembre:159-170.

LESLIE, J.A.K., *A Survey of Dar es Salaam,* Published on behalf of East African Institute of Social Research by Oxford University Press, London, New York and Nairobi, 1963.

LEWINSON, Anne S., « Renovating the modern home: Gender, marriage and weddings among professionals in Dar es Salaam", in CREIGHTON, Colin and C.K. OMARI (edited by), *Gender, Family and Household in Tanzania*, Aldershot, Brookfield USA, Hong Kong, Singapore, Sidney: Avebury, 2000: 266-292.

LISTER, R., *Citizenship. A Feminist Perspective*, London: Macmillan, 1997.

LOCOH, Thérèse, Annie LABOURIE-RACAPÉ, Christine TICHIT (edité par), *Genre et développement : des pistes à suivre*, Documents et Manuels du CEPED no 5, EHESS_INED_INSEE_ORSTOM-Université Paris V1, 1996.

LUGALLA, J., *Socialist Contribution and the urbanization Process in Tanzania: An Analysis of Urban Poverty and Politics*, PhD thesis, Bremen: University of Bremen, *1990.*

MACKINNON, Catherine, *Towards a Feminist Theory of the State*, Cambridge, Massachusetts: Harvard University Press, 1989.

MADUNAGU, Bene E., "Programme d'action des femmes pour la justice entre hommes et femmes, les expériences des femmes africaines", in VERSCHUUR, Christine et Fenneke REYSOO (dirigé par), *Genre, mondialisation et pauvreté*, Cahiers genre et développement, no. 3, iuéd-efi, Genève, l'Harmattan, 2002 : 167-177.

MANNATHOKO, Changu, "Feminist Theories and the Study of Gender Issues in Southern Africa", in *Gender in Southern Africa. Conceptual and Theoretical issues*, Ruth MEENA (ed), Harare: Sapes Books, 1992: 71-91.

MASCERENHAS, Ophelia and Marjorie MBILINYI, *Women in Tanzania : an Analytical Bibliography,* Uppasala: The Scandinavian Institute for African Studies, 1983.

MBA, Nina, "Kaba and Khaki: Women and the Militarised State in Nigeria", in Jane L. PARPART and Kathleen A. STAUDT (eds), *Women and the State in Africa,* Boulder: Lynne Rienner, 1989.

MBILINYI, M., *Gender and Structural Adjustment*, TGNP Seminar Series, Dar es Salaam, 1994.

MBILINYI, Marjorie, "Research methodologies in Gender Issues", in *Gender in Southern Africa. Conceptual and Theoretical issues*, in Ruth Meena (ed), Harare: Sapes Books, 1992: 31-70.

MBILINYI, Marjorie, *Big Slavery*, Dar es Salaam University Press, Dar es Salaam, Tanzania, 1991.

MBILINYI, Marjorie, "Research Priorities in Women's Studies in Eastern Africa", in *Women's Studies International Forum*, vol.7, No 4, 1984: 289-300.

MBILINYI, Marjorie, "Women in Development Ideology: the Promotion of Competition and Exploitation", in *Africa Development*, vol. 11, No 7, 1984:19-33.

MEENA, Ruth, "Gender Research/Studies in Southern Africa: An Overview", in MEENA, Ruth (ed), *Gender in Southern Africa. Conceptual and Theoretical issues,* Harare: Sapes Books, 1992:1-30.

MIES, Maria, *Patriarchy and Accumulation on a World Scale: Women in the International Division of Labour*, London: Zed Press, 1986.

MIKELL, Gwendolyn , "Introduction", in *African Feminism. The Politics of Survival in Sub-Saharan Africa*, Gwendolyn Mikell (ed), Philadelphia: University of Philadelphia Press, 1997: 1-52.

MITTER, Swasti and Sheila ROWBOTHAM (eds), *Women Encounter Technology*. Changing patterns of Employment in the Third World, London and New York: the United Nations University INTEC Institute for New technologies, published in association with the UNU Press, 1995.

MOGHADAM, Valentine M. (ed), *Patriarchy and Economic Development*. Women's Positions at the End of the Twentieth Century, A study prepared for the World Institute for Development Economics research of the United Nations University (UNU/WIDER), Oxford: Clarendon Press, 1996.

MOGHADAM, Valentine M., "Patriarchy and the Politics of Gender in Modernizing Societies: Iran, Pakistan and Afghanistan", in *International Sociology*, Vol. 7, No. 1. March 1992: 35-53.

MOSER, Caroline, *Confronting Crisis: A Comparative Study of Household Responses to Poverty and Vulnerability in Four Urban Communities*, Environmental Sustainable Development Studies and Monograph Series 8, Washington D.C.: World Bank, 1996.

MWENESI, Halima Abdullah, "Women and Decision-Making for their Children's Health Care" in Pandu WIJEYARATNE, Lori Jones ARSENAULT, Janet HATCHER ROBERTS, and Jennifer KITTS (eds), *Gender, Health and Sustainable Development*, Proceedings of a Workshop held in Nairobi, Kenya, 5-8 October 1993: Ottawa, Cairo, Dakar, Johannesburg, Montevideo, Nairobi, New Delhi, Singapore: International Development Research Centre: 117-129.

NARAYAN, Deepa, Robert CHAMBERS, Meera Kaul SHAH, Patti PETESCH, *Voices of the Poor. Crying Out for Change*, published by the Oxford University Press for the World Bank, World Bank, 2000.

NARAYAN, Deepa, *Voices of the Poor.* Poverty and Social capital in Tanzania, Environmental and Socially Sustainable Development and Monographs Series 20, Washington D.C.: The World Bank, 1997.

NDUNGU, Njoki S., "Gender-Based Violence Within the African Region, An overview", in *Newsletter for Women in Law and Development in Africa*, WILDAF News, Number 1, Harare: 1999: 7-10.

OBBO, Christina, *African Women. Their Struggle for Economic Independence,* London: Zed Press, 1981.

OBRIST VAN EEUWIJK, Brigit, *Struggling for Health in the City.* An Anthropological Inquiry in Dar es Salaam, Tanzania, Ethnologisches Seminar der Universitat Basel, Schweizerisches Tropeninstitut, Basel, Habilitationsschrift, Juni 2000.

OHENEBA-SAKYI, Yaw, *Female Autonomy, Family Decision making, and Demographic Behaviour in Africa,* with contributions from Kofi AWUSABO-ASARE, Studies in African Economic and Social development, Volume 12, Lewiston, Queenston, Lampeter: The Edwin Mellen Press, 1999.

OJWANG, J.B., "Death and Burial in Modern Kenya", in *The S.M. Otieno Case: Death and Burial in Modern Kenya,* by J.B. Ojwang and J.N.K. Mugambi (eds), Nairobi: Nairobi University Press, 1989.

OMARI, C.K., "Decision-making and the household: case studies from Tanzania", in CREIGHTON, Colin and C.K. OMARI (edited by), *Gender, Family and Household in Tanzania,* Aldershot, Brookfield USA, Hong Kong, Singapore, Sidney: Avebury, 1995: 203-221.

OMARI, C.K., "Fertility rates and the status of women in Tanzania", in CREIGHTON, Colin and C.K. OMARI (edited by), *Gender, Family and Work in Tanzania,* Aldershot, Brookfield USA, Hong Kong, Singapore, Sidney: Avebury, 1995: 253-269.

OMARI, C.K. AND D.A.S. MBILINYI, "Born to be less equal: The predicament of the girl child in Tanzania", in CREIGHTON, Colin and C.K. OMARI (edited by), *Gender, Family and Work in Tanzania,* Aldershot, Brookfield USA, Hong Kong, Singapore, Sidney: Avebury, 2000: 292-315.

OPPONG, C., *Sex Roles, Population and Development in Africa. Policy-Related Studies on Work and Demographic Issues,* Portsmouth (N.H.), Heinemann and London: James Currey, 1987.

OPPONG, C. (ed): *Female and male in West Africa,* London: George Allen and Unwin, 1983.

PARPART, Jane, "Gender, Patriarchy, and Development in Africa: The Zimbabwean Case", in MOGHADAM, Valentine M. (edited by), *Patriarchy and Economic Development.* Women's Positions at the End of the Twentieth Century, A study prepared for the World Institute for Development Economics research of the United Nations University (UNU/WIDER), Oxford: Clarendon Press, 1996: 145-169.

PARPART, Jane L. and Kathleen A. STAUDT (eds), *Women and the State in Africa,* Boulder: Lynne Rienner, 1989.

PARPART, Jane L., "Women and the State in Africa", in ROTHCHILD, Donald and Naomi CHAZAN (eds), *The Precarious Balance: State and Society in Africa*, Boulder: Westview, 1988.

PILON, Marc, "Genre et scolarisation des enfants en Afrique sub-saharienne", in LOCOH, Thérèse, Annie LABOURIE-RACAPÉ, Christine TICHIT (edité par), *Genre et développement : des pistes à suivre,*

Documents et Manuels du CEPED no 5, EHESS_INED_INSEE_ORSTOM-Université Paris V1, 1996 :25-35.

RAIKES, Alanagh, « Women's Health in East Africa », in *Social Sciences & Medicine,* Vol. 28, No.5, 1989 :447-459.

ROBERTSON, Claire and Iris BERGER (eds), *Women and Class in Africa*, Claire Robertson and Iris Berger (eds), New York: Africana, 19

RODRIGUEZ-TORRES, Deyssi, "À chacun son trottoir: l'appropriation des espaces publics par les jeunes de Nairobi", in F. Grignon et H. Maupeu (sous le direction de*), l'Afrique orientale. Annuaire 2000*: 325-351.

RODRIGUEZ-TORRES, Deyssi, "A chacun son trottoir: l'appropriation des espaces publics par les jeunes de Nairobi", in F. Grignon et H. Maupeu (sous le direction de*), l'Afrique orientale. Annuaire 2000*, PARIS: l'Harmattan, 2000 : 325-351.

RODRIGUEZ-TORRES, D., "La libre entreprise au féminin. Une typologie de la prostitution à Nairobi, Kenya », in DE LAME, Danielle et Chantal ZABUS (sous la direction de), *Changements au féminin en Afrique noire*. Anthropologie et littérature, Volume 1 : Anthropologie, Paris : l'Harmattan, Montréal : l'Harmattan Inc., 1999 : 115-147.

RUTASHOBYA, Lettice, « Women in business in Tanzania », in CREIGHTON, Colin and C.K. OMARI (edited by), *Gender, Family and Household in Tanzania*, Aldershot, Brookfield USA, Hong Kong, Singapore, Sidney: Avebury, 1995: 269-282.

SHAIDI, Joyce, "Sexual Harassment of Women in the Formal Sector: The Case of Tanzania", OSSREA Gender Research Competition Paper, 1991.

SHELDON, Kathleen (ed), *Courtyards, Markets, City Streets. Urban Women in Africa,* USA: Westview Press, a Division of Harper Collins Publishers, 1996.

SHIFFERAW, Maigenet, "African Women and Reproduction of Knowledge Through Formal Schooling- A Case Study of Zambian Female Education in Secondary Schools" in *Association des femmes Africaines pour la recherche et le Developpment (AFARD) and Association of African Women for research and Development (AAWORD),* Occasional Paper Series No 5, Dakar, 1992: 79-111.

SHIP, Susan, *Women's Empowerment in Tanzania : Towards a Feminist Vision of Development (l'accroissement des pouvoirs des femmes en*

Tanzanie : vers une vision féministe du développement), mémoire présenté à l'Université du Québec à Montréal comme exigence partielle de la maîtrise en science politique, Université du Québec, juin 1988.

SILBERSCHMIDT, Margrethe, *Gender Identity: A neglected dimension in the study of reproductive and sexual behaviour in urban Tanzania,* CDR Project Proposal 95.8, 1995.

SNYDER, Margaret and Mary TADESSE, *African Women and Development. A history*, Johannesburg: Witwatersrand University Press and London and New Jersey: Zed Books, 1995.

SPRING, Anita and Barbara E. MCDADE (edited by), *African Entrepreneurship.* Theory and Reality, Gainesville, Tallahassee, Tampa, Boca Raton, Pensacola, Orlando, Miami, Jacksonville: University Press of Florida, 1998.

STAMP, Patricia, "Kikuyu Women's Self-Help Groups: Toward an Understanding of the relations Between Sex-Gender System and Mode of production in Africa", in *Women and Class in Africa*, Claire Robertson and Iris Berger (eds), New York: Africana, 19?????

Statistics Bureau, *Women and Men in Tanzania*, Dar es Salaam, Tanzania, 1992.

STEENBEEK, Gerdien, Annelou YPEIJ and Fenneke REYSOO, "Genre et mondialisation: exploration d'un débat", in VESCHUUR, Christine with Fenneke REYSOO, *Genre, mondialisation et pauvreté,* Cahiers genre et développement, No. 3, iuéd-efi, Genève: l'Harmattan, 2002: 23-35.

SWANTZ, Lloyd W., "The Zaramo of Dar es Salaam: a study of continuity and change", in *Dar es Salaam. City, Port and Region*, J.E.G. Sutton (ed), Tanzania Notes and Records, The Journal of Tanzania Society, Number 71, 1970:157-164.

TALL, Kadidia, "Une association féminine entreprend la gestion de l'environnement dans un quartier de Ouagadougou", in HAINARD, François et Christine VERSCHUUR (éds), *Femmes dans les crises urbaines.* Relations de genre et environnement précaires, Paris: Karthala, 2001.

EAST AFRICAN STATISTICAL DEPARTMENT, *African Population of Tanganyika,* Geographical and Tribal Studies 1948, Government Printer, Dar es Salaam, 1953.

TANZANIA GENDER NETWORKING PROGRAMME, *Gender Profile of Tanzania,* Dar es Salaam, Tanzania Gender Networking Programme, 1993.

TIMAUS, Ian M. and Louisiana LUSH, "Intra-urban differentials in child health" in *Health Transition Review 5,* 1995:163-190.

TRANBERG HANSEN, Karen, "Gender and difference: youth, bodies and clothing in Zambia", in GODDARD, Victoria Ann (edited by), *Gender, Agency and Change. Anthropological Perspectives*, London and New York: Routledge, 2000: 32-56.

Tripp, Aili Mari, "Urban Women's Movement and Political Liberalisation in East Africa", in *Courtyards, Markets, City Streets. Urban Women in Africa,* Kathleen Sheldon (ed), USA: Westview Press, a Division of Harper Collins Publishers, 1996:285-308.

TRIPP, Aili Mari, "Urban Women's Movement and Political Liberalisation in East Africa", in *Courtyards, Markets, City Streets. Urban Women in Africa,* Kathleen Sheldon (ed), Westview Press, a Division of Harper Collins Publishers, USA, 1996:285-308.

TRIPP, A.M., "Women and the Changing Household Economy in Urban Tanzania", in *The Journal of Modern Africa Studies* 27 (4), 1992: 601-623.

TRIPP, A.M., "The Impact of Crisis and Economic reform on Women in Tanzania", in L. BENERIA and S. FELDMAN, *Unequal Burden: Economic Crises, Persistent Poverty and Women's Work,* Boulder, Colorado: Westview Press, 1992.

TSIKATA, Dzodzi and Joanna KERR with cathy BLACKLOCK and Jocelyne LAFORCE (eds), *Demanding Dignity: Women Confronting Economic Reforms in Africa,* Ottawa: Renouf Publishing Co. Ltd., Accra: the North-South Institute and Third World Network-Africa, 2000.

TUNGARAZA, Felician S.K., "The family and social policy in Tanzania", in CREIGHTON, Colin and C.K. OMARI (edited by), *Gender, Family and Household in Tanzania*, Aldershot, Brookfield USA, Hong Kong, Singapore, Sidney: Avebury, 1995: 299-317.

TUNGARAZA, Felician S.K., « Changes in Traditional Social Security Systems and their Impact on Women in Tanzania », in Klemp, Lutgera (ed*), Gender and Social Policy Experiences of Tanzania*, Published by the Friedrich Ebert Stiftung Women's project, Dar es Salaam, 1994, 12-35.

UNITED NATIONS CHILDREN'S FUND AND THE GOVERNMENT OF THE UNITED REPUBLIC OF TANZANIA, *Women and Children in Tanzania.* A Situation Analysis, Dar es Salaam, Tanzania, 1990,

UNITED NATIONS CHILDREN'S FUND AND THE GOVERNMENT OF THE UNITED REPUBLIC OF TANZANIA, *Situation Analysis of Children in Tanzania*, Dar es Salaam, Tanzania, 2001.

VANCE, Carole S., "Social construction Theory and Sexuality", in Maurice BERGER, Brian WALLIS and Simon WATSON (eds), *Constructing Masculinity*, New York and London: Routledge, 1995:37-48.

VANGROENWEGHE, Daniel, *Sida et sexualité en Afrique,* EPO éditions, 2000.

VAN HOLZEN, Nadia, Nadel-Report on The Practical Assistance at UHP/PAU Dar es Salaam Tanzania, 6/5/1994-3/2/1995, Dar es Salaam urban Health Project, January 1995.

VANISTENDAEL, S., *Clés pour devenir : la résilience*, les Vendredis de Châteauvallon. Novembre 1998, BICE, Bureau International Catholique de l'Enfance, les cahiers du BICE, Genève, 1998.

VERSCHUUR, Christine et Fenneke REYSOO (dirigé par), *Genre, mondialisation et pauvreté*, Cahiers genre et développement, no. 3, iuéd-efi, Genève, l'Harmattan, 2002.

VUORELA, U., *The Women's Question and the Modes of Human Reproduction: an Analysis of a Tanzanian Village*, Helsinki: Finnish Society for Development Studies, Monograph 1, 1987.

WALBY, Sylvia, « The 'Declining Significance' or the 'Changing Forms' of Patriarchy? », in MOGHADAM, Valentine M. (edited by), *Patriarchy and Economic Development.* Women's Positions at the End of the Twentieth Century, a study prepared for the World Institute for Development Economics Research of the United Nations University (UNU/WIDER), Oxford, Clarendon Press, 1996: 19-34.

WEBER, Max, *The Theory of Economic and Social Organization*, New York Cambridge University Press, 1947.

WOMEN MOVING HUMAN RIGHTS CENTRE STAGE, *The Tribune. A Women and Development Quarterly*, International Women's Tribune Centre, Newsletter 58, May New York, 1999.

WORLD BANK, *Tanzania. A Poverty Profile*, Population and Human Resources Division, Eastern Africa Department, Africa Region, Report No. 12298-TA, December1993.

WORLD BANK, Women in the urban labour market of Africa: the case of Tanzania, World Bank Working Paper, no 380, Washington, 1980.

WYSS, Kaspar et al, *Health Statistics Dar es Salaam 1995,* Dar es Salaam Urban Health Project (DUHP), City Medical office of Health, Dar es Salaam City Council, Dar es Salaam, Tanzania, 1995.

Appendix: Study methodology

Research was conducted in the three districts of Dar es Salaam, using an anthropological and inductive approach. The study was separated into several partly overlapping components and employed a range of research techniques. Interviews, life histories and participant observation, depending on the issues, were used. The methodology is anthropological, and favours the understanding of people and the meaningful world they create in different social, environmental and historical contexts.

A review of current and recent research on the state of women in Dar es Salaam and Tanzania was carried out to identify relevant findings and avoid duplication. On the basis of this review some women's groups or individuals were selected for a closer study. This provides more factual data on the social milieu.

Background information was collected specifically on environmental and demographic details, recent history, basic services and infrastructure, and community composition and organisation. This information facilitated the development of tools for the field study, which focuses on women's perception of their identity.

As the first activity, semi-structured interviews were conducted with women of all classes and age groups who earned more money than their husbands. This gave us information on the individual's life and personal involvement in productive activities, socialisation, and gender relations through daily attitudes and individual practices.

An assistant researcher conducted the first set of interviews with various women from diverse wards[1] of Dar es Salaam, involved in different productive activities. The number of interviews carried out was 68. Interviewees were questioned about their productive activity histories, educational background, their self-perception, and suggestions or practical solutions for improving the lives of women and girls. These data provided an ethnographic background to help understand women's lives in an urban environment. Information was

[1] It refers to an administrative structure of the city.

collected on the sexual division of labour, sexual power relations and emotional relationships.

The second activity mainly consisted of a set of semi-structured interviews with men from different social categories, living in diverse parts of Dar es Salaam. It was completed with a few interviews with men from the village of Mtava in the Mara region. Questions focused mainly on men's social status, and their perception and representation of women's ideal behaviour and attitudes, and of femininity. Men were asked to describe some components of good feminine and masculine behaviours, and of gender relations, and to propose solutions for ameliorating gender relations in the context of the urban environment.

The third activity involved 70 students at Form 1V level[2] studying in a public school in Dar es Salaam. They were asked to write a dissertation on four different issues. This activity was conducted within the framework of a course called "Civic and Community Issues." Four different topics were proposed to participants, and they had to choose one on which to give their point of view:

- Is marriage important for you? Explain the reasons for your answer. What do you expect from your wife/husband?
- What do you think of a woman who earns more money than her husband? How should the money be used?
- Do women have to respect men in general? Does this come from a specific tradition or belief? Can you explain this tradition or belief? Where did you learn it?
- Many women say that men are the cause of their underdevelopment and that men humiliate women. Is this true?

This method was used in order to compare young people's point of view with what was expressed by older men and women.

The fourth activity was related to women's life histories. The aim was to study the transformation over the period from the 1940s to

---

[2] The age of students in Form 1V varies from 18 to 22 years. Children start primary school at the age of 7 and most of them complete their primary education, if they do not have to repeat, by the age of 14. Form IV is the fourth year of the secondary level, which supposes that students are mostly aged 18 or above.

today, as experienced and told by women themselves. Long interviews of two to four hours aimed to capture the social perspective of women and the strategies they use in day-to-day living through their personal biographies. In-depth interviews were conducted with four women of different ages in order to establish an inter-generational comparison. Three of the interviewed women identified themselves as Christians and only one as Muslim. These four women were not included in the first group of 68 participants.

Several sessions were used in order to achieve in-depth interviews. They were tape-recorded, translated into English and transcribed.

The question of generalisation is an important one and must be considered in the national context. Many conclusions must be drawn and programmes based on data from one city or a small region. Thus, life histories or case studies are seen as a small step toward grand generalisation. This method facilitated an understanding of the "identity detours" between social and professional identity, or family and personal identity. It focused on complexities, since qualitative research is based on a holistic view of social practice. It notes that social phenomena, human dilemmas, and the nature of cases are situational and influenced by events of many kinds (Lahire, 1998). Participant observation, through informal conversations, home visits, confidences and/or personal communication with colleagues on different occasions, was the way to obtain additional data on gender relations. In the city, it is difficult to capture the complete picture of an actor as he or she embraces multiple roles in diverse places. The occupational diversity of the city, without emphasising its intra-ethnic diversity, was taken into account. In Tanzania ethnicity is not a criterion for defining people, and heterogeneity and mixing has been encouraged since the Independence.

Objectives and relevance of the research

The research investigated structural and historical changes that shape the social experience of people and hence their gender relations. People as active social actors are endowed with *agency*; they shape their lives under various circumstances. By their actions they reproduce or change collective meanings, notions, values and rules.

What kind of strategies do they use in a social structure that expresses various social constraints?

The study also tried to measure the impact of women earning more money than their husbands on gender relations. It aimed to gather and analyse information about gender relations in Dar es Salaam and to provide up-to-date, reliable, representative and empirical data for analysis. The purpose was to:

- Identify *l'etat des lieux* of women in Dar es Salaam who are earning more money than their husbands.
- Evaluate the changing role and status of women and men in terms of their perception and representation of personal power and gender interactions.
- Assess the impact of social and economic factors on daily life, which influence the decision-making process.
- Theorise about determinants that have greater influence on the choices and opportunities open to individuals.

Conceptual framework: Action and plural actor

The concepts of social action, agency, habitus and habits, plural actor, and resilience were used to understand gender relations in the urban context of Dar es Salaam.

Social structure and agency

From an anthropological point of view, people's lives can be captured by taking into account 1) the structure into which they are inserted and, 2) people's *agency*, which means their capacity to insert themselves specifically into that structure. Labrecque (2001: 11) noted that it is the core of the Gidden's theory of "structuration," which focuses on actors' "situated practices" (Lamphere *ET al.* 1997:5).

The concept of structure refers to a historical construction. It is related "to the intractability of the social world" (Connell, 1995:92). It expresses the constraints that exist within a given form of a social organisation that restrains social practice. Of course, the structure contributes to building a certain type of subjects. Nevertheless, it does not mean that the subjects are without *agency* (Giddens, 1987). Individuals are still able to act and to project themselves in action.

Women as individuals are collectively engaged in an "action regime." By using their mental and bodily repertoire, individuals are collectively engaged in an action regime that reactivates a specific part of social life. Thus, it is through their *agency* that they develop new habits and become more resilient. The action regime leads them to change and to new analyses of their social environment.

Thus, the concept of *agency* contains history, inasmuch as the subjects can consider himself/herself in the present through his/her experience and daily life; in the past through the constituted structure of multiple experiences; and in the future by his/her capacity or resistance for transforming the structure (Labrecque, idem). The social actor, through the *habit* defined as an incorporated scheme, records social memory that is registered in larger and powerful processes. An incorporated scheme can also be registered in the form of concrete gestures.

The field of gender relations refers to the cultural construction of male and female identities and the design of the cultural categories of male and female in a specific historical time. Gender identities are divided between various structures. Connell has identified 1) the sexual division of labour, 2) attitudes to power, authority and coercion, and 3) the emotional and daily links that exist between people (1987:95), each of which generates its own form of oppression and has its own historical trajectory.

For women of Dar es Salaam, in what kind of situation are their practices constrained? Does the social structure ultimately determine the lives of women involved in economic and productive activities in an urban environment? Can new habits help women to escape from the social structure of male dominance that has been established by patriarchy? Are men and women using and negotiating new meanings in action and interaction? Or do they conform to the so-called tradition?

Social life, agency and new practices: habitus and habits of the "plural actor"

In the social sciences, theories of social action mainly focus on two sets of models:

- The first is centred on the past and future, for instance the concept of "habitus." It neglects interactions and the immediate and pragmatic context of action.

- The "acting present" preoccupies the second set of models. Action is analysed without reference to the past; actors are seen as being motivated only by the logic of present action. The model takes out all aspects of present action that have been influenced by past experience and/or knowledge (Lahire, 1998:53).

These two points of view, which differ in their underlying determinism and subjects' initiative, should be seen as complementary and not opposed. The first model describes social life (Bourdieu, 1980) as a mutually constituting interaction of structures, dispositions and actions, whereby social structures and the embodied knowledge of those structures produce orientations towards action which, in turn, are constitutive of social structures. These orientations both shape and are shaped by social practice. Practice results from a process of improvisation, personal trajectories and the ability to play the game of social interaction (Calhoun, LiPuma and Postone, 1993:4).

For Bourdieu, practices and strategies are embedded in the human capacity for structured improvisation, which is called *habitus*. It is defined as:

> *...a system of general schemes that are both durable (inscribed in the social construction of the self) and transportable (from one field to another), function on an unconscious plane, and take place within a structured space of possibilities (defined by the intersection of material conditions and fields of operation). In fact, it is a system of dispositions that is both objective and subjective. So conceived, the habitus is the dynamic*

intersection of structure and action, society and the individual. The notion of habitus enables Bourdieu to analyse the behaviour of agents as objectively coordinated and regular without being the producer of rules on the one hand, or conscious rationality on the other. It is meant to capture the practical mastery that people have of their social situation, while grounding that mastery itself socially (Postone, LiPuma, and Calhoun, 1993: 4).

The *habitus* is both an internalisation and incorporation of culture. For Bourdieu, "strategy" is that practice which is the product of a practical sense of a particular social game. It results from constant invention or improvisation. It cannot be achieved by mechanical obedience or codified rules. Nevertheless, people reproduce the system because of a durably installed generative principle of regulated improvisation, which tends to reproduce regularities. Most actions of human beings are ruled by "practical logic."

Kaufmann (2001) reactivated the old concept of "*habit*" which links the past and the capacity of individuals to project into the future. The concept is defined as "incorporated schemes regulating action." Habits are multiform, dynamic and visualised as tools for building and regulating action. Habits register social memory in mobile and powerful processes; they are expressed through concrete gestures that not only reproduce the old but also record changes. Social contradiction is at the core of the habit; a lack of coincidence between previously incorporated and new socialisation schemes is at the origin of individualisation, and as societies tend not to reproduce in identical ways, the contradiction generates resistance and reflection. New social trajectories are opened; a constant movement of *habits* is opposed to the stability of *habitus*.

The individual is a plural actor, confronted with multiple situations, who carries out various action schemes. Is the social actor acting more in conformity with acquired schemes, or according to a more complex context in which action schemes are not determined? In reality, most past experiences are active in present action; but the actor also has the ability to project him or herself into the future. All these aspects are linked to the internal plurality of the actor, which correlatives with the plurality of logics of action (Lahire, 1998:53 and Kaufmann, 2001).

However, the habitus model of Bourdieu cannot be used to explain the complexity of men and women's behaviours in Dar es Salaam. For instance, to what extent is male control over female involvement in the economy non-negotiable if men realise that their behaviour threatens women's incomes—and ultimately their ability to develop their own productive activities and fulfil all the family's needs? How can men justify their power in the decision-making process when they barely earn a livelihood and cannot support their family members? To what extent do men lack a feeling of responsibility for their own family but still support their family of origin, allowing their own children to suffer? How can men justify their behaviour by reference to tradition, when in fact they are ignorant of the so-called tradition and cannot explain where it comes from? Why are some women able to succeed in a world where compromises are so hard to negotiate?

People are not influenced just by their past experience. As indicated by Lahire, "the production of homogeneous *habitus* in all spheres of life is a fiction" (1998:34). Women and men are not products of homogenous social conditions of existence. They experience new situations that are completely different from past ones, and they do not simply reproduce the old order.

The material and cultural conditions of stability, existence and socialisation principles produce individuals that are guided by action schemes. But in today's urban areas, these action schemes or habits are no longer coherent and homogeneous. People no longer live in moral and intellectual uniformity. Contemporary Dar es Salaam society is complex and heterogeneous. People are confronted with heterogeneous situations and influenced not only by the family but also by school, peer or work groups, multiple cultural institutions, information media and the cinema, and so on. These influences are sometimes in contradiction with each other in terms of the socialisation principles they develop.

The multiplicity of social contexts leads to a complexity of repertoires of *habits*. In urban areas, people live simultaneously and successively in different social contexts. Moreover, homogeneity of an institution cannot be assumed. For example, configurations within a family are not homogenous from a cultural and moral point of view. Many children experience contradictory socialisation principles, and through their different sets of relatives are confronted by various attitudes and behaviours. Their situation may contain contradictory elements, especially in extensive families where several generations live under the same roof (Lahire, 1998:41).

It seems impossible to diagnose the social behaviour of an individual because of the social complexity of a situation, which is never identical with one that has previously been experienced by the actor. But complexity is also generated because the "plural actor" is the product of the experience, often early, of socialisation in heterogeneous contexts. The actor participates in various social universes while occupying different positions, and incorporates a multiplicity of action schemes and habits that could be organised in as many repertoires as there are social contexts to be identified and names (Lahire, 1998:42).

Women and resiliency

Power relations cannot be seen as structurally obvious if we understand power as exercised or sustained throughout local circumstances of social interaction. For instance, Tanzanian women cannot be presented solely as victims of their society. Certain women could be seen as marginal in a society that allows them little room to manoeuvre; while others are able to overcome society's constraints and succeed in organising and managing their lives as well as they can in the Tanzanian context of 2001. We could refer to the concept of resiliency as defined by S. Vanistendael (1998) and Boris Cyrulnik (1999).

In the social sciences, this term means the capacity to succeed, to live and to develop personally in an acceptable social way, in spite of stress or adversity which usually carries a heavy risk of a negative result (Cyrulnik, 1999:10). The idea is that people can overcome and triumph over difficult circumstances. Resilience is a natural process, in which what we are is connected to our ecological, affective and verbal milieu. The more difficult life is, the more demands it makes on an individual. But resilience shows that it is possible to escape from a bad situation—"history is not destiny." Women's resilience is expressed through their capacity to act in contexts whose social and economic structures are detrimental to them.

Women are thus aware of the prevailing oppressive gender relations and challenge these conditions in a variety of ways. It is a misconception to view feminism merely as a Western ideology, which reflects Western culture simply because feminist theories, just like other theories, have been influenced by external pressures resulting from colonialism and imperialism (Mannathoko, 1992:72). Feminism also has roots in the African condition, and has affected development strategies by forcing governments to incorporate practical and strategic gender needs within mainstream development. Women's consciousness has been raised as they have overcome difficult situations. These are not superwomen; they are women who have developed survival strategies, which satisfy certain needs while leaving others, unmet (Mbilinyi, 1992:67).

New pictures of women

In Dar es Salaam, a new picture of women is emerging. Women today know they must struggle to create their own space. Women's resistance to oppressive gender relations is growing; they have been radicalised by existing material conditions (Mannathoko, idem: 82). The Structural Adjustment Programme, focusing only on efficiency, affected the feminist struggle for social justice, equality and human rights as it shifted the costs of reproduction from the state to the household and thus increased women's burden (idem: 87). The SAP undermined the minimal achievements of the 1970s and early 1980s. Nevertheless, "today more African women are willing to use the term 'feminist' to describe their new mode of operation and their goals for achieving a new gender compact. For the most part, they are concerned about how to reconcile this approach with African culture in assertive and positive ways as they seek solutions to the many problems facing them, their communities and their states" (Mikell, 1997:28). The challenge, for African women, is to reconcile the new gender picture with African culture.

Feminist political economy

The anthropological approach of this study derives from "feminist political economy." This approach stresses the importance of context and locates the anthropological subject simultaneously in history and in contingency (everyday occurrences), in the global and local situation, in structure and in action (Labrecque, 2001). This approach, as proposed by Stamp (1986), combines Marx's rigorous, historical, materialist method with radical feminism's insight that the personal is political and that gender oppression cuts across class lines. Gender relations are viewed in their specificity, while taking into account the effects of such things such as class and race (Gordon, 1996:16).

> *Stamp roots gender oppression in the way societies are organised to produce and distribute the necessities of life. Although economics is essential to understanding women's status, there is a complex interaction between the economical, political and ideological aspects of society. For instance, the ideology and practices of kinship is not merely the superstructure determined by relations of production; they help shape productive relations. Economic work and the fulfilment of kinship obligations become inseparable, as are the often-dichotomised public and private spheres. In other words, the sex-gender system is closely related to the relations of production but it is separate from them and not reducible to them (Gordon, idem).*

Gender inequality cannot be understood without the concept of patriarchy, defined by Ehrenreich (1995:284) as:

> *In the original sense of the word, as the intimate power of men over women, a power which is historically exercised within the family by the male as breadwinner, property owner, or armed defender of women and children. This is the traditional meaning of patriarchy: the rule of the father, including the rule of older men over younger men and of fathers over the daughters, as well as husbands over wives.*

Femininity or masculinity is not just ideas or personal identities. Gender relations are enmeshed in the history of institutions and social structures. The constructions are often made by configurations of practice structured by gender relations; they are inherently historical, and their making and remaking is a political process affecting the balance of interests within society and the direction of social change (Connell, 1987:44). To understand gender relations requires a critique of the real and not just a reflection of it.

CPSIA information can be obtained at www.ICGtesting.com
225349LV00004B/91/A

9 789987 417544